POEMS
TO READ ALOUD

POEMS

TO

SELECTED AND EDITED

READ ALOUD

BY *Edward Hodnett*

New York

W · W · NORTON & COMPANY · INC ·

COPYRIGHT © 1957 BY EDWARD HODNETT

Since this page cannot legibly accommodate all the copyright notices, the four pages following constitute an extension of the copyright page.

110342

Library of Congress Catalogue Card No. 57-10633

PRINTED IN THE UNITED STATES OF AMERICA
FOR THE PUBLISHERS BY THE VAIL-BALLOU PRESS
3 4 5 6 7 8 9

For Carolyn and Grey

Contents

CONTENTS

To the Reader

You ARE not likely to find a way of spending your leisure that is so pleasant, so easy, so inexpensive, and so rewarding as reading poetry aloud. It is a pity it is not more widely enjoyed. *Poems to Read Aloud* aims to make that enjoyment more accessible, for as far as I can discover, this anthology is the first one specifically devoted to poems to be read aloud by the general reader.

Happily, poetry readings, public and private, are growing in popularity. In the last few years the public response to dramatic and verse readings has been surprising. The visits of the Welsh poet, the late Dylan Thomas, stirred excitement among multitudes of people for whom poetry had not previously been exciting. As evidence of this change of climate, the production and sale of poetry recordings have increased enormously. Of course reading poetry aloud did not stop with Ben Jonson and his fellow poets at the Mermaid Tavern nor with Grandma's memories of winter evenings about the fireside with "Evangeline" and "Thanatopsis." The recent flame of interest rises from a fire that has never died out.

The delights of reading poetry aloud are double—reading and listening. They can be simple and childlike or complex and sophisticated. The appeal of Tennyson's "*Revenge*" or Noyes' "Barrel-Organ" or Carroll's "Walrus and the Carpenter" is as direct and irresistible as Dixieland music or a Disney fantasy. Then there are delights as exquisite as those that arise from the baroque splendors of Shakespeare's sonnets, the disenchantments of A. E. Housman, and the falcon flights of Gerard Manley Hopkins.

Your pleasure in reading poetry aloud need not be labored or precious. As in chamber music, your appreciation grows by association with the best. After enough years of listening to the Budapest or Griller quartets play Mozart, you cannot fail to appreciate the mastery of the composer and the performers. So with poetry. If you give your ears a chance, they will grow accustomed to excellence. In time your ears will sense how deftly a first-rate poet complies with the imperatives of rhythm and rime and yet transcends them by infinite variety and unflagging invention. The pre-eminence accorded Chaucer, Shakespeare, and Milton in English poetry derives in no small part from the incredible skill with which they maintain flexibility and freshness within fixed patterns of verse through thousands of lines of narrative.

From what may at first seem only a hum of words, in time your ears will pick single words, phrases, and lines that are so fresh and right that the dew stays on them, as it were, forever. Today, no less than when first I read it long ago, Housman's line "Star and coronal and bell" seems magic—as utterly lovely as those notes of Bach commonly called "Air for the G String." Sometimes these items are elegant dandies, like Shakespeare's "Not marble, nor the gilded monuments of princes." Some are plain, yet they have an incandescent glow, like Shakespeare's "golden lads and girls" in

> Golden lads and girls all must,
> As chimney sweepers, come to dust.

Your ears tell you that the effect is intensified by the homely "as chimney sweepers" followed by the pebble-dropping finality of "come to dust."

Besides the immediate delight that comes from reading aloud —and the blessed forgetfulness of mundane affairs—other benefits are worth noting. First is the fact of participation. In a day when millions of Americans spend millions of hours in a state of hypnosis in cars, in movies, and before television sets, it is no minor triumph to prove that you are alive. Reading poetry—and to a lesser degree listening to it—keeps you alert. To lift the poet's words off the printed page and clothe them in meaning and emotion is to share in the creative act, quite as truly as to play a piano is.

Reading aloud is the best way to understand the meaning of a poem. Listening to it being read is next best. No one can read a poem aloud skilfully without understanding what the words are meant to communicate. There are, of course, many different ways of reading a poem well, for words have a much wider range of possible interpretation than musical notes have. Words have literal meanings, they have emotional connotations, and when read aloud they have sound. Having to read a poem aloud willy-nilly puts you in collaboration with the author. It quickens your sense of his over-all purpose, of the relation of the parts of his poem to each other, and of the special contribution of every word and phrase. You never acquire this completeness of understanding through the eye alone. And naturally as you develop this comprehensive understanding of one poem, you find it easier to understand the next one— and the next.

To increase your understanding of poetry is to increase your understanding of life. Poets are peculiarly equipped to give you insights into the profound aspects of human experience. A poem is a confrontation. The poet confronts life, and he has what the rest of us may not have, the sensitivity and the wisdom and the command of language to react intelligently and to snare his reactions in a net of words. He often confronts a problem and gives his answer. It is your problem and my problem. But though the poet, like the composer of music, is the recorder of some of the subtlest and most complex experiences of the human spirit, he is likewise the recorder of all of the simplest and most delightful of those common experiences that make our days agreeable.

The poet must try unceasingly to catch in words the precise shape and significance of experience if what he has seen and felt and thought are to come alive for you. If the poet does have a shining vision to record, he often entrusts it to words that are too tired from service to other poets to do the job he requires. It is no small achievement to write a good poem. As one of the secondary benefits, therefore, you will in time discover that reading poetry aloud will improve your own writing and speaking. The very tests that consign most poems to oblivion insure that the best of those that survive are models of economy, exactness, and grace of expression.

*   *   *   *   *

Three things have determined the choice of poems in *Poems to Read Aloud*—readability, literary excellence, and variety.

All poems can be read aloud. Almost all of them were written to be read aloud, though many modern poems seem meant for the eye alone. With study an experienced reader can read almost any poem aloud with a reasonable degree of effectiveness. But the experienced reader is the first to grant as self-evident that the degrees vary widely. Open a volume of Walt Whitman. In my edition "When Lilacs Last in the Dooryard Bloomed" comes right before "O Captain! My Captain!" They are Whitman's best-known poems, written at the same time about the same subject—the death of Lincoln. Any schoolboy can aspire to give a fair rendition of "O Captain! My Captain!"—and most of them have. Considerable virtuosity is needed to seize and sustain the solemn yet delicate music of the grief-struck elegy, "When Lilacs Last in the Dooryard Bloomed." One of the great poems of the English language, it is one whose greatness is peculiarly dependent on actual sound. It is one of your adventures in reading aloud.

Many excellent poems do not seem to fit this collection because they lack a certain fluency, tension, and eloquence—the qualities peculiarly necessary to make reading aloud a pleasure. For example, Hart Crane's "The Bridge" is one of the major modern poems, and it gains much from being heard. Yet it is a difficult poem to keep in flight. On the other hand, the anthologies and volumes of collected works are full of poems easy to read fluently. But all too frequently they lack the kind of tension and eloquence that gives reading aloud a lift. Take "The Sheaves" by Edwin Arlington Robinson. It is a good poem, and it is easy to read. It begins:

> Where long the shadows of the wind had rolled,
> Green wheat was yielding to the change assigned.

Somehow—perhaps because the poem is a low-key reflective sonnet—the lift is lacking. Yet reflective poems can be charged with an intensity that makes them eloquent. In "For a Dead Lady" Robinson wonders

> what inexorable cause
> Makes Time so vicious in the reaping.

That has intensity and eloquence.

To choose poems that have literary excellence as well as readability is easier to do than to defend specific instances. Yet readability is not enough. Most narrative poems, love lyrics, and children's verses are easy to read, but most of them are shot through with mediocrity of thought and mediocrity of execution. Poems for children contain a depressing amount of simpering sentimentality, pedestrian versification, and lackluster imagery. To achieve distinction, a poem must be excellent *of its kind*. By one system of evaluation Wordsworth's "Westminster Bridge" is a "better" poem than Edmund Waller's "Go, Lovely Rose" or Lewis Carroll's "Jabberwocky" because it deals with more elevated matter in a more serious way. But "Go, Lovely Rose" is a superb example of the Cavalier accent —a blend of cool artifice and thrush-song sincerity—and "Jabberwocky" is a superb example of language play of the highest order. Both are excellent of their kind.

Some poems achieve fame without achieving literary distinction. Whitman's "O Captain! My Captain!"—to use the same example again—strikes me as trite and maudlin. Yet I have included Scott's "Soldier, Rest!" It is sentimental. But it is not banal. You ask, therefore, only that a poem be excellent within the conventions of its type, just as you do a detective story or a folksong.

The third basis for selecting poems for *Poems to Read Aloud* is variety. This is a book to meet the taste of all sorts of readers, moods, and occasions. "Sir Patrick Spence," "The Old Vicarage," "Grantchester," "The Love Song of J. Alfred Prufrock," "The Ballad of Fisher's Boardinghouse," "The Rose of the World," "Five Bells," "Casey at the Bat," "The Shooting of Dan McGrew"—famous and little-known, humorous, romantic, and philosophic—they all seem wonderful to me and all deserve to be here. At the end of the book is a list of poems that children like. Not all are written for children, and children as they grow older and read more will range far beyond them. On the other hand, no poem in the book is selected exclusively for children. What grownup can resist "Custard the Dragon"? A time comes when the mood calls for you to read Eliot's "Prufrock," and no less inevitably an occasion will demand that you let yourself go with "The Shooting of Dan McGrew."

Regretfully I have had to omit some poems that require explanatory comment. It spoils the fun to stop reading to throw in footnotes. I have not included excerpts from long poems, passages from plays (except songs), poems with very familiar musical settings, or selections from the Bible. Some poets— especially Herrick, Dickinson, Browning, Kipling, Housman, Masefield, Yeats, Millay, Eliot, and Cummings—have written many more excellent read-aloud poems than can be offered here.

But you will inevitably be exploring the complete works of these poets and of many more and adding a lot of poems to your personal repertory.

*   *   *   *   *

Some common-sense suggestions about the technique of reading aloud may come in handy. Let me confess that I belong to the be-natural school of reading. Perhaps I should call it the read-for-meaning school. Or if I may twist the phrase, I advise that you read *from* meaning. If you search first for meaning, expression will follow. If you concentrate primarily on the way you are reading, you will put yourself between the poet and the listener—and you may sound silly.

Let's see what reading from meaning is. Let's take a relatively difficult poem—John Donne's "A Hymn to God the Father." Read it aloud before you read what I say about it. Here it is:

A Hymn to God the Father

Wilt Thou forgive that sin where I begun,
   Which was my sin, though it were done before?
Wilt Thou forgive that sin through which I run,
   And do run still, though still I do deplore?
     When Thou hast done, Thou hast not done,
       For I have more.

Wilt Thou forgive that sin which I have won
   Others to sin, and made my sins their door?
Wilt Thou forgive that sin which I did shun
   A year or two, but wallowed in a score?
     When Thou hast done, Thou hast not done,
       For I have more.

I have a sin of fear, that when I have spun
   My last thread, I shall perish on the shore;
Swear by Thyself that at my death Thy Son
   Shall shine as He shines now and heretofore;
     And having done that, Thou hast done;
       I fear no more.

First of all, the *tone*. The title of the poem and your first silent glance over it tell you the tone is religious. Further acquaintance tells you it is not a hymn so much as a prayer. At least John Donne is talking to God, and he is talking with profound earnestness. To carry conviction, you estimate that your voice will have to range from quiet seriousness to intense fervor.

The first step is to catch the tone—the general spirit of the poem. Since you do not have to read a poem aloud at sight, you come to assurance about this and other estimates only after several private trials.

Next you look to see how the *thought* of the poem *develops*. The three stanzas reveal a simple one-two-three progression. In the first stanza Donne asks God if He will forgive two kinds of sin and adds that he has more to ask forgiveness for. In the second stanza he asks God to forgive him for two more kinds of sin and adds again that he is not through. In the third stanza he signals a change in the kind of thing he is going to say by changing the formula he has been following. Each of the previous four confessions of sin has been introduced by the signal "Wilt Thou forgive," and each has been cast in the form of a question. Now Donne switches from question to statement—"I have a sin of fear." And the two lines devoted to it are followed, not by another sin as in the previous stanzas, but by a petition of a wholly new sort. With the curious intimacy of the mystic, he asks God to swear that at his death Christ "Shall shine as He shines now and heretofore." And he parallels the shift in the first line of the stanza by dropping the refrain that he has used to end both of the first two stanzas. Now God has done, and the poet fears no more. (You doubtless have caught the pun on his name that Donne injects.)

No matter what your impression the first time over, you see that "A Hymn to God the Father" is logical in its thought development. Now what cue to your reading do you get from this one-two-three pattern? You see that stanzas one and two are almost identical in what they say. These two stanzas serve to build up suspense for the third by reason of the incompleteness announced in the refrain. The third stanza is the culmination. Donne clearly expects an affirmative answer to his petition to God. For the Dean of St. Paul's the certainty that Christ shall live and be his Savior is unassailably true, even though Hell was a lot closer three hundred and fifty years ago than it is today.

So the pattern of Donne's thought yields you a pattern for your reading. The despair in the first two stanzas you convey by whatever means you can manage with your voice, but in any case you are not going to read loud, fast, or "expressively." Sincerity rather than showmanship befits a prayer. You might even decide to adopt something close to a monotone. The despair vanishes in the third stanza. Then even the statement of the sin in the first two lines seems to call for a stronger voice. The rhetorical request to God in the third and fourth lines is suffused with mystic conviction. It is really an affirmation of faith, and it demands resonance and energy. The last two lines tell you that the problem is resolved, the tension relaxed. They call for quiet positiveness. Of course, you may read this poem differently. That is where the creativeness of reading comes in.

Now let's have a look at the *rhythm*. The basic unit or foot that Donne uses is the commonest one in English. It is represented by the word *begun*—two syllables with the accent on the second. In the first four lines of each stanza there are five *beats*—five feet with the accent on the second syllable. This five-beat line is called iambic pentameter. Because of its dignity and flexibility, it has been the favorite since Chaucer introduced it to England nearly six hundred years ago. For songs and vigorous story-telling shorter lines and different accenting are often used to pick up the tempo.

But in a sense you ignore the beat. If the poet has done his job properly, the beat takes care of itself. In the first line of "A Hymn to God the Father" Donne is asking God a plain question, and you read it in a straightforward manner, not in the jerky rhythm of a child jumping rope. Now read that first line again:

> Wilt Thou forgive that sin where I begun,

If the line in English poetry were as regular as it is often imagined to be, you would have to read the first foot [wltTHOU]. But *wilt* is a decisive kind of word, and you are unable to swallow that *lt* combination, as you do the [buh] in *begun*. If you say WILT THOU with even emphasis, you do only what comes naturally, and if you do not notice anything awkward about the rhythm, the question of whether or not the line scans is irrelevant. If you go through the poem line by line, you will discover numerous other deviations from a mechanical German-band one-TWO, one-TWO beat. This crafty varying of the accent is not merely poetic license. It is poetic necessity. It accounts for the tireless ease you feel in reading familiar masterpieces. The lack of variation helps explain why reading inferior poetry is so wearisome.

Much contemporary verse (by no means all) deviates even more. It does not even start with a line of regular or approximately regular feet. It simply breaks into groups of words according to sense, and the rhythm is the *cadence* of the voice in natural speech. What eloquence you give it in your reading derives from your sense of the eloquence daily speech can give the concentrated, elliptical, metaphorical statements of poetic thought. This seems the place to note the modern use of partial rimes of two sorts—*assonance* and *dissonance*. In *assonance* the accented vowels (and any following ones) have the same sound, but the following consonants (and sometimes the preceding ones, too) do not—*moan–mole, moan–yolk*. In *dissonance* the accented vowels are different, but either the preceding or the following consonants, or both, are the same—*stir–star, stir–stab, fir–star*. Pairs of words that look as though they rime but do not—*heath–death*—are a form of dissonance. These partial rimes enrich much modern verse by occurring within the line as well as at the end. And in old and new verse the read-aloud quality depends greatly on the echoing of similar sounds, apart from rimes.

The next clue to the rhythm is the way the sentences are put together. To a considerable degree, this is outlined for you by the *punctuation*. Look at the first stanza of Donne's poem. At the end of the first line is a comma. It is followed by the short, almost parenthetic clause, "which was my sin," and then the question is completed by a "though" clause. The third and fourth lines follow exactly the same pattern. It can be diagrammed thus:

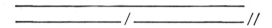

These three lines represent your fundamental grouping of words by meaning. And these are your fundamental groups in reading.

Look now at the second stanza. Here Donne has varied the grouping, but both questions again follow an identical pattern.

In the first stanza you break your reading at the end of the first line. In the second stanza you do not pause until the middle of the second line. In the third stanza you will not be surprised to discover that the change in the nature of the ideas already noted is matched by fairly drastic variations from the patterns of the previous stanzas. How long you pause when you do pause cannot be specified. A question mark or period signals the completion of a significant unit of thought and calls for a significant break in the rhythm. You will often track larger units of thought through several sentences until you come to a major break. In the fourteen lines of a sonnet, for instance, the most important break in the thought usually comes at the end of the eighth line, for the first eight lines often present a problem and the last six give an answer.

Now that you see how Donne gives you a guide to the flow of his thought in "A Hymn to God the Father," suppose we go on to the last step—the *word-for-word* reading. We can take only a few points. Just as a subtle variety among stressed and unstressed syllables keeps the beat from becoming tiresomely regular, so a similar variety exists among words. It is self-evident that the beat must fall on chief words—never on servant words like *a, the, of, with, and,* or (except for humorous effect) on unaccented syllables like *be* in *begun.* Only stilted grammar-school reading—as [ayee] instead of [uh] for *a,* and [thee] instead of [thuh] for *the*—will lead you into trouble with unstressed syllables. The poet takes care of you.

Where the poet is unable to help and you must make an independent judgment is in the distinctions of emphasis among the chief words. Take the opening words of the third stanza— "I have a sin of fear." How will reading from meaning guide you here? Clearly, *I have* has no key significance. If you read the words rather than the meaning, you will probably read, "I have a SIN of fear." But Donne has been talking about sin before. What your listeners are waiting to hear is the name of the new sin. *Fear* is a blurry sound. If you read the line mechanically, you will let your voice drop after emphasizing *sin,* and the sense of the passage will not register. Reading from the meaning, you read, "I have a sin of FEAR"—not in the exaggerated way it looks here but so firmly that *fear* emerges as important. All the rest of the two-line passage is the answer to the question about the identity of the new sin and should be read with equal clarity.

Emphasis, of course, is not gained only by loudness. Lowering the voice and pauses can each be just as effective. Change in the quality of your voice and change in your tempo produce emphasis through contrast, and the variety keeps your reading from becoming soporific. But again, you can achieve this variety best by being sensitive to the shifting meanings of the words you are uttering. Many poems like this one of Donne's are conversational. No matter how special the language, basically someone is talking—generally the poet to the reader or the world at large. If you put yourself in the place of the speaker and say what he has to say to the people who are listening to *you*, you will come out better than if you start with a preconceived notion of how poetry *should* sound and try for those effects.

Now I can borrow Donne's words and say, "I have done." I have no more to say about "A Hymn to God the Father." Most of the poems in *Poems to Read Aloud* are easier to understand and easier to read. If you have followed the analysis of this poem, you should be able to apply the same approach to any other poem.

* * * * *

American speech tends to be flat, harsh, and slovenly. You do not have to affect a pseudo-British accent to make your reading sound more musical than a telephone conversation. By all odds the most important thing for you to do is to speak clearly and naturally. Singsong rhythm and letting your voice die at the end of a line or a sentence show you are not following the meaning. You also prevent your listeners from hearing the words. Since final words tend to be important, you might even correct this common tendency to drop the voice at the end of lines and sentences by raising your inflection a little. In addition, without getting into the mysteries of phonetics, you can settle for precision of enunciation to bring out the full flavor of a word. For instance, *sin* should not be slurred to [sn], *did* to [dud], *wallowed* to [wallud], *thread* to [thrud], or *perish* to [purush]. Do not abandon your native dialect if you are fond of it. But one of the by-products of your reading aloud will be a general improvement in your everyday speech, including correction of regional or personal variations from generally accepted good usage. For example, New Yorkers often pronounce *fine* somewhat like [faheen], New Englanders, *idea* like [idear], and Ohioans, *caught* like [caht]. You do not have to sport an excessively broad *a* and mispronounce *last*, [lawhst] to avoid the ugly draggy nasal pronunciation of *a* common all over the United States. Shorn of parochialism and affectation, our English tongue is lovely and various. To draw from the printed poem the music and rich savor of the language that the poet incorporated in it, you must make some effort. In this effort, as in that of penetrating to the meaning and pattern of the poem, you are being creative, and you enhance your own delight and that of your listeners.

At this point we might think a bit about how to *listen* to poetry. First, put yourself in a receptive mood. Do not be defensive. You will not have to take an exam at the end of the reading. If you have not acquired a taste for poetry, do not make apologetic remarks to the reader. You will make him uncomfortable, and you may sound as though you are bragging about your ignorance. Ignorance of any of the arts is something to regret and remedy, not something to say trite things about. On the other hand, poems are to be enjoyed—they are not vitamin pills to be swallowed because they are good for you. Relax, then, and be receptive.

Try to follow the sense as well as the sound of the poems. Almost all in this book are comprehensible with little effort. But if the meaning of a poem escapes you at first, or if your mind wanders, do not be severe with yourself. Just as in listening to music or looking at paintings, you will find that all you have to do is give yourself a chance. A poem that seems at first hearing to be only a jumble of pleasant sounds will on further acquaintance, like a Schubert quartet or a painting by Braque, grow familiar and ingratiating. This is all there really is to it. Except—if you are going to listen to someone read poetry, do remember your manners. Pray do not fidget, look at magazines, fetch people ashtrays, offer extended commentaries after each poem, or start irrelevant conversations when the reader pauses.

To increase your listening pleasure and your skill in reading, you simply must listen to the poetry recordings now abundant. Hearing Robert Frost, Edna St. Vincent Millay, T. S. Eliot, and W. H. Auden read from their own works is instantly to gain an insight into the nature of their poems not possible in any other way. The recordings of Dylan Thomas have perhaps more than any other single factor made the sound of poetry thrilling to a significant new public.

34

But listening to poetry is only a third or less of the fun. You must read aloud yourself to get your full measure of it. It is altogether possible to read aloud to yourself. But it is more fun to have a listener, and you read better. Exchanging roles as reader and listener shares the profits. A poetry-reading party is a civilized form of entertainment. When you invite new guests, take a few reasonable precautions. First make clear to them what they are in for—a whole afternoon or evening of nothing but poetry. Give them a fair chance to get out of coming. Then if they accept, have them bring poems they like, with the understanding they will read some. Let your guests take turns reading. After an evening or two the stiffness—and the stiffs—will depart. You can vary the pattern indefinitely—include records, read from one poet, one type, or one period, take turns reading from a long poem, bring in a guest poet, read original manuscripts, and try group reading in unison or antiphonally. Such evenings can be an exhilarating way to combine sociability, group activity, and inward satisfaction.

Meanwhile, go ahead reading *Poems to Read Aloud* and building up your own library of poetry books and recordings. With practice you can read poetry aloud with the same ease that you waltz, play bridge, or tell a rose-breasted grosbeak from a towhee, and your rewards will be much more enduring.

POEMS
TO READ ALOUD

CONRAD AIKEN

1889–

All Lovely Things

All lovely things will have an ending,
All lovely things will fade and die,
And youth, that's now so bravely spending,
Will beg a penny by and by.

Fine ladies all are soon forgotten,
And goldenrod is dust when dead,
The sweetest flesh and flowers are rotten
And cobwebs tent the brightest head.

Come back, true love! Sweet youth, return!—
But time goes on, and will, unheeding,
Though hands will reach, and eyes will yearn,
And the wild days set true hearts bleeding.

Come back, true love! Sweet youth, remain!—
But goldenrod and daisies wither,
And over them blows autumn rain,
They pass, they pass, and know not whither.

Music I Heard with You

Music I heard with you was more than music,
And bread I broke with you was more than bread;
Now that I am without you, all is desolate;
All that was once so beautiful is dead.

Your hands once touched this table and this silver,
And I have seen your fingers hold this glass.
These things do not remember you, beloved—
And yet your touch upon them will not pass.

For it was in my heart you moved among them,
And blessed them with your hands and with your eyes;
And in my heart they will remember always—
They knew you once, O beautiful and wise!

ANONYMOUS

Sir Patrick Spence

The king sits in Dumferling town,
  Drinking his blood-red wine;
"Oh where will I get a good sailor
  To sail this ship of mine?"

Up and spake an eldern knight,
  Sat at the king's right knee:
"Sir Patrick Spence is the best sailor
  That sails upon the sea."

The king has written a broad letter,
  And signed it wi' his hand,
And sent it to Sir Patrick Spence,
  Was walking on the sand.

The first line that Sir Patrick read,
  A loud laugh laughed he;
The next line that Sir Patrick read,
  The tear blinded his ee.

"Oh who is this has done this deed,
  This ill deed done to me,
To send me out this time o' the year,
  To sail upon the sea!

"Make haste, make haste, my merry men all,
  Our good ship sails the morn!"
"Oh say not so, my master dear,
  For I fear a deadly storm.

"Late, late yestreen I saw the new moon
  Wi' the old moon in her arm,
And I fear, I fear, my dear master,
  That we will come to harm."

Oh our Scots nobles were right loath
  To wet their cork-heeled shoon;
But long ere a' the play were played,
  Their hats they swam aboon.

Oh long, long may their ladies sit
  Wi' their fans into their hand,
Or e'er they see Sir Patrick Spence
  Come sailing to the land.

Oh long, long may the ladies stand
  Wi' their gold combs in their hair,
Waiting for their own dear lords,
  For they'll see them na mair.

Half o'er, half o'er to Aberdour
  It's fifty fathom deep,
And there lies good Sir Patrick Spence
  Wi' the Scots lords at his feet.

ANONYMOUS

Edward, Edward

"Why does your brand so drop wi' blood,
                  Edward, Edward?
Why does your brand so drop wi' blood,
  And why so sad gang ye O?"
"Oh I have killed my hawk so good,
                  Mother, mother,
Oh I have killed my hawk so good,
  And I had no more but he O."

"Your hawk's blood was never so red,
                  Edward, Edward,
Your hawk's blood was never so red,
  My dear son, I tell thee O."
"Oh I have killed my red-roan steed,
                  Mother, mother,
Oh I have killed my red-roan steed,
  That erst was so fair and free O."

"Your steed was old, and ye have got more,
                  Edward, Edward,
Your steed was old, and ye have got more;

Some other dole ye dree O."
"Oh I have killed my father dear,
                    Mother, mother,
Oh I have killed my father dear,
    Alas, and woe is me O."

"And what penance will ye dree for that,
                    Edward, Edward?
And what penance will ye dree for that?
    My dear son, now tell me O."
"I'll set my feet in yonder boat,
                    Mother, mother,
I'll set my feet in yonder boat,
    And I'll fare over the sea O."

"And what will ye do wi' your towers and your hall,
                    Edward, Edward?
And what will ye do wi' your towers and your hall,
    That were so fair to see O?"
"I'll let them stand till they down fall,
                    Mother, mother,
I'll let them stand till they down fall,
    For here never more shall I be O."

"And what will ye leave to your bairns and your wife,
                    Edward, Edward?
And what will ye leave to your bairns and your wife,
    When ye gang over the sea O?"
"The world's room—let them beg through life,
                    Mother, mother,
The world's room—let them beg through life,
    For them never more will I see O."

"And what will ye leave to your own mother dear,
                    Edward, Edward?
And what will ye leave to your own mother dear?
    My dear son, now tell me O."
"The curse of hell from me shall ye bear,
                    Mother, mother,
The curse of hell from me shall ye bear,
    Such counsels ye gave to me O."

ANONYMOUS

Back and Side Go Bare

But if that I may have truly
    Good ale my belly full,
I shall look like one, by sweet Saint John,
    Were shorn against the wool.
Though I go bare, take you no care—
    I am nothing cold,
I stuff my skin so full within
    Of jolly good ale and old.
        Back and side go bare, go bare,
            Both hand and foot go cold;
        But belly, God send thee good ale enough,
            Whether it be new or old!

I cannot eat but little meat—
    My stomach is not good;
But sure I think that I could drink
    With him that weareth an hood.
Drink is my life; although my wife
    Sometime do chide and scold,
Yet spare I not to ply the pot
    Of jolly good ale and old.
        Back and side, etc.

I love no roast but a brown toast,
    Or a crab in the fire;
A little bread shall do me stead,
    Much bread I never desire.
Nor frost nor snow nor wind, I trow,
    Can hurt me if it wold,
I am so wrapped within and lapped
    With jolly good ale and old.
        Back and side, etc.

I care right nought, I take no thought
    For clothes to keep me warm;
Have I good drink, I surely think

Nothing can do me harm.
For truly than I fear no man,
   Be he never so bold,
When I am armed and throughly warmed
   With jolly good ale and old.
      Back and side, etc.

But now and than I curse and ban,
   They make their ale so small.
God give them care and evil to fare!
   They stry the malt and all.
Such peevish pew, I tell you true,
   Not for a crown of gold
There cometh one sip within my lip,
   Whether it be new or old.
      Back and side, etc.

Good ale and strong maketh me among
   Full jocund and full light,
That oft I sleep and take no keep
   From morning until night.
Then start I up and flee to the cup—
   The right way on I hold;
My thirst to staunch, I fill my paunch
   With jolly good ale and old.
      Back and side, etc.

And Kit my wife, that as her life
   Loveth well good ale to seek,
Full oft drinketh she, that ye may see
   The tears run down her cheek.
Then doth she troll to me the bowl,
   As a good maltworm shold,
And say, "Sweetheart, I have take my part
   Of jolly good ale and old."
      Back and side, etc.

They that do drink till they nod and wink,
   Even as good fellows should do,
They shall not miss to have the bliss
   That good ale hath brought them to.
And all poor souls that scour black bowls
   And them hath lustily trolled,
God save the lives of them and their wives,
   Whether they be young or old!
      Back and side, etc.

ANONYMOUS

Yet If His Majesty

Yet if his Majesty, our sovereign lord,
    Should of his own accord
    Friendly himself invite
And say, "I'll be your guest tomorrow night,"
How should we stir ourselves, call and command
All hands to work! "Let no man idle stand!

"Set me fine Spanish tables in the hall—
    See they be fitted all;
    Let there be room to eat,
And order taken that there want no meat.
See every sconce and candlestick made bright,
That without tapers they may give a light.

"Look to the presence: are the carpets spread
    The dais o'er the head,
    The cushions in the chairs,
And all the candles lighted on the stairs?
Perfume the chambers, and in any case
Let each man give attendance in his place!"

Thus if the king were coming would we do,
    And 'twere good reason, too;
    For 'tis a duteous thing
To show all honor to an earthly king,
And after all our travail and our cost,
So he be pleased, to think no labor lost.

But at the coming of the King of Heaven
    All's set at six and seven;
    We wallow in our sin;
Christ cannot find a chamber in the inn.
We entertain him always like a stranger,
And, as at first, still lodge him in the manger.

ANONYMOUS

The Bells of London

Gay go up, and gay go down,
To ring the bells of London town!

Bull's eyes and targets,
Say the bells of St. Marg'ret's.

Brickbats and tiles,
Say the bells of St. Giles'.

Ha'pence and farthings
Say the bells of St. Martin's.

Oranges and lemons,
Say the bells of St. Clement's.

Pancakes and fritters,
Say the bells of St. Peter's.

Two sticks and an apple,
Say the bells at Whitechapel.

Old Father Baldpate,
Say the slow bells at Aldgate.

Maids in white aprons,
Say the bells of St. Cath'rine's.

Pokers and tongs,
Say the bells at St. John's.

Kettles and pans,
Say the bells at St. Ann's.

You owe me ten shillings,
Say the bells at St. Helen's.

When will you pay me?
Say the bells at Old Bailey.

When I grow rich,
Say the bells at Shoreditch.

When will that be?
Say the bells at Stepney.

I am sure I don't know,
Says the great bell at Bow.

When I am old,
Say the bells at St. Paul's.

MATTHEW ARNOLD

1822–1888

Dover Beach

The sea is calm tonight,
The tide is full, the moon lies fair
Upon the straits—on the French coast the light
Gleams and is gone; the cliffs of England stand,
Glimmering and vast, out in the tranquil bay.
Come to the window; sweet is the night-air!
Only, from the long line of spray
Where the sea meets the moon-blanched land,
Listen! you hear the grating roar
Of pebbles which the waves draw back, and fling,
At their return, up the high strand,
Begin, and cease, and then again begin,
With tremulous cadence slow, and bring
The eternal note of sadness in.

Sophocles long ago
Heard it on the Aegean and it brought
Into his mind the turbid ebb and flow
Of human misery; we
Find also in the sound a thought,
Hearing it by this distant northern sea.

The sea of faith
Was once, too, at the full, and round earth's shore
Lay like the folds of a bright girdle furled.
But now I only hear

Its melancholy, long, withdrawing roar,
Retreating, to the breath
Of the night-wind, down the vast edges drear
And naked shingles of the world.

Ah love, let us be true
To one another! for the world, which seems
To lie before us like a land of dreams,
So various, so beautiful, so new,
Hath really neither joy, nor love, nor light,
Nor certitude, nor peace, nor help for pain;
And we are here as on a darkling plain
Swept with confused alarms of struggle and flight,
Where ignorant armies clash by night.

Requiescat

Strew on her roses, roses,
    And never a spray of yew!
In quiet she reposes;
    Ah would that I did too!

Her mirth the world required;
    She bathed it in smiles of glee.
But her heart was tired, tired,
    And now they let her be.

Her life was turning, turning,
    In mazes of heat and sound.
But for peace her soul was yearning,
    And now peace laps her round.

Her cabined, ample spirit,
    It fluttered and failed for breath.
Tonight it doth inherit
    The vasty hall of death.

The Last Word

Creep into thy narrow bed,
Creep, and let no more be said!

Vain thy onset! all stands fast.
Thou thyself must break at last.

Let the long contention cease!
Geese are swans, and swans are geese.
Let them have it how they will!
Thou art tired; best be still.

They out-talked thee, hissed thee, tore thee?
Better men fared thus before thee;
Fired their ringing shot and passed,
Hotly charged—and sank at last.

Charge once more, then, and be dumb!
Let the victors, when they come,
When the forts of folly fall,
Find thy body by the wall!

W. H. AUDEN

1907–

Musée des Beaux Arts

About suffering they were never wrong,
The Old Masters: how well they understood
Its human position; how it takes place
While someone else is eating or opening a window or just walking
      dully along;
How, when the aged are reverently, passionately waiting
For the miraculous birth, there always must be
Children who did not specially want it to happen, skating
On a pond at the edge of the wood:
They never forgot
That even the dreadful martyrdom must run its course
Anyhow in a corner, some untidy spot
Where the dogs go on with their doggy life and the torturer's horse
Scratches its innocent behind on a tree.

In Brueghel's *Icarus*, for instance: how everything turns away
Quite leisurely from the disaster; the ploughman may

Have heard the splash, the forsaken cry,
But for him it was not an important failure; the sun shone
As it had to on the white legs disappearing into the green
Water; and the expensive delicate ship that must have seen
Something amazing, a boy falling out of the sky,
Had somewhere to get to and sailed calmly on.

Something Is Bound to Happen

Doom is dark and deeper than any sea-dingle.
Upon what man it fall
In spring, day-wishing flowers appearing,
Avalanche sliding, white snow from rock-face,
That he should leave his house,
No cloud-soft hand can hold him, restraint by women;
But ever that man goes
Through place-keepers, through forest trees,
A stranger to strangers over undried sea,
Houses for fishes, suffocating water,
Or lonely on fell as chat,
By pot-holed becks
A bird stone-haunting, an unquiet bird.

There head falls forward, fatigued at evening,
And dreams of home,
Waving from window, spread of welcome,
Kissing of wife under single sheet;
But waking sees
Bird-flocks nameless to him, through doorway voices
Of new men making another love.

Save him from hostile capture,
From sudden tiger's spring at corner;
Protect his house,
His anxious house where days are counted;
From thunderbolt protect,
From gradual ruin spreading like a stain;
Converting number from vague to certain,
Bring joy, bring day of his returning,
Lucky with day approaching, with leaning dawn.

The Unknown Citizen

(To JS/o7/M/378
This Marble Monument
Is Erected by the State)

He was found by the Bureau of Statistics to be
One against whom there was no official complaint;
And all the reports on his conduct agree
That, in the modern sense of an old-fashioned word, he was a saint,
For in everything he did he served the Greater Community.
Except for the War, till the day he retired
He worked in a factory and never got fired,
But satisfied his employers, Fudge Motors Inc.
Yet he wasn't a scab or odd in his views,
For his Union reports that he paid his dues,
(Our report on his Union shows it was sound)
And our Social Psychology workers found
That he was popular with his mates and liked a drink.
The Press are convinced that he bought a paper every day
And that his reactions to advertisements were normal in every way.
Policies taken out in his name prove that he was fully insured,
And his Health-card shows he was once in hospital but left it cured.
Both Producers Research and High-Grade Living declare
He was fully sensible to the advantages of the Installment Plan
And had everything necessary to the Modern Man—
A phonograph, a radio, a car and a frigidaire.
Our researchers into Public Opinion are content
That he held the proper opinions for the time of year:
When there was peace, he was for peace; when there was war, he
    went.
He was married and added five children to the population,
Which our Eugenist says was the right number for a parent of his
    generation,
And our teachers report that he never interfered with their edu-
    cation.
Was he free? Was he happy? The question is absurd:
Had anything been wrong, we should certainly have heard.

Jumbled in the Common Box

Jumbled in the common box
Of their dark stupidity,

Orchid, swan, and Caesar lie;
Time that tires of everyone
Has corroded all the locks—
Thrown away the key for fun.

In its cleft the torrent mocks
Prophets who in days gone by
Made a profit on each cry,
Persona grata now with none;
And a jackass language shocks
Poets who can only pun.

Silence settles on the clocks;
Nursing mothers point a sly
Index finger at a sky,
Crimson with the setting sun;
In the valley of the fox
Gleams the barrel of a gun.

Once we could have made the docks,
Now it is too late to fly;
Once too often you and I
Did what we should not have done;
Round the rampant rugged rocks
Rude and ragged rascals run.

Now Through Night's Caressing Grip

Now through night's caressing grip
Earth and all her oceans slip,
Capes of China slide away
From her fingers into day,
And the Americas incline
Coasts toward her shadow line.
Now the ragged vagrants creep
Into crooked holes to sleep;
Just and unjust, worst and best,
Change their places as they rest;
Awkward lovers lie in fields
Where disdainful beauty yields;
While the splendid and the proud
Naked stand before the crowd,
And the losing gambler gains,
And the beggar entertains.

May sleep's healing power extend
Through these hours to each friend;
Unpursued by hostile force,
Traction engine, bull or horse,
Or revolting succubus;
Calmly till the morning break
Let them lie, then gently wake.

Over the Heather

Over the heather the wet wind blows,
I've lice in my tunic and a cold in my nose.

The rain comes pattering out of the sky;
I'm a Wall soldier, I don't know why.

The mist creeps over the hard grey stone;
My girl's in Tungria, I sleep alone.

Aulus goes hanging around her place;
I don't like his manners, I don't like his face.

Piso's a Christian, he worships a fish;
There'd be no kissing if he had his wish.

She gave me a ring but I diced it away;
I want my girl and I want my pay.

When I'm a veteran with only one eye
I shall do nothing but look at the sky.

STEPHEN VINCENT BENÉT

1898–1943

The Ballad of William Sycamore

(1790–1871)

My father, he was a mountaineer,
His fist was a knotty hammer;

He was quick on his feet as a running deer,
And he spoke with a Yankee stammer.

My mother, she was merry and brave,
And so she came to her labor,
With a tall green fir for her doctor grave
And a stream for her comforting neighbor.

And some are wrapped in the linen fine,
And some like a godling's scion;
But I was cradled on twigs of pine
In the skin of a mountain lion.

And some remember a white, starched lap
And a ewer with silver handles;
But I remember a coonskin cap
And the smell of bayberry candles,

The cabin logs, with the bark still rough,
And my mother, who laughed at trifles,
And the tall, lank visitors, brown as snuff,
With their long, straight squirrel-rifles.

I can hear them dance, like a foggy song,
Through the deepest one of my slumbers,
The fiddle squeaking the boots along,
And my father calling the numbers;

The quick feet shaking the puncheon floor,
And the fiddle squeaking and squealing,
Till the dried herbs rattled above the door
And the dust went up to the ceiling.

There are children lucky from dawn till dusk,
But never a child so lucky!
For I cut my teeth on "Money Musk"
In the Bloody Ground of Kentucky!

When I grew tall as the Indian corn,
My father had little to lend me,
But he gave me his great old powderhorn
And his woodsman's skill to befriend me.

With a leather shirt to cover my back,
And a redskin nose to unravel
Each forest sign, I carried my pack
As far as a scout could travel.

Till I lost my boyhood and found my wife,
A girl like a Salem clipper!
A woman straight as a hunting-knife
With eyes as bright as the Dipper!

We cleared our camp where the buffalo feed,
Unheard-of streams were our flagons;
And I sowed my sons like the apple-seed
On the trail of the Western wagons.

They were right, tight boys, never sulky or slow,
A fruitful, a goodly muster.
The eldest died at the Alamo;
The youngest fell with Custer.

The letter that told it burned my hand.
Yet we smiled and said, "So be it!"
But I could not live when they fenced the land,
For it broke my heart to see it.

I saddled a red, unbroken colt
And rode him into the day there;
And he threw me down like a thunderbolt
And rolled on me as I lay there.

The hunter's whistle hummed in my ear
As the city men tried to move me,
And I died in my boots like a pioneer
With the whole wide sky above me.

Now I lie in the heart of the fat, black soil,
Like the seed of a prairie-thistle;
It has washed my bones with honey and oil
And picked them clean as a whistle.

And my youth returns, like the rains of Spring,
And my sons, like the wild-geese flying;
And I lie and hear the meadowlark sing,
And I have much content in my dying.

Go play with the towns you have built of blocks,
The towns where you would have bound me!
I sleep in the earth like a tired fox,
And my buffalo have found me.

WILLIAM BLAKE

1757–1827

Mad Song

The wild winds weep,
  And the night is a-cold;
Come hither, Sleep,
  And my griefs unfold:
But lo! the morning peeps
Over the eastern steeps,
And the rustling beds of dawn
The earth do scorn.

Lo! to the vault
  Of pavéd heaven,
With sorrow fraught,
  My notes are driven:
They strike the ear of night,
Make weep the eyes of day;
They make mad the roaring winds,
And with tempests play.

Like a fiend in a cloud,
  With howling woe
After night I do crowd,
  And with night will go;
I turn my back to the east
From whence comforts have increased;
For light doth seize my brain
With frantic pain.

The Tiger

Tiger! tiger! burning bright
In the forests of the night,
What immortal hand or eye
Could frame thy fearful symmetry?

In what distant deeps or skies
Burned the fire of thine eyes?
On what wings dare he aspire?
What the hand dare seize the fire?

And what shoulder, and what art,
Could twist the sinews of thy heart?
And when thy heart began to beat,
What dread hand? and what dread feet?

What the hammer? what the chain?
In what furnace was thy brain?
What the anvil? what dread grasp
Dare its deadly terrors clasp?

When the stars threw down their spears
And watered heaven with their tears,
Did he smile his work to see?
Did he who made the Lamb make thee?

Tiger! tiger! burning bright
In the forests of the night,
What immortal hand or eye
Dare frame thy fearful symmetry?

And Did Those Feet in Ancient Time

And did those feet in ancient time
    Walk upon England's mountains green?
And was the holy Lamb of God
    On England's pleasant pastures seen?

And did the Countenance Divine
    Shine forth upon our clouded hills?
And was Jerusalem builded here
    Among these dark Satanic mills?

Bring me my bow of burning gold!
    Bring me my arrows of desire!
Bring me my spear! O clouds, unfold!
    Bring me my chariot of fire!

I will not cease from mental fight,
    Nor shall my sword sleep in my hand,
Till we have built Jerusalem
    In England's green and pleasant land.

RUPERT BROOKE
1887–1915

Heaven

Fish (fly-replete, in depth of June,
Dawdling away their wat'ry noon)
Ponder deep wisdom, dark or clear,
Each secret fishy hope or fear.
Fish say, they have their Stream and Pond;
But is there anything Beyond?
This life cannot be All, they swear,
For how unpleasant, if it were!
One may not doubt that, somehow, Good
Shall come of Water and of Mud;
And, sure, the reverent eye must see
A purpose in Liquidity.
We darkly know, by Faith we cry,
The future is not Wholly Dry.
Mud unto mud—Death eddies near—
Not here the appointed End, not here!
But somewhere, beyond Space and Time,
Is wetter water, slimier slime!
And there (they trust) there swimmeth One
Who swam ere rivers were begun,
Immense, of fishy form and mind,
Squamous, omnipotent, and kind;
And under that Almighty Fin,
The littlest fish may enter in.
Oh never fly conceals a hook,
Fish say, in the Eternal Brook,
But more than mundane weeds are there,
And mud, celestially fair;
Fat caterpillars drift around,
And paradisal grubs are found;
Unfading moths, immortal flies,
And the worm that never dies.
And in that Heaven of all their wish,
There shall be no more land, say fish.

Oh Death Will Find Me

Oh death will find me, long before I tire
   Of watching you; and swing me suddenly
Into the shade and loneliness and mire
   Of the last land! There, waiting patiently,

One day, I think, I'll feel a cool wind blowing,
   See a slow light across the Stygian tide,
And hear the Dead about me stir, unknowing,
   And tremble. And I shall know that you have died,

And watch you, a broad-browed and smiling dream,
   Pass, light as ever, through the lightless host,
Quietly ponder, start, and sway, and gleam—
   Most individual and bewildering ghost!—

And turn, and toss your brown delightful head
Amusedly, among the ancient Dead.

The Soldier

If I should die, think only this of me:
   That there's some corner of a foreign field
That is forever England. There should be
   In that rich earth a richer dust concealed;
A dust whom England bore, shaped, made aware,
   Gave, once, her flowers to love, her ways to roam,
A body of England's, breathing English air,
   Washed by the rivers, blest by suns of home.

And think, this heart, all evil shed away,
   A pulse in the eternal mind, no less
      Gives somewhere back the thoughts by England given;
Her sights and sounds; dreams happy as her day;
   And laughter, learnt of friends; and gentleness,
      In hearts at peace, under an English heaven.

The Old Vicarage, Grantchester
(*Café des Westens, Berlin, May 1912*)

Just now the lilac is in bloom,
All before my little room;
And in my flower-beds, I think,
Smile the carnation and the pink;
And down the borders, well I know,
The poppy and the pansy blow . . .
Oh there the chestnuts, summer through,
Beside the river make for you
A tunnel of green gloom, and sleep
Deeply above; and green and deep
The stream mysterious glides beneath,
Green as a dream and deep as death.
—Oh damn! I know it! and I know
How the May fields all golden show,
And when the day is young and sweet,
Gild gloriously the bare feet
That run to bathe . . .
                  Du lieber Gott!

Here am I, sweating, sick, and hot,
And there the shadowed waters fresh
Lean up to embrace the naked flesh.
Temperamentvoll German Jews
Drink beer around—and *there* the dews
Are soft beneath a morn of gold.
Here tulips bloom as they are told;
Unkempt about those hedges blows
An English unofficial rose;
And there the unregulated sun
Slopes down to rest when day is done,
And wakes a vague unpunctual star,
A slippered Hesper; and there are
Meads towards Haslingfield and Coton
Where *das Betreten's* not *verboten.*

Would I were, would I were
In Grantchester, in Grantchester!—
Some, it may be, can get in touch
With Nature there, or Earth, or such.

60

And clever modern men have seen
A Faun a-peeping through the green,
And felt the Classics were not dead,
To glimpse a Naiad's reedy head,
Or hear the Goat-foot piping low . . .
But these are things I do not know.
I only know that you may lie
Day long and watch the Cambridge sky,
And flower-lulled in sleepy grass,
Hear the cool lapse of hours pass,
Until the centuries blend and blur
In Grantchester, in Grantchester . . .
Still in the dawnlit waters cool
His ghostly Lordship swims his pool,
And tries the strokes, essays the tricks,
Long learnt on Hellespont, or Styx.
Dan Chaucer hears his river still
Chatter beneath a phantom mill.
Tennyson notes with studious eye
How Cambridge waters hurry by . . .
And in that garden, black and white,
Creep whispers through the grass all night;
And spectral dance, before the dawn,
A hundred Vicars down the lawn;
Curates, long dust, will come and go
On lissom, clerical, printless toe;
And oft between the boughs is seen
The sly shade of a Rural Dean . . .
Till, at a shiver in the skies,
Vanishing with Satanic cries,
The prim ecclesiastic rout
Leaves but a startled sleeper-out,
Grey heavens, a first bird's drowsy calls,
The falling house that never falls.

God! I will pack, and take a train,
And get me to England once again!
For England's the one land, I know,
Where men with Splendid Hearts may go;
And Cambridgeshire, of all England,
The shire for Men who Understand;
And of *that* district I prefer
The lovely hamlet Grantchester.
For Cambridge people rarely smile,

Being urban, squat, and packed with guile;
And Royston men in the far South
Are black and fierce and strange of mouth;
At Over they fling oaths at one,
And worse than oaths at Trumpington,
And Ditton girls are mean and dirty,
And there's none in Harston under thirty,
And folks in Shelford and those parts
Have twisted lips and twisted hearts,
And Barton men make Cockney rimes,
And Coton's full of nameless crimes,
And things are done you'd not believe
At Madingley on Christmas Eve.
Strong men have run for miles and miles,
When one from Cherry Hinton smiles;
Strong men have blanched, and shot their wives,
Rather than send them to St. Ives;
Strong men have cried like babes, bydam,
To hear what happened at Babraham.
But Grantchester! ah Grantchester!
There's peace and holy quiet there,
Great clouds along pacific skies,
And men and women with straight eyes,
Lithe children lovelier than a dream,
A bosky wood, a slumbrous stream,
And little kindly winds that creep
Round twilight corners, half asleep.
In Grantchester their skins are white;
They bathe by day, they bathe by night;
The women there do all they ought;
The men observe the Rules of Thought.
They love the Good; they worship Truth;
They laugh uproariously in youth;
(And when they get to feeling old,
They up and shoot themselves, I'm told) . . .

Ah God! to see the branches stir
Across the moon at Grantchester!
To smell the thrilling-sweet and rotten
Unforgettable, unforgotten
River smell, and hear the breeze
Sobbing in the little trees.
Say, do the elm-clumps greatly stand
Still guardians of that holy land?

The chestnuts shade, in reverent dream,
The yet unacademic stream?
Is dawn a secret shy and cold
Anadyomene, silver-gold?
And sunset still a golden sea
From Haslingfield to Madingley?
And after, ere the night is born,
Do hares come out about the corn?
Oh is the water sweet and cool,
Gentle and brown, above the pool?
And laughs the immortal river still
Under the mill, under the mill?
Say, is there Beauty yet to find?
And Certainty? and Quiet Kind?
Deep meadows yet, for to forget
The lies, and truths, and pain? . . . oh yet
Stands the Church clock at ten to three?
And is there honey still for tea?

ELIZABETH BARRETT BROWNING

1806–1861

How Do I Love Thee?

How do I love thee? Let me count the ways.
I love thee to the depth and breadth and height
My soul can reach, when feeling out of sight
For the ends of being and ideal grace.
I love thee to the level of every day's
Most quiet need, by sun and candlelight.
I love thee freely, as men strive for right;
I love thee purely, as men turn from praise.
I love thee with the passion put to use
In my old griefs, and with my childhood's faith.
I love thee with a love I seemed to lose
With my lost saints—I love thee with the breath,
Smiles, tears of all my life!—and, if God choose,
I shall but love thee better after death.

ROBERT BROWNING

1812–1890

Meeting at Night

The grey sea and the long black land;
And the yellow half-moon large and low;
And the startled little waves that leap
In fiery ringlets from their sleep,
As I gain the cove with pushing prow,
And quench its speed i' the slushy sand.

Then a mile of warm sea-scented beach;
Three fields to cross till a farm appears;
A tap at the pane, the quick sharp scratch
And blue spurt of a lighted match,
And a voice less loud, through its joys and fears,
Than the two hearts beating each to each!

Home Thoughts from Abroad

Oh to be in England
Now that April's there,
And whoever wakes in England
Sees, some morning, unaware,
That the lowest boughs and the brushwood sheaf
Round the elm-tree bole are in tiny leaf,
While the chaffinch sings on the orchard bough
In England—now!

And after April, when May follows,
And the whitethroat builds, and all the swallows!
Hark, where my blossomed pear-tree in the hedge
Leans to the field and scatters on the clover
Blossoms and dewdrops—at the bent spray's edge—
That's the wise thrush; he sings each song twice over,
Lest you should think he never could recapture
The first fine careless rapture!

And though the fields look rough with hoary dew,
All will be gay when noontide wakes anew
The buttercups, the little children's dower—
Far brighter than this gaudy melon-flower!

Up at a Villa—Down in the City
As Distinguished by an Italian Person of Quality

Had I but plenty of money, money enough and to spare,
The house for me, no doubt, were a house in the city-square;
Ah such a life, such a life, as one leads at the window there!

Something to see, by Bacchus, something to hear, at least!
There the whole day long one's life is a perfect feast;
While up at a villa one lives, I maintain it, no more than a beast.
Well now, look at our villa! stuck like the horn of a bull
Just on a mountain-edge as bare as the creature's skull,
Save a mere shag of a bush with hardly a leaf to pull!
—I scratch my own, sometimes, to see if the hair's turned wool!

But the city, oh the city—the square with the houses! Why?
They are stone-faced, white as a curd, there's something to take the
        eye!
Houses in four straight lines, not a single front awry;
You watch who crosses and gossips, who saunters, who hurries by;
Green blinds, as a matter of course, to draw when the sun gets high;
And the shops with fanciful signs which are painted properly.

What of a villa? Though winter be over in March by rights,
'Tis May perhaps ere the snow shall have withered well off the
        heights:
You've the brown ploughed land before, where the oxen steam and
        wheeze,
And the hills over-smoked behind by the faint grey olive-trees.

Is it better in May, I ask you? You've summer all at once;
In a day he leaps complete, with a few strong April suns.
'Mid the sharp short emerald wheat, scarce risen three fingers well,
The wild tulip, at end of its tube, blows out its great red bell
Like a thin clear bubble of blood, for the children to pick and sell.

Is it ever hot in the square? There's a fountain to spout and splash!
In the shade it sings and springs; in the shine such foam-bows flash

On the horses with curling fish-tails, that prance and paddle and
    pash
Round the lady atop in her conch—fifty gazers do not abash,
Though all that she wears is some weeds round her waist in a sort of
    sash.

All the year long at the villa, nothing to see though you linger,
Except yon cypress that points like death's lean lifted forefinger!
Some think fireflies pretty, when they mix 'i the corn and mingle,
Or thrid the stinking hemp till the stalks of it seem a-tingle,
Late August or early September, the stunning cicala is shrill,
And the bees keep their tiresome whine round the resinous firs on
    the hill.
Enough of the seasons! I spare you the months of the fever and
    chill.

Ere you open your eyes in the city, the blesséd church-bells begin;
No sooner the bells leave off than the diligence rattles in:
You get the pick of the news, and it costs you never a pin.
By and by there's the traveling doctor gives pills, lets blood, draws
    teeth;
Or the Pulcinello-trumpet breaks up the market beneath.
At the post-office such a scene-picture—the new play, piping hot!
And a notice how, only this morning, three liberal thieves were shot.
Above it, behold the Archbishop's most fatherly of rebukes,
And beneath, with his crown and his lion, some little new law of
    the Duke's!
Or a sonnet with flowery marge, to the Reverend Don So-an-so,
Who is Dante, Boccaccio, Petrarca, Saint Jerome, and Cicero,
"And moreover," (the sonnet goes riming), "the skirts of Saint Paul
    has reached,
Having preached us those six Lent-lectures more unctuous than ever
    he preached."
Noon strikes—here sweeps the procession! our Lady borne smiling
    and smart
With a pink gauze gown all spangles, and seven swords stuck in her
    heart!
Bang-whang-whang goes the drum, *tootle-te-tootle* the fife;
No keeping one's haunches still: it's the greatest pleasure in life.

But bless you, it's dear—it's dear! fowls, wine, at double the rate.
They have clapped a new tax upon salt, and what oil pays passing
    the gate
It's a horror to think of. And so, the villa for me, not the city.
Beggars can scarcely be choosers: but still—ah the pity, the pity!

Look, two and two go the priests, then the monks with cowls and
    sandals,
And the penitents dressed in white shirts, a-holding the yellow
    candles;
One, he carries a flag up straight, and another a cross with handles,
And the Duke's guard brings up the rear, for the better prevention
    of scandals:
Bang-whang-whang goes the drum, *tootle-te-tootle* the fife.
Oh a day in the city-square, there is no such pleasure in life!

The Patriot

It was roses, roses, all the way,
    With myrtle mixed in my path like mad:
The house-roofs seemed to heave and sway,
    The church-spires flamed, such flags they had,
A year ago on this very day.

The air broke into a mist with bells,
    The old walls rocked with the crowd and cries.
Had I said, "Good folk, mere noise repels—
    But give me your sun from yonder skies!"
They had answered, "And afterwards, what else?"

Alack, it was I who leaped at the sun
    To give it my loving friends to keep!
Naught man could do, have I left undone;
    And you see my harvest, what I reap
This very day, now a year is run.

There's nobody on the housetops now—
    Just a palsied few at the windows set;
For the best of the sight is, all allow,
    At the Shambles' Gate—or, better yet,
By the very scaffold's foot, I trow.

I go in the rain, and more than needs,
    A rope cuts both my wrists behind;
And I think, by the feel, my forehead bleeds,
    For they fling, whoever has a mind,
Stones at me for my year's misdeeds.

Thus I entered, and thus I go!
    In triumphs people have dropped down dead.

"Paid by the world, what dost thou owe
   Me?" God might question. Now instead,
'Tis God shall repay: I am safer so.

Prospice

Fear death?—to feel the fog in my throat,
   The mist in my face,
When the snows begin, and the blasts denote
   I am nearing the place,
The power of the night, the press of the storm,
   The post of the foe;
Where he stands, the Arch Fear in a visible form,
   Yet the strong man must go:
For the journey is done, and the summit attained,
   And the barriers fall,
Though a battle's to fight ere the guerdon be gained,
   The reward of it all.
I was ever a fighter, so—one fight more,
   The best and the last!
I would hate that death bandaged my eyes, and forebore,
   And bade me creep past.
No! let me taste the whole of it, fare like my peers,
   The heroes of old,
Bear the brunt, in a minute pay glad life's arrears
   Of pain, darkness, and cold.
For sudden the worst turns the best to the brave,
   The black minute's at end,
And the elements' rage, the fiend-voices that rave,
   Shall dwindle, shall blend,
Shall change, shall become first a peace out of pain,
   Then a light, then thy breast,
O thou soul of my soul! I shall clasp thee again,
   And with God be the rest!

GEORGE GORDON, LORD BYRON
1788–1824

Stanzas for Music

There be none of beauty's daughters
   With a magic like thee;
And like music on the waters
   Is thy sweet voice to me:
When, as if its sound were causing
The charmèd ocean's pausing,
The waves lie still and gleaming,
And the lulled winds seem dreaming.

And the midnight moon is weaving
   Her bright chain o'er the deep;
Whose breast is gently heaving,
   As an infant's asleep:
So the spirit bows before thee,
To listen and adore thee;
With a full but soft emotion,
Like the swell of summer's ocean.

So We'll Go No More A-Roving

So we'll go no more a-roving
   So late into the night,
Though the heart be still as loving,
   And the moon be still as bright.

For the sword outwears its sheath,
   And the soul wears out the breast,
And the heart must pause to breathe,
   And love itself have rest.

Though the night was made for loving,
   And the day returns too soon,
Yet we'll go no more a-roving
   By the light of the moon.

69

THOMAS CAMPION

1567–1620

Thrice Toss These Oaken Ashes

Thrice toss these oaken ashes in the air,
Thrice sit thou mute in this enchanted chair,
Then thrice three times tie up this true love's knot,
And murmur soft, She will, or she will not.

Go burn these pois'nous weeds in yon blue fire,
These screech-owl's feathers and this prickling brier,
This cypress gathered at a dead man's grave,
That all thy fears and cares an end may have.

Then come, you fairies, dance with me a round;
Melt her hard heart with your melodious sound.
In vain are all the charms I can devise:
She hath an art to break them with her eyes.

When Thou Must Home

When thou must home to shades of underground,
    And there arrived, a new admiréd guest,
The beauteous spirits do engirt thee round,
    White Iope, blithe Helen, and the rest,
To hear the stories of thy finished love
From that smooth tongue whose music hell can move;

Then wilt thou speak of banqueting delights,
    Of masques and revels which sweet youth did make,
Of tourneys and great challenges of knights,
    And all these triumphs for thy beauty's sake;
When thou hast told these honors done to thee,
Then tell, oh tell, how thou didst murder me.

(after Propertius)

My Sweetest Lesbia

My sweetest Lesbia, let us live and love,
And though the sager sort our deeds reprove,
Let us not weigh them. Heaven's great lamps do dive
Into their west and straight again revive,
But soon as once set is our little light,
Then must we sleep one ever-during night.

If all would lead their lives in love like me,
Then bloody swords and armor should not be;
No drum nor trumpet peaceful sleeps should move,
Unless alarm came from the camp of love.
But fools do live and waste their little light,
And seek with pain their ever-during night.

When timely death my life and fortune ends,
Let not my hearse be vexed with mourning friends,
But let all lovers, rich in triumph, come
And with sweet pastimes grace my happy tomb;
And Lesbia, close up thou my little light,
And crown with love my ever-during night.

(after Catullus)

Now Winter Nights Enlarge

Now winter nights enlarge
   The number of their hours,
And clouds their storms discharge
   Upon the airy towers.
Let now the chimneys blaze,
   And cups o'erflow with wine;
Let well-tuned words amaze
   With harmony divine.
Now yellow waxen lights
   Shall wait on honey love;
While youthful revels, masques, and courtly sights,
   Sleep's leaden spells remove.

This time doth well dispense
   With lovers' long discourse;
Much speech hath some defence,
   Though beauty no remorse.

All do not all things well:
   Some measures comely tread,
Some knotted riddles tell,
   Some poems smoothly read.
The summer hath his joys,
   And winter his delights;
Though love and all his pleasures are but toys,
   They shorten tedious nights.

The Man of Life Upright

The man of life upright,
   Whose guiltless heart is free
From all dishonest deeds,
   Or thought of vanity;

The man whose silent days
   In harmless joys are spent,
Whom hopes cannot delude,
   Nor sorrow discontent;

That man needs neither towers
   Nor armor for defence,
Nor secret vaults to fly
   From thunder's violence.

He only can behold
   With unaffrighted eyes
The horrors of the deep
   And terrors of the skies.

Thus, scorning all the cares
   That fate or fortune brings,
He makes the heaven his book,
   His wisdom heavenly things,

Good thoughts his only friends,
   His wealth a well-spent age,
The earth his sober inn
   And quiet pilgrimage.

(after Horace)

THOMAS CAREW

1598?–1639?

Ask Me No More

Ask me no more where Jove bestows,
When June is past, the fading rose;
For in your beauty's orient deep
These flowers, as in their causes, sleep.

Ask me no more whither do stray
The golden atoms of the day;
For in pure love heaven did prepare
Those powders to enrich your hair.

Ask me no more whither doth haste
The nightingale when May is past;
For in your sweet dividing throat
She winters, and keeps warm her note.

Ask me no more where those stars light
That downwards fall in dead of night;
For in your eyes they sit, and there
Fixed become as in their sphere.

Ask me no more if east or west
The phœnix builds her spicy nest;
For unto you at last she flies,
And in your fragrant bosom dies.

LEWIS CARROLL

1832–1898

Father William

"You are old, Father William," the young man said,
    "And your hair has become very white;

And yet you incessantly stand on your head—
    Do you think, at your age, it is right?"

"In my youth," Father William replied to his son,
    "I feared it might injure the brain;
But now that I'm perfectly sure I have none,
    Why, I do it again and again."

"You are old," said the youth, "as I mentioned before,
    And have grown most uncommonly fat;
Yet you turned a back-somersault in at the door—
    Pray, what is the reason of that?"

"In my youth," said the sage, as he shook his grey locks,
    "I kept all my limbs very supple
By the use of this ointment—one shilling the box—
    Allow me to sell you a couple?"

"You are old," said the youth, "and your jaws are too weak
    For anything tougher than suet;
Yet you finished the goose, with the bones and the beak—
    Pray, how did you manage to do it?"

"In my youth," said his father, "I took to the law,
    And argued each case with my wife;
And the muscular strength which it gave to my jaw
    Has lasted the rest of my life."

"You are old," said the youth, "one would hardly suppose
    That your eye was as steady as ever;
Yet you balanced an eel on the end of your nose—
    What made you so awfully clever?"

"I have answered three questions, and that is enough,"
    Said his father; "don't give yourself airs!
Do you think I can listen all day to such stuff?
    Be off, or I'll kick you downstairs."

Jabberwocky

'Twas brillig, and the slithy toves
    Did gyre and gimble in the wabe,
All mimsy were the borogoves,
    And the mome raths outgrabe.

"Beware the Jabberwock, my son!
  The jaws that bite, the claws that catch!
Beware the Jubjub bird, and shun
  The frumious Bandersnatch!"

He took his vorpal sword in hand:
  Long time the manxome foe he sought—
So rested he by the Tumtum tree,
  And stood awhile in thought.

And as in uffish thought he stood,
  The Jabberwock, with eyes of flame,
Came whiffling through the tulgey wood,
  And burbled as it came!

One, two! One, two! And through and through
  The vorpal blade went snicker-snack!
He left it dead, and with its head
  He went galumphing back.

"And hast thou slain the Jabberwock?
  Come to my arms, my beamish boy!
O frabjous day! Callooh! Callay!"
  He chortled in his joy.

'Twas brillig, and the slithy toves
  Did gyre and gimble in the wabe;
All mimsy were the borogoves,
  And the mome raths outgrabe.

The Walrus and the Carpenter

The sun was shining on the sea,
  Shining with all his might;
He did his very best to make
  The billows smooth and bright—
And this was odd, because it was
  The middle of the night.

The moon was shining sulkily,
  Because she thought the sun
Had got no business to be there
  After the day was done—
"It's very rude of him," she said,
  "To come and spoil the fun!"

The sea was wet as wet could be,
　　The sands were dry as dry.
You could not see a cloud, because
　　No cloud was in the sky;
No birds were flying overhead—
　　There were no birds to fly.

The Walrus and the Carpenter
　　Were walking close at hand;
They wept like anything to see
　　Such quantities of sand:
"If this were only cleared away,"
　　They said, "it would be grand!"

"If seven maids with seven mops
　　Swept it for half a year,
Do you suppose," the Walrus said,
　　"That they could get it clear?"
"I doubt it," said the Carpenter,
　　And shed a bitter tear.

"O Oysters, come and walk with us!"
　　The Walrus did beseech.
"A pleasant walk, a pleasant talk,
　　Along the briny beach;
We cannot do with more than four,
　　To give a hand to each."

The eldest Oyster looked at him,
　　But never a word he said;
The eldest Oyster winked his eye,
　　And shook his heavy head—
Meaning to say he did not choose
　　To leave the oyster-bed.

But four young Oysters hurried up,
　　All eager for the treat;
Their coats were brushed, their faces washed,
　　Their shoes were clean and neat—
And this was odd, because, you know,
　　They hadn't any feet.

Four other Oysters followed them,
　　And yet another four;
And thick and fast they came at last,

And more, and more, and more—
All hopping through the frothy waves,
  And scrambling to the shore.

The Walrus and the Carpenter
  Walked on a mile or so,
And then they rested on a rock
  Conveniently low:
And all the little Oysters stood
  And waited in a row.

"The time has come," the Walrus said,
  "To talk of many things:
Of shoes—and ships—and sealing-wax—
  Of cabbages—and kings—
And why the sea is boiling hot—
  And whether pigs have wings."

"But wait a bit," the Oysters cried,
  "Before we have our chat;
For some of us are out of breath,
  And all of us are fat!"
"No hurry!" said the Carpenter.
  They thanked him much for that.

"A loaf of bread," the Walrus said,
  "Is what we chiefly need;
Pepper and vinegar besides
  Are very good indeed—
Now, if you're ready, Oysters dear,
  We can begin to feed."

"But not on us!" the Oysters cried,
  Turning a little blue.
"After such kindness that would be
  A dismal thing to do!"
"The night is fine," the Walrus said.
  "Do you admire the view?

"It was so kind of you to come!
  And you are very nice!"
The Carpenter said nothing but:
  "Cut us another slice.
I wish you were not quite so deaf—
  I've had to ask you twice!"

"It seems a shame," the Walrus said,
  "To play them such a trick,
After we've brought them out so far,
  And made them trot so quick!"
The Carpenter said nothing but,
  "The butter's spread too thick!"

"I weep for you," the Walrus said;
  "I deeply sympathize."
With sobs and tears he sorted out
  Those of the largest size,
Holding his pocket-handkerchief
  Before his streaming eyes.

"O Oysters," said the Carpenter,
  "You've had a pleasant run!
Shall we be trotting home again?"
  But answer came there none—
And this was scarcely odd, because
  They'd eaten every one.

CHARLES EDWARD CARRYL

1841–1920

Robinson Crusoe's Story

The night was thick and hazy
  When the "Piccadilly Daisy"
Carried down the crew and captain in the sea;
  And I think the water drowned 'em;
  For they never, never found 'em.
And I know they didn't come ashore with me.

Oh 'twas very sad and lonely
  When I found myself the only
Population on this cultivated shore;
  But I've made a little tavern
  In a rocky little cavern
And I sit and watch for people at the door.

I spent no time in looking
For a girl to do my cooking,
As I'm quite a clever hand at making stews;
But I had that fellow Friday,
Just to keep the tavern tidy,
And to put a Sunday polish on my shoes.

I have a little garden
That I'm cultivating lard in,
As the things I eat are rather tough and dry;
For I live on toasted lizards,
Prickly pears, and parrot gizzards,
And I'm really very fond of beetle-pie.

The clothes I had were furry,
And it made me fret and worry
When I found the moths were eating off the hair;
And I had to scrape and sand 'em,
And I boiled 'em and I tanned 'em,
Till I got the fine morocco suit I wear.

I sometimes seek diversion
In a family excursion
With the few domestic animals you see;
And we take along a carrot
As refreshment for the parrot,
And a little can of jungleberry tea.

Then we gather as we travel,
Bits of moss and dirty gravel,
And we chip off little specimens of stone;
And we carry home as prizes
Funny bugs, of handy sizes,
Just to give the day a scientific tone.

If the roads are wet and muddy,
We remain at home and study—
For the goat is very clever at a sum—
And the dog, instead of fighting,
Studies ornamental writing,
While the cat is taking lessons on the drum.

We retire at eleven,
And we rise again at seven;
And I wish to call attention, as I close,
To the fact that all the scholars
Are correct about their collars,
And particular in turning out their toes.

GEOFFREY CHAUCER

1340?–1400

Patient Griselda

Griselda's dead, and so's her patience,
And both lie buried in a Lombard dale;
And thus I cry in open audience—
No wedded man should recklessly assail
His wife's patience in hope to find
Griselda's, for certainly he will fail.

O noble wives, full of high prudence,
Let not humility your sharp tongues nail,
Nor let a clerk misread your diffidence
And write of you so marvelous a tale
As of Griselda, patient, meek, and kind,
Lest a monster swallow you in its entrail.

Follow Echo, that tolerates no silence,
But ever answers with a counter hail;
Be not befuddled by your innocence,
But firmly make your tyranny prevail.
Imprint full well this lesson in your mind
For common profit, since it may avail.

You super-wives, stand up to your defence,
Since you're as strong as a camel or a whale;
Nor suffer men to do the least offence.
And puny wives, in struggle weak and frail,
Be fierce as Indian tiger toward mankind,
And clatter like a windmill at every male;

Nor dread them not, nor do them reverence,
For though your husband arméd be in mail,
The arrows of your crabbéd eloquence
Shall pierce his breast and headpiece, without fail.
Take this advice: use jealousy to bind,
And you shall make him cower as does a quail.

If you are fair, wherever crowds are dense
Show off your clothes and boldly your charms unveil;
If you are homely, be lavish of expense;
To win admiration spare no travail;
And light as linden leaf be unconfined—
And let him mope, and wring his hands, and wail.

G. K. CHESTERTON
1874–1936

Lepanto

White founts falling in the courts of the sun,
And the Soldan of Byzantium is smiling as they run;
There is laughter like the fountains in that face of all men feared,
It stirs the forest darkness, the darkness of his beard,
It curls the blood-red crescent, the crescent of his lips,
For the inmost sea of all the earth is shaken with his ships.
They have dared the white republics up the capes of Italy,
They have dashed the Adriatic round the Lion of the Sea,
And the Pope has cast his arms abroad for agony and loss,
And called the kings of Christendom for swords about the Cross.
The cold queen of England is looking in the glass;
The shadow of the Valois is yawning at the Mass;
From evening isles fantastical rings faint the Spanish gun,
And the Lord upon the Golden Horn is laughing in the sun.

Dim drums throbbing, in the hills half heard,
Where only on a nameless throne a crownless prince has stirred,
Where, risen from a doubtful seat and half-attainted stall,
The last knight of Europe takes weapons from the wall,
The last and lingering troubadour to whom the bird has sung,
That once went singing southward when all the world was young.
In that enormous silence, tiny and unafraid,
Comes up along a winding road the noise of the crusade.
Strong gongs groaning as the guns boom far,
Don John of Austria is going to the war,
Stiff flags straining in the night-blasts cold

In the gloom black-purple, in the glint old-gold,
Torchlight crimson on the copper kettle-drums,
Then the tuckets, then the trumpets, then the cannon, and he
    comes.
Don John laughing in the brave beard curled,
Spurning of his stirrups like the thrones of all the world,
Holding his head up for a flag of all the free.
Love-light of Spain—hurrah!
Death-light of Africa!
Don John of Austria
Is riding to the sea.

Mahound is in his paradise above the evening star,
(*Don John of Austria is going to the war.*)
He moves a mighty turban on the timeless houri's knees,
His turban that is woven of the sunset and the seas.
He shakes the peacock gardens as he rises from his ease,
And he strides among the tree-tops and is taller than the trees,
And his voice through all the garden is a thunder sent to bring
Black Azrael and Ariel and Ammon on the wing.
Giants and the genii,
Multiplex of wing and eye,
Whose strong obedience broke the sky
When Solomon was king.

They rush in red and purple from the red clouds of the morn,
From temples where the yellow gods shut up their eyes in scorn;
They rise in green robes roaring from the green hells of the sea
Where fallen skies and evil hues and eyeless creatures be;
On them the sea-valves cluster and the grey sea-forests curl,
Splashed with a splendid sickness, the sickness of the pearl;
They swell in sapphire smoke out of the blue cracks of the ground—
They gather and they wonder and give worship to Mahound.
And he saith, "Break up the mountains where the hermit-folk may
    hide,
And sift the red and silver sands lest bone of saint abide,
And chase the Giaours flying night and day, not giving rest,
For that which was our trouble comes again out of the west.
We have set the seal of Solomon on all things under sun,
Of knowledge and of sorrow and endurance of things done,
But a noise is in the mountains, in the mountains, and I know
The voice that shook our palaces—four hundred years ago:
It is he that saith not "Kismet"; it is he that knows not Fate;
It is Richard, it is Raymond, it is Godfrey in the gate!
It is he whose loss is laughter when he counts the wager worth,
Put down your feet upon him, that our peace be on the earth."

For he heard drums groaning and he heard guns jar,
(*Don John of Austria is going to the war.*)
Sudden and still—hurrah!
Bolt from Iberia!
Don John of Austria
Is gone by Alcalar.

St. Michael's on his mountain in the sea-roads of the north
(*Don John of Austria is girt and going forth.*)
Where the grey seas glitter and the sharp tides shift.
And the sea folk labor and the red sails lift.
He shakes his lance of iron and he claps his wings of stone;
The noise is gone through Normandy; the noise is gone alone;
The North is full of tangled things and texts and aching eyes
And dead is all the innocence of anger and surprise,
And Christian killeth Christian in a narrow dusty room,
And Christian dreadeth Christ that hath a newer face of doom,
And Christian hateth Mary that God kissed in Galilee,
But Don John of Austria is riding to the sea.
Don John calling through the blast and the eclipse,
Crying with the trumpet, with the trumpet of his lips,
Trumpet that sayeth ha!
    Domino gloria!
Don John of Austria
Is shouting to the ships.

King Philip's in his closet with the Fleece about his neck
(*Don John of Austria is armed upon the deck.*)
The walls are hung with velvet that is black and soft as sin,
And little dwarfs creep out of it and little dwarfs creep in.
He holds a crystal phial that has colors like the moon,
He touches, and it tingles, and he trembles very soon,
And his face is as a fungus of a leprous white and grey
Like plants in the high houses that are shuttered from the day,
And death is in the phial, and the end of noble work,
But Don John of Austria has fired upon the Turk.
Don John's hunting, and his hounds have bayed—
Booms away past Italy the rumor of his raid.
Gun upon gun, ha! ha!
Gun upon gun, hurrah!
Don John of Austria
Has loosed the cannonade.

The Pope was in his chapel before day or battle broke,
(*Don John of Austria is hidden in the smoke.*)
The hidden room in a man's house where God sits all the year,

The secret window whence the world looks small and very dear.
He sees as in a mirror on the monstrous twilight sea
The crescent of his cruel ships whose name is mystery;
They fling great shadows foe-wards, making Cross and Castle dark,
They veil the pluméd lions on the galleys of St. Mark;
And above the ships are palaces of brown, black-bearded chiefs,
And below the ships are prisons, where with multitudinous griefs,
Christian captives sick and sunless, all a laboring race repines
Like a race in sunken cities, like a nation in the mines.
They are lost like slaves that swat, and in the skies of morning hung
The stairways of the tallest gods when tyranny was young.
They are countless, voiceless, hopeless as those fallen or fleeing on
Before the high Kings' horses in the granite of Babylon.
And many a one grows witless in his quiet room in hell
Where a yellow face looks inward through the lattice of his cell,
And he finds his God forgotten, and he seeks no more a sign—
(*But Don John of Austria has burst the battle-line!*)
Don John pounding from the slaughter-painted poop,
Purpling all the ocean like a bloody pirate's sloop,
Scarlet running over on the silvers and the golds,
Breaking of the hatches up and bursting of the holds,
Thronging of the thousands up that labor under sea
White for bliss and blind for sun and stunned for liberty.
Vivat Hispania!
Domino Gloria!
Don John of Austria
Has set his people free!

Cervantes on his galley sets the sword back in the sheath
(*Don John of Austria rides homeward with a wreath.*)
And he sees across a weary land a straggling road in Spain,
Up which a lean and foolish knight forever rides in vain,
And he smiles, but not as Sultans smile, and settles back the
blade. . . .
(*But Don John of Austria rides home from the crusade.*)

SAMUEL TAYLOR COLERIDGE

1772–1834

Kubla Khan

In Xanadu did Kubla Khan
A stately pleasure-dome decree:
Where Alph, the sacred river, ran
Through caverns measureless to man
    Down to a sunless sea.
So twice five miles of fertile ground
With walls and towers were girdled round:
And there were gardens bright with sinuous rills,
Where blossomed many an incense-bearing tree;
And here were forests ancient as the hills,
Enfolding sunny spots of greenery.

But oh that deep romantic chasm which slanted
Down the green hill athwart a cedarn cover!
A savage place! as holy and enchanted
As e'er beneath a waning moon was haunted
By woman wailing for her demon-lover!
And from this chasm, with ceaseless turmoil seething,
As if this earth in fast thick pants were breathing,
A mighty fountain momently was forced;
Amid whose swift half-intermitted burst
Huge fragments vaulted like rebounding hail,
Or chaffy grain beneath the thresher's flail:
And 'mid these dancing rocks at once and ever
It flung up momentarily the sacred river.
Five miles meandering with a mazy motion
Through wood and dale the sacred river ran,
Then reached the caverns measureless to man,
And sank in tumult to a lifeless ocean:
And 'mid this tumult Kubla heard from far
Ancestral voices prophesying war!

    The shadow of the dome of pleasure
    Floated midway on the waves,
    Where was heard the mingled measure

From the fountain and the caves.
It was a miracle of rare device,
A sunny pleasure-dome with caves of ice!

A damsel with a dulcimer
In a vision once I saw:
It was an Abyssinian maid,
And on her dulcimer she played,
Singing of Mount Abora.
Could I revive within me
Her symphony and song,
To such a deep delight 'twould win me
That with music loud and long
I would build that dome in air,
That sunny dome! those caves of ice!
And all who heard should see them there,
And all should cry: "Beware! beware!
His flashing eyes, his floating hair!
Weave a circle round him thrice,
And close your eyes with holy dread,
For he on honey-dew hath fed,
And drunk the milk of Paradise."

PADRAIC COLUM

1881–

An Old Woman of the Roads

Oh to have a little house!
To own the hearth and stool and all!
The heaped up sods upon the fire,
The pile of turf against the wall!

To have a clock with weights and chains
And pendulum swinging up and down!
A dresser filled with shining delph,
Speckled and white and blue and brown!

I could be busy all the day
Clearing and sweeping hearth and floor,
And fixing on their shelf again
My white and blue and speckled store!

I could be quiet there at night
Beside the fire and by myself,
Sure of a bed and loath to leave
The ticking clock and the shining delph!

Och! but I'm weary of mist and dark,
And roads where there's never a house nor bush,
And tired I am of bog and road,
And the crying wind and the lonesome hush!

And I am praying to God on high,
And I am praying Him night and day,
For a little house—a house of my own—
Out of the wind's and the rain's way.

WILLIAM JOHNSON CORY

1823–1892

Heraclitus

They told me, Heraclitus, they told me you were dead,
They brought me bitter news to hear and bitter tears to shed.
I wept as I remembered how often you and I
Had tired the sun with talking and sent him down the sky.

And now that thou art lying, my dear old Carian guest,
A handful of grey ashes, long, long ago at rest,
Still are thy pleasant voices, thy nightingales, awake;
For Death, he taketh all away, but them he cannot take.

(*after Callimachus*)

E. E. CUMMINGS
1894–

What If a Much of a Which of a Wind

what if a much of a which of a wind
gives the truth to summer's lie;
bloodies with dizzying leaves the sun
and yanks immortal stars awry?
Blow king to beggar and queen to seem
(blow friend to fiend: blow space to time)
—when skies are hanged and oceans drowned,
the single secret will still be man

what if a keen of a lean wind flays
screaming hills with sleet and snow:
strangles valleys by ropes of thing
and stifles forests in white ago?
Blow hope to terror; blow seeing to blind
(blow pity to envy and soul to mind)
—whose hearts are mountains, roots are trees,
it's they shall cry hello to the spring

what if a dawn of a doom of a dream
bites this universe in two,
peels forever out of his grave
and sprinkles nowhere with me and you?
Blow soon to never and never to twice
(blow life to isn't: blow death to was)
—all nothing's only our hugest home;
the most who die, the more we live

All In Green Went My Love Riding

All in green went my love riding
on a great horse of gold
into the silver dawn.

four lean hounds crouched low and smiling
the merry deer ran before.

Fleeter be they than dappled dreams
the swift sweet deer
the red rare deer.

Four red roebuck at a white water
the cruel bugle sang before.

Horn at hip went my love riding
riding the echo down
into the silver dawn.

four lean hounds crouched low and smiling
the level meadows ran before.

Softer be they than slippered sleep
the lean lithe deer
the fleet flown deer.

Four fleet does at a gold valley
the famished arrow sang before.

Bow at belt went my love riding
riding the mountain down
into the silver dawn.

four lean hounds crouched low and smiling
the sheer peaks ran before.

Paler be they than daunting death
the sleek slim deer
the tall tense deer.

Four tall stags at a green mountain
the lucky hunter sang before.

All in green went my love riding
on a great horse of gold
into the silver dawn.

four lean hounds crouched low and smiling
my heart fell dead before.

If I Have Made, My Lady

if i have made,my lady,intricate
imperfect various things chiefly which wrong
your eyes(frailer than most deep dreams are frail)
songs less firm than your body's whitest song
upon my mind—if i have failed to snare
the glance too shy—if through my singing slips
the very skillful strangeness of your smile
the keen primeval silence of your hair

—let the world say "his most wise music stole
nothing from death"—
                              you only will create
(who are so perfectly alive)my shame:
lady through whose profound and fragile lips
the sweet small clumsy feet of April came

into the ragged meadow of my soul.

SIR WILLIAM D'AVENANT

1606–1668

The Lark Now Leaves His Wat'ry Nest

The lark now leaves his wat'ry nest,
    And climbing shakes his dewy wings;
He takes this window for the east,

And to implore your light he sings:
Awake, awake, the morn will never rise
Till she can dress her beauty at your eyes.

The merchant bows unto the seaman's star,
    The plowman from the sun his season takes;
But still the lover wonders what they are
    Who look for day before his mistress wakes.
Awake, awake, break through your veils of lawn!
Then draw your curtains, and begin the dawn.

C. DAY LEWIS

1904–

Do Not Expect Again a Phoenix Hour

Do not expect again a phoenix hour,
The triple-towered sky, and dove complaining,
Sudden the rain of gold and heart's first ease
Tranced under trees by the eldritch light of sundown.

By a blazed trail our joy will be returning:
One burning hour throws light a thousand ways,
And hot blood stays into familiar gestures.
The best years wait, the body's plenitude.

Consider then, my lover, this is the end
Of the lark's ascending, the hawk's unearthly hover:
Spring season is over soon and first heatwave;
Grave-browed with cloud ponders the huge horizon.

Draw up the dew. Swell with pacific violence.
Take shape in silence. Grow as the clouds grew.
Beautiful brook the cornlands, and you are heavy;
Leafy the boughs—they also hide big fruit.

WALTER DE LA MARE

1873–1956

The Listeners

"Is there anybody there?" said the Traveler,
    Knocking on the moonlit door;
And his horse in the silence champed the grasses
    Of the forest's ferny floor:
And a bird flew up out of the turret,
    Above the Traveler's head:
And he smote upon the door again a second time;
    "Is there anybody there?" he said.
But no one descended to the Traveler;
    No head from the leaf-fringed sill
Leaned over and looked into his grey eyes,
    Where he stood perplexed and still.
But only a host of phantom listeners
    That dwelt in the lone house then
Stood listening in the quiet of the moonlight
    To that voice from the world of men:
Stood thronging the faint moonbeams on the dark stair,
    That goes down to the empty hall,
Hearkening in an air stirred and shaken
    By the lonely Traveler's call.
And he felt in his heart their strangeness,
    Their stillness answering his cry,
While his horse moved, cropping the dark turf,
    'Neath the starred and leafy sky;
For he suddenly smote on the door, even
    Louder, and lifted his head—
"Tell them I came, and no one answered,
    That I kept my word," he said.
Never the least stir made the listeners,
    Though every word he spake
Fell echoing through the shadowiness of the still house
    From the one man left awake:
Ay, they heard his foot upon the stirrup,
    And the sound of iron on stone,

And how the silence surged softly backward,
When the plunging hoofs were gone.

EMILY DICKINSON

1830–1886

A Bird Came down the Walk

A bird came down the walk:
He did not know I saw;
He bit an angleworm in halves
And ate the fellow, raw.

And then he drank a dew
From a convenient grass,
And then hopped sidewise to the wall
To let a beetle pass.

He glanced with rapid eyes
That hurried all around—
They looked like frightened beads, I thought—
He stirred his velvet head

Like one in danger; cautious,
I offered him a crumb,
And he unrolled his feathers
And rowed him softer home

Than oars divide the ocean,
Too silver for a seam,
Or butterflies, off banks of noon,
Leap, plashless, as they swim.

The Gentian Weaves Her Fringes

The gentian weaves her fringes,
The maple's loom is red,

My departing blossoms
    Obviate parade.

A brief but patient illness,
An hour to prepare,
And one below, this morning
Is where the angels are.
It was a short procession:
The bobolink was there,
An agéd bee addressed us,
And then we knelt in prayer.
We trust that she was willing;
We ask that we may be.
Summer—sister—seraph!
Let us go with thee!

In the name of the bee—
And of the butterfly—
And of the breeze—amen!

I Know Some Lonely Houses

I know some lonely houses off the road
A robber'd like the look of—
Wooden barred,
And windows hanging low,
Inviting to
A portico,
Where two could creep,
One hand the tools,
The other peep
To gauge the sleep—
Old-fashioned eyes,
Not easy to surprise!

How orderly the kitchen'd look by night
With just a clock—
But they could gag the tick—
And mice won't bark;
And so the walls don't tell,
None will.

A pair of spectacles ajar just stir;
An almanac's aware.

94

Was it the mat winked,
Or a nervous star?
The moon slides down the stair
To see who's there!

There's plunder—where?—
Tankard or spoon,
Earring or stone,
A watch, some antique brooch
To match the grandmama,
Staid, sleeping there.

Day rattles too;
Stealth's slow;
The sun has got as far
As the third sycamore.
Screams chanticleer,
"Who's there?"

And echoes, trains away,
Sneer, "Where!"
While the old couple, just astir,
Fancy the sunrise left the door ajar!

If You Were Coming in the Fall

If you were coming in the fall,
I'd brush the summer by
With half a smile and half a spurn,
As housewives do a fly.

If I could see you in a year,
I'd wind the months in balls,
And put them each in separate drawers,
For fear the numbers fuse.

If only centuries delayed,
I'd count them on my hand,
Substracting till my fingers dropped
Into Van Diemen's Land.

If certain, when this life was out,
That yours and mine should be,
I'd toss it yonder like a rind,
And taste eternity.

But now, uncertain of the length
Of this that is between,
It goads me, like the goblin bee,
That will not state its sting.

Success Is Counted Sweetest

Success is counted sweetest
By those who ne'er succeed.
To comprehend a nectar
Requires sorest need.

Not one of all the purple host
Who took the flag today
Can tell the definition,
So clear, of victory,

As he, defeated, dying,
On whose forbidden ear
The distant strains of triumph
Burst, agonized and clear.

I Years Had Been from Home

I years had been from home,
And now, before the door
I dared not open, lest a face
I never saw before

Stare vacant into mine
And ask my business there,
(My business—just a life I left;
Was such still dwelling there?)

I fumbled at my nerve,
I scanned the windows o'er;
The silence like an ocean rolled
And broke against my ear.

I laughed a wooden laugh
That I could fear a door,
Who danger and the dead had faced,
But never quaked before.

I fitted to the latch
My hand, with trembling care,
Lest back the awful door should spring
And leave me standing there.

I moved my fingers off
As cautiously as glass,
And held my ears, and like a thief
Fled gasping from the house.

I Felt a Funeral in My Brain

I felt a funeral in my brain,
And mourners to and fro
Kept treading, treading, till it seemed
That sense was breaking through.

And when they all were seated,
A service like a drum
Kept beating, beating, till I thought
My mind was going numb.

And then I heard them lift a box
And creak across my soul
With those same boots of lead again;
Then space began to toll

As all the heavens were a bell,
And Being but an ear,
And I and silence some strange race
Wrecked, solitary, here.

And then a plank in reason broke,
And I dropped down and down,
And hit a world at every crash,
And got through knowing then.

I Heard a Fly Buzz

I heard a fly buzz when I died;
The stillness in the room

Was like the stillness in the air
Between the heaves of storm.

The eyes around had wrung them dry,
And breaths were gathering firm
For that last onset, when the king
Be witnessed in the room.

I willed my keepsakes, signed away
What portion of me be
Assignable—and then it was
There interposed a fly,

With blue, uncertain, stumbling buzz,
Between the light and me;
And then the windows failed, and then
I could not see to see.

AUSTIN DOBSON

1840–1921

The Ladies of St. James's

The ladies of St. James's
   Go swinging to the play;
Their footmen run before them,
   With a "Stand by! Clear the way!"
But Phyllida, my Phyllida!
   She takes her buckled shoon,
When we go out a-courting
   Beneath the harvest moon.

The ladies of St. James's
   Wear satin on their backs;
They sit all night at *Ombre*,
   With candles all of wax:
But Phyllida, my Phyllida!
   She dons her russet gown,
And runs to gather May dew
   Before the world is down.

98

The ladies of St. James's!
   They are so fine and fair,
You'd think a box of essences
   Was broken in the air:
But Phyllida, my Phyllida!
   The breath of heath and furze
When breezes blow at morning,
   Is not so fresh as hers.

The ladies of St. James's!
   They're painted to the eyes;
Their white it stays forever
   Their red it never dies:
But Phyllida, my Phyllida!
   Her color comes and goes;
It trembles to a lily—
   It wavers to a rose.

The ladies of St. James's!
   You scarce can understand
The half of all their speeches,
   Their phrases are so grand:
But Phyllida, my Phyllida!
   Her shy and simple words
Are clear as after raindrops
   The music of the birds.

The ladies of St. James's!
   They have their fits and freaks;
They smile on you—for seconds,
   They frown on you—for weeks:
But Phyllida, my Phyllida!
   Come either storm or shine,
From Shrovetide unto Shrovetide,
   Is always true—and mine.

My Phyllida! my Phyllida!
   I care not though they heap
The hearts of all St. James's,
   And give me all to keep;
I care not whose the beauties
   Of all the world may be,
For Phyllida—for Phyllida
   Is all the world to me!

JOHN DONNE
1573–1631

The Good-Morrow

I wonder by my troth what thou and I
Did till we loved? Were we not weaned till then
But sucked on country pleasures, childishly?
Or snorted we in the seven sleepers den?
'Twas so; but this, all pleasures fancies be.
If ever any beauty I did see,
Which I desired, and got, 'twas but a dream of thee.

And now good-morrow to our waking souls,
Which watch not one another out of fear;
For love, all love of other sights controls,
And makes one little room an everywhere.
Let sea-discoverers to new worlds have gone,
Let maps to other, worlds on worlds have shown,
Let us possess one world—each hath one and is one.

My face in thine eye, thine in mine appears,
And true plain hearts do in the faces rest;
Where can we find two better hemispheres
Without sharp north, without declining west?
Whatever dies was not mixed equally;
If our two loves be one, or thou and I
Love so alike that none do slacken, none can die.

Go and Catch a Falling Star

Go and catch a falling star,
    Get with child a mandrake root,
Tell me where all past years are,
    Or who cleft the Devil's foot;
Teach me to hear mermaids singing,
Or to keep off envy's stinging
            And find

What wind
Serves to advance an honest mind.

If thou be'st born to strange sights,
    Things invisible to see,
Ride ten thousand days and nights
    Till age snow white hairs on thee;
Thou, when thou return'st, wilt tell me
All strange wonders that befell thee,
            And swear
            No where
Lives a woman true and fair.

If thou find'st one, let me know;
    Such a pilgrimage were sweet.
Yet do not; I would not go,
    Though at next door we might meet.
Though she were true when you met her,
And last till you write your letter,
            Yet she
            Will be
False, ere I come, to two or three.

The Bait

Come live with me and be my love,
And we will some new pleasures prove
Of golden sands and crystal brooks,
With silken lines and silver hooks.

There will the river whispering run
Warmed by thy eyes, more than the sun.
And there th' enamored fish will stay,
Begging themselves they may betray.

When thou wilt swim in that live bath,
Each fish, which every channel hath,
Will amorously to thee swim,
Gladder to catch thee, than thou him.

If thou to be so seen be'st loath
By sun or moon, thou darkenest both,
And if myself have leave to see,
I need not their light, having thee.

Let others freeze with angling reeds,
And cut their legs with shells and weeds,
Or treacherously poor fish beset,
With strangling snare or windowy net:

Let coarse bold hands, from slimy nest
The bedded fish in banks outwrest,
Or curious traitors, sleeve-silk flies,
Bewitch poor fishes' wand'ring eyes.

For thee, thou need'st no such deceit,
For thou thyself art thine own bait;
That fish, that is not catched thereby,
Alas, is wiser far than I.

The Funeral

Whoever comes to shroud me, do not harm
    Nor question much
That subtle wreath of hair about mine arm;
The mystery, the sign you must not touch,
    For 'tis my outward soul,
Viceroy to that which, unto heaven being gone,
    Will leave this to control
And keep these limbs, her provinces, from dissolutión.

For if the sinewy thread my brain lets fall
    Through every part
Can tie those parts, and make me one of all,
These hairs, which upward grew and strength and art
    Have from a better brain,
Can better do't—except she meant that I
    By this should know my pain,
As prisoners then are manacled when they're condemned to die.

Whate'er she meant by't, bury it with me,
    For since I am
Love's martyr, it might breed idolatry
If into others' hands these reliques came.
    As 'twas humility
T' afford to it all that a soul can do,
    So 'tis some bravery
That since you would have none of me, I bury some of you.

102

Death, Be Not Proud

Death, be not proud, though some have called thee
Mighty and dreadful, for thou art not so;
For those whom thou think'st thou dost overthrow
Die not, poor Death; nor yet canst thou kill me.
From rest and sleep, which but thy picture be,
Much pleasure; then from thee much more must flow;
And soonest our best men with thee do go—
Rest of their bones and souls' delivery!
Thou'rt slave to fate, chance, kings, and desperate men,
And dost with poison, war, and sickness dwell;
And poppy or charms can make us sleep as well
And better than thy stroke. Why swell'st thou then?
One short sleep past, we wake eternally,
And Death shall be no more; Death, thou shalt die!

A Hymn to God the Father

Wilt Thou forgive that sin where I begun,
    Which was my sin, though it were done before?
Wilt Thou forgive that sin through which I run,
    And do run still, though still I do deplore?
        When Thou hast done, Thou has not done,
            For I have more.

Wilt Thou forgive that sin which I have won
    Others to sin, and made my sins their door?
Wilt Thou forgive that sin which I did shun
    A year or two, but wallowed in a score?
        When Thou hast done, Thou hast not done,
            For I have more.

I have a sin of fear, that when I have spun
    My last thread, I shall perish on the shore;
Swear by Thyself that at my death Thy Son
    Shall shine as He shines now and heretofore;
        And having done that, Thou hast done;
            I fear no more.

H. D. (HILDA DOOLITTLE)
1886–

Lethe

Nor skin nor hide nor fleece
  Shall cover you,
Nor curtain of crimson nor fine
Shelter of cedar-wood be over you,
  Nor the fir-tree,
  Nor the pine.

Nor sight of whin nor gorse
  Nor river-yew,
Nor fragrance of flowering bush,
Nor wailing of reed-bird to waken you,
  Nor of linnet,
  Nor of thrush.

Nor word nor touch nor sight
  Of lover. You
Shall long through the night but for this:
The roll of the full tide to cover you
  Without question,
  Without kiss.

ERNEST DOWSON
1867–1900

Cynara

Last night, ah yesternight, betwixt her lips and mine
There fell thy shadow, Cynara! thy breath was shed
Upon my soul between the kisses and the wine;

And I was desolate and sick of an old passion,
    Yea, I was desolate and bowed my head:
I have been faithful to thee, Cynara! in my fashion.

All night upon mine heart I felt her warm heart beat,
Night-long within mine arms in love and sleep she lay;
Surely the kisses of her bought red mouth were sweet;
But I was desolate and sick of an old passion,
    When I awoke and found the dawn was grey:
I have been faithful to thee, Cynara! in my fashion.

I have forgot much, Cynara! gone with the wind,
Flung roses, roses riotously with the throng,
Dancing, to put thy pale, lost lilies out of mind;
But I was desolate and sick of an old passion,
    Yea, all the time, because the dance was long:
I have been faithful to thee, Cynara! in my fashion.

I cried for madder music and for stronger wine,
But when the feast is finished and the lamps expire,
Then falls thy shadow, Cynara! the night is thine;
And I am desolate and sick of an old passion,
    Yea, hungry for the lips of my desire:
I have been faithful to thee, Cynara! in my fashion.

They Are Not Long

They are not long, the weeping and the laughter,
    Love and desire and hate:
I think they have no portion in us after
    We pass the gate.

They are not long, the days of wine and roses:
    Out of a misty dream
Our path emerges for a while, then closes
    Within a dream.

MICHAEL DRAYTON
1563–1631

Ballad of Agincourt

Fair stood the wind for France,
When we our sails advance,
Nor now to prove our chance
    Longer will tarry;
But putting to the main,
At Caux, the mouth of Seine,
With all his martial train
    Landed King Harry;

And taking many a fort,
Furnished in warlike sort,
Marcheth towards Agincourt
    In happy hour,
Skirmishing day by day
With those that stopped his way,
Where the French gen'ral lay
    With all his power;

Which, in his height of pride,
King Henry to deride,
His ransom to provide
    To the King sending;
Which he neglects the while,
As from a nation vile,
Yet with an angry smile,
    Their fall portending.

And turning to his men,
Quoth our brave Henry then:
    "Though they to one be ten,
    Be not amazéd!
Yet have we well begun;
Battles so bravely won
Have ever to the sun
    By Fame been raiséd!

"And for myself," quoth he,
"This my full rest shall be:
England ne'er mourn for me,
   Nor more esteem me!
Victor I will remain,
Or on this earth lie slain;
Never shall she sustain
   Loss to redeem me.

"Poitiers and Cressy tell,
When most their pride did swell,
Under our swords they fell.
   No less our skill is,
Than when our grandsire great,
Claiming the regal seat,
By many a warlike feat
   Lopped the French lilies."

The Duke of York so dread
The eager vanguard led;
With the main Henry sped
   Amongst his henchmen;
Exeter had the rear,
A braver man not there;
O Lord, how hot they were
   On the false Frenchmen!

They now to fight are gone;
Armor on armor shone,
Drum now to drum did groan,
   To hear was wonder;
That with cries they make
The very earth did shake,
Trumpet to trumpet spake,
   Thunder to thunder.

Well it thine age became,
O noble Erpingham,
Which didst the signal aim
   To our hid forces;
When from a meadow by,
Like a storm suddenly,
The English archery
   Stuck the French horses,

With Spanish yew so strong,
Arrows a cloth-yard long,

That like to serpents stung,
   Piercing the weather;
None from his fellow starts,
But playing manly parts,
And like true English hearts,
   Stuck close together.

When down their bows they threw,
And forth their bilboes drew,
And on the French they flew,
   Not one was tardy;
Arms were from shoulders sent,
Scalps to the teeth were rent,
Down the French peasants went;
   Our men were hardy.

This while our noble King,
His broadsword brandishing,
Down the French host did ding,
   As to o'erwhelm it;
And many a deep wound lent,
His arms with blood besprent,
And many a cruel dent
   Bruiséd his helmet.

Gloster, that Duke so good,
Next of the royal blood,
For famous England stood
   With his brave brother;
Clarence in steel so bright,
Though but a maiden knight,
Yet in that furious fight
   Scarce such another.

Warwick in blood did wade,
Oxford the foe invade,
And cruel slaughter made,
   Still as they ran up;
Suffolk his ax did ply,
Beaumont and Willoughby
Bare them right doughtily,
   Ferrers and Fanhope.

Upon Saint Crispin's day
Fought was this noble fray,
Which fame did not delay
   To England to carry.

Oh when shall Englishmen
With such acts fill a pen,
Or England breed again
　　Such a King Harry?

JOHN DRINKWATER
1882–

Moonlit Apples

At the top of the house the apples are laid in rows,
And the skylight lets the moonlight in, and those
Apples are deep-sea apples of green. There goes
　　A cloud on the moon in the autumn night.

A mouse in the wainscot scratches, and scratches, and then
There is no sound at the top of the house of men
Or mice; and the cloud is blown, and the moon again
　　Dapples the apples with deep-sea light.

They are lying in rows there, under the gloomy beams;
On the sagging floor; they gather the silver streams
Out of the moon, those moonlit apples of dreams,
　　And quiet is the steep stair under.

In the corridors under there is nothing but sleep,
And stiller than ever on orchard boughs they keep
Tryst with the moon, and deep is the silence, deep
　　On moon-washed apples of wonder.

SIR EDWARD DYER

1543–1607

The Lowest Trees

The lowest trees have tops, the ant her gall,
　The fly her spleen, the little sparks their heat;
The slender hairs cast shadows, though but small,
　And bees have stings, although they be not great;
Seas have their source, and so have shallow springs;
And love is love, in beggars as in kings.

Where rivers smoothest run, deep are the fords;
　The dial stirs, yet none perceives it move;
The firmest faith is in the fewest words;
　The turtles cannot sing, and yet they love:
True hearts have eyes and ears, no tongues to speak;
They hear and see, and sigh, and then they break.

T. S. ELIOT

1888–

The Love Song of J. Alfred Prufrock

Let us go then, you and I,
When the evening is spread out against the sky
Like a patient etherized upon a table;
Let us go, through certain half-deserted streets,
The muttering retreats
Of restless nights in one-night cheap hotels
And sawdust restaurants with oyster-shells:
Streets that follow like a tedious argument
Of insidious intent
To lead you to an overwhelming question . . .

Oh do not ask, "What is it?"
Let us go and make our visit.

In the room the women come and go
Talking of Michelangelo.

The yellow fog that rubs its back upon the window-panes,
The yellow smoke that rubs its muzzle on the window-panes
Licked its tongue into the corners of the evening,
Lingered upon the pools that stand in drains,
Let fall upon its back the soot that falls from chimneys,
Slipped by the terrace, made a sudden leap,
And seeing that it was a soft October night,
Curled once about the house, and fell asleep.

And indeed there will be time
For the yellow smoke that slides along the street,
Rubbing its back upon the window-panes;
There will be time, there will be time
To prepare a face to meet the faces that you meet;
There will be time to murder and create,
And time for all the works and days of hands
That lift and drop a question on your plate;
Time for you and time for me,
And time yet for a hundred indecisions,
And for a hundred visions and revisions,
Before the taking of a toast and tea.

In the room the women come and go
Talking of Michelangelo.

And indeed there will be time
To wonder, "Do I dare?" and, "Do I dare?"
Time to turn back and descend the stair,
With a bald spot in the middle of my hair—
[They will say: "How his hair is growing thin!"]
My morning coat, my collar mounting firmly to the chin,
My necktie rich and modest, but asserted by a simple pin—
[They will say: "But how his arms and legs are thin!"]
Do I dare
Disturb the universe?
In a minute there is time
For decisions and revisions which a minute will reverse.

For I have known them all already, known them all—
Have known the evenings, mornings, afternoons,

I have measured out my life with coffee spoons;
I know the voices dying with a dying fall
Beneath the music from a farther room.
　　　So how should I presume?

And I have known the eyes already, known them all—
The eyes that fix you in a formulated phrase,
And when I am formulated, sprawling on a pin,
When I am pinned and wriggling on the wall,
Then how should I begin
To spit out all the butt-ends of my days and ways?
　　　And how should I presume?

And I have known the arms already, known them all—
Arms that are braceleted and white and bare
[But in the lamplight, downed with light brown hair!]
Is it perfume from a dress
That makes me so digress?
Arms that lie along a table, or wrap about a shawl.
　　　And should I then presume?
　　　And how should I begin?

　　　　　. . . . .

Shall I say, I have gone at dusk through narrow streets
And watched the smoke that rises from the pipes
Of lonely men in shirt-sleeves, leaning out of windows? . . .

I should have been a pair of ragged claws
Scuttling across the floors of silent seas.

　　　　　. . . . .

And the afternoon, the evening, sleeps so peacefully!
Smoothed by long fingers,
Asleep . . . tired . . . or it malingers,
Stretched on the floor, here beside you and me.
Should I, after tea and cakes and ices,
Have the strength to force the moment to its crisis?
But though I have wept and fasted, wept and prayed,
Though I have seen my head [grown slightly bald] brought in upon
　　　a platter,
I am no prophet—and here's no great matter;
I have seen the moment of my greatness flicker,
And I have seen the eternal Footman hold my coat, and snicker,
And in short, I was afraid.

And would it have been worth it, after all,
After the cups, the marmalade, the tea,
Among the porcelain, among some talk of you and me,

112

Would it have been worth while,
To have bitten off the matter with a smile,
To have squeezed the universe into a ball
To roll it toward some overwhelming question,
To say: "I am Lazarus, come from the dead,
Come back to tell you all, I shall tell you all"—
If one, settling a pillow by her head,
      Should say: "That is not what I meant at all.
      That is not it, at all."

And would it have been worth it, after all,
Would it have been worth while,
After the sunsets and the dooryards and the sprinkled streets,
After the novels, after the teacups, after the skirts that trail along
      the floor—
And this, and so much more?—
It is impossible to say just what I mean!
But as if a magic lantern threw the nerves in patterns on a screen:
Would it have been worth while
If one, settling a pillow or throwing off a shawl,
And turning toward the window, should say:
      "That is not it at all,
      That is not what I meant, at all."

            . . . . .

No! I am not Prince Hamlet, nor was meant to be;
Am an attendant lord, one that will do
To swell a progress, start a scene or two,
Advise the prince; no doubt, an easy tool,
Deferential, glad to be of use,
Politic, cautious, and meticulous;
Full of high sentence, but a bit obtuse;
At times, indeed, almost ridiculous—
Almost, at times, the Fool.

I grow old. . . . I grow old. . . .
I shall wear the bottoms of my trousers rolled.

Shall I part my hair behind? Do I dare to eat a peach?
I shall wear white flannel trousers, and walk upon the beach.
I have heard the mermaids singing, each to each.

I do not think that they will sing to me.

I have seen them riding seaward on the waves
Combing the white hair of the waves blown back
When the wind blows the water white and black.

We have lingered in the chambers of the sea
By sea-girls wreathed with seaweed red and brown
Till human voices wake us, and we drown.

Macavity: the Mystery Cat

Macavity's a Mystery Cat; he's called the Hidden Paw—
For he's the master criminal who can defy the Law.
He's the bafflement of Scotland Yard, the Flying Squad's despair:
For when they reach the scene of crime—*Macavity's not there!*

Macavity, Macavity, there's no one like Macavity,
He's broken every human law, he breaks the law of gravity.
His powers of levitation would make a fakir stare,
And when you reach the scene of crime—*Macavity's not there!*
You may seek him in the basement, you may look up in the air—
But I tell you once and once again, *Macavity's not there!*
Macavity's a ginger cat, he's very tall and thin;
You would know him if you saw him, for his eyes are sunken in.
His brow is deeply lined with thought, his head is highly domed;
His coat is dusty from neglect, his whiskers are uncombed.
He sways his head from side to side, with movements like a snake;
And when you think he's half asleep, he's always wide awake.

Macavity, Macavity, there's no one like Macavity,
For he's a fiend in feline shape, a monster of depravity.
You may meet him in a by-street, you may see him in the square—
But when a crime's discovered, then *Macavity's not there!*

He's outwardly respectable. (They say he cheats at cards.)
And his footprints are not found in any file of Scotland Yard's.
And when the larder's looted, or the jewel-case is rifled,
Or when the milk is missing, or another Peke's been stifled,
Or the greenhouse glass is broken, and the trellis past repair—
Ay, there's the wonder of the thing! *Macavity's not there!*

And when the Foreign Office find a Treaty's gone astray,
Or the Admiralty lose some plans and drawings by the way,
There may be a scrap of paper in the hall or on the stair—
But it's useless to investigate—*Macavity's not there!*
And when the loss has been disclosed, the Secret Service say:
"It *must* have been Macavity!"—but he's a mile away.
You'll be sure to find him resting, or a-licking of his thumbs,
Or engaged in doing complicated long division sums.

Macavity, Macavity, there's no one like Macavity,
There never was a Cat of such deceitfulness and suavity.
He always has an alibi, and one or two to spare:
At whatever time the deed took place—MACAVITY WASN'T THERE!
And they say that all the Cats whose wicked deeds are widely known
(I might mention Mungojerrie, I might mention Griddlebone)
Are nothing more than agents for the Cat who all the time
Just controls their operations: the Napoleon of Crime!

ELIZABETH I

1558–1603

When I Was Fair and Young

When I was fair and young, and favor gracéd me,
    Of many was I sought, their mistress for to be;
But I did scorn them all, and answered them therefore,
    "Go, go, go, seek some otherwhere,
        Impórtune me no more!"

How many weeping eyes I made to pine with woe,
    How many sighing hearts, I have no skill to show;
Yet I the prouder grew, and answered them therefore,
    "Go, go, go, seek some otherwhere,
        Impórtune me no more!"

Then spake fair Venus' son, that proud victorious boy,
    And said: "Fine dame, since that you be so coy,
I will so pluck your plumes that you shall say no more,
    Go, go, go, seek some otherwhere,
        Impórtune me no more!"

When he had spake these words, such change grew in my breast
    That neither night nor day since that, I could take any rest.
Then lo! I did repent that I had said before,
    "Go, go, go, seek some otherwhere,
        Impórtune me no more!"

RALPH WALDO EMERSON

1803–1882

Brahma

If the red slayer think he slays,
   Or if the slain think he is slain,
They know not well the subtle ways
   I keep, and pass, and turn again.

Far or forgot to me is near;
   Shadow and sunlight are the same;
The vanished gods to me appear;
   And one to me are shame and fame.

They reckon ill who leave me out;
   When me they fly, I am the wings;
I am the doubter and the doubt,
   And I the hymn the Brahmin sings.

The strong gods pine for my abode,
   And pine in vain the sacred Seven;
But thou, meek lover of the good!
   Find me, and turn thy back on heaven.

KENNETH FEARING

1902–

Dirge

1–2–3 was the number he played but today the number came 3–2–1;
   bought his Carbide at 30 and it went to 29; had the favorite at
   Bowie but the track was slow—

O executive type, would you like to drive a floating power, knee-
   action, silk-upholstered six? Wed a Hollywood star? Shoot the
   course in 58? Draw to the ace, king, jack?

O fellow with a will who won't take no, watch out for three cig-
arettes on the same, single match; O democratic voter born in
August under Mars, beware of liquidated rails—

Dénouement to dénouement, he took a personal pride in the cer-
tain, certain way he lived his own, private life,
but nevertheless, they shut off his gas; nevertheless, the bank fore-
closed; nevertheless, the landlord called; nevertheless, the radio
broke,

And twelve o'clock arrived just once too often,
just the same he wore one grey tweed suit, bought one straw hat,
drank one straight Scotch, walked one short step, took one long
look, drew one deep breath,
just one too many,

And wow he died as wow he lived,
going whop to the office and blooie home to sleep and biff got
married and bam had children and oof got fired,
zowie did he live and zowie did he die,

With who the hell are you? at the corner of his casket, and where
the hell we going? on the right hand silver knob, and who the
hell cares? walking second from the end with an American
Beauty wreath from why the hell not?

Very much missed by the circulation staff of the *New York Evening
Post*; deeply, deeply mourned by the B.M.T.,

Wham, Mr. Roosevelt; pow, Sears Roebuck; awk, big dipper; bop,
summer rain;
bong, Mr., bong, Mr., bong, Mr., bong!

Minnie and Mrs. Hoyne

She could die laughing,
On Sunday noon, back of the pawnshop, under the smoke-
stack, with Mrs. Hoyne.
She could hide her face in rags and die laughing on the street.
She could snicker in the broom closet. In the dark of the
movies. In bed.
Die, at the way some people talk.
The things they talk about and believe and do.
She and Mrs. Hoyne could sit together and laugh.

Minnie could nicker in the dark alone.
Jesus, what do they mean?
> Girls trying to be in love.
> People worried about other people. About the world. Do
>   they own it?
> People that don't believe a street is what it looks like. They
>   think there's more.
> There isn't any more, the coo-coos.
> She could die laughing.
> Free milk for babies, Mrs. Hoyne!
Crazy liars, all of them, and what next?
> Minnie will be a millionaire.
> Mrs. Hoyne will fly a balloon.
> Give my regards to the Queen of France when you get there.
> Ask her if she remembers me: "Say, Queen,
> Have you got any old bloomers you don't want, for Minnie
>   Spohr?"
> She could die, grinning among the buckets at midnight,
> Snicker, staring down the elevator shaft;
> Minnie doesn't care. Get the money!
> She could die laughing some time
> Alone in the broom closet on the forty-third floor.

THOMAS HORNSBY FERRIL

1896–

Wood

> There was a dark and awful wood
> Where increments of death accrued
> To every leaf and antlered head
> Until it withered and was dead,
> And lonely there I wandered
> And wandered and wandered.

> But once a myth-white moon shone there
> And you were kneeling by a flower,
> And it was practical and wise
> For me to kneel and you to rise,

And me to rise and turn to go,
And you to turn and whisper *no*,
And seven wondrous stags that I
Could not believe walked slowly by.

EUGENE FIELD

1850–1895

Wynken, Blynken, and Nod

Wynken, Blynken, and Nod one night
  Sailed off in a wooden shoe—
Sailed on a river of crystal light
  Into a sea of dew.
"Where are you going, and what do you wish?"
  The old moon asked the three.
"We have come to fish for the herring fish
  That live in this beautiful sea;
  Nets of silver and gold have we!"
      Said Wynken,
      Blynken,
      And Nod.

The old moon laughed and sang a song,
  As they rocked in the wooden shoe;
And the wind that sped them all night long
  Ruffled the waves of dew.
The little stars were the herring fish
  That lived in that beautiful sea—
"Now cast your nets wherever you wish—
  Never afeard are we!"
  So cried the stars to the fishermen three,
      Wynken,
      Blynken,
      And Nod.

All night long their nets they threw
  To the stars in the twinkling foam—
Then down from the skies came the wooden shoe,

Bringing the fishermen home.
'Twas all so pretty a sail, it seemed
   As if it could not be;
And some folk thought 'twas a dream they'd dreamed
   Of sailing that beautiful sea;
   But I shall name you the fishermen three:
       Wynken,
       Blynken,
       And Nod.

Wynken and Blynken are two little eyes,
   And Nod is a little head,
And the wooden shoe that sailed the skies
   Is a wee one's trundle-bed;
So shut your eyes while Mother sings
   Of wonderful sights that be,
And you shall see the beautiful things
   As you rock in the misty sea
   Where the old shoe rocked the fishermen three—
       Wynken,
       Blynken,
       And Nod.

The Duel

The gingham dog and the calico cat
Side by side on the table sat;
'Twas half-past twelve, and (what do you think!)
Nor one nor t'other had slept a wink!
   The old Dutch clock and the Chinese plate
   Appeared to know as sure as fate
There was going to be a terrible spat.
   (I wasn't there; I simply state
   What was told to me by the Chinese plate!)

The gingham dog went, "Bow-wow-wow!"
And the calico cat replied, "Mee-ow!"
The air was littered, an hour or so,
With bits of gingham and calico,
   While the old Dutch clock in the chimney-place
   Up with its hands before its face,
For it always dreaded a family row!

(Now mind: I'm only telling you
What the old Dutch clock declares is true!)

The Chinese plate looked very blue,
And wailed, "Oh dear! What shall we do!"
But the gingham dog and the calico cat
Wallowed this way and tumbled that,
    Employing every tooth and claw
    In the awfullest way you ever saw—
And oh how the gingham and calico flew!
    (Don't fancy I exaggerate—
    I got my news from the Chinese plate!)

Next morning, where the two had sat
They found no trace of dog or cat;
And some folks think unto this day
That burglars stole that pair away!
    But the truth about the cat and pup
    Is this: *They ate each other up!*
Now what do you really think of that?
    (The old Dutch clock, it told me so,
    And that is how I came to know.)

JAMES ELROY FLECKER

1884–1915

To a Poet a Thousand Years Hence

I who am dead a thousand years,
    And wrote this sweet archaic song,
Send you my words for messengers
    The way I shall not pass along.

I care not if you bridge the seas,
    Or ride secure the cruel sky,
Or build consummate palaces
    Of metal or of masonry.

But have you wine and music still,
    And statues and a bright-eyed love,

And foolish thoughts of good and ill,
    And prayers to them who sit above?

How shall we conquer? Like a wind
    That falls at eve, our fancies blow,
And old Maeonides the blind
    Said it three thousand years ago.

O friend unseen, unborn, unknown,
    Student of our sweet English tongue,
Read out my words at night, alone:
    I was a poet, I was young.

Since I can never see your face,
    And never shake you by the hand,
I send my soul through time and space
    To greet you. You will understand.

The Old Ships

I have seen old ships sail like swans asleep
Beyond the village which men still call Tyre,
With leaden age o'ercargoed, dipping deep
For Famagusta and the hidden sun
That rings black Cyprus with a lake of fire;
And all those ships were certainly so old,
Who knows how oft with squat and noisy gun,
Questing brown slaves or Syrian oranges,
The pirate Genoese
Hell-raked them till they rolled
Blood, water, fruit, and corpses up the hold.
But now through friendly seas they softly run,
Painted the mid-sea blue or shore-sea green,
Still patterned with the vine and grapes in gold.

But I have seen,
Pointing her shapely shadows from the dawn,
An image tumbled on a rose-swept bay,
A drowsy ship of some yet older day;
And, wonder's breath indrawn,
Thought I—who knows—who knows—but in that same
(Fished up beyond Aeaea, patched up new
—Stern painted brighter blue—)
That talkative, bald-headed seaman came

(Twelve patient comrades sweating at the oar)
From Troy's doom-crimson shore,
And with great lies about his wooden horse
Set the crew laughing, and forgot his course.

It was so old a ship—who knows—who knows?
—And yet so beautiful, I watched in vain
To see the mast burst open with a rose,
And the whole deck put on its leaves again.

JOHN FLETCHER
1579–1625

To Sleep

Care-charming Sleep, thou easer of all woes,
Brother to Death, sweetly thyself dispose
On this afflicted prince; fall like a cloud,
In gentle showers; give nothing that is loud
Or painful to his slumbers—easy, light,
And as a purling stream, thou son of Night,
Pass by his troubled senses; sing his pain
Like hollow murmuring wind or silver rain;
Into this prince gently, oh gently slide,
And kiss him into slumbers like a bride!

ROBERT FROST
1875–

Birches

When I see birches bend to left and right
Across the lines of straighter darker trees,

I like to think some boy's been swinging them.
But swinging doesn't bend them down to stay.
Ice-storms do that. Often you must have seen them
Loaded with ice a sunny winter morning
After a rain. They click upon themselves
As the breeze rises, and turn many-colored
As the stir cracks and crazes their enamel.
Soon the sun's warmth makes them shed crystal shells
Shattering and avalanching on the snow-crust—
Such heaps of broken glass to sweep away
You'd think the inner dome of heaven had fallen.
They are dragged to the withered bracken by the load,
And they seem not to break; though once they are bowed
So low for long, they never right themselves:
You may see their trunks arching in the woods
Years afterwards, trailing their leaves on the ground
Like girls on hands and knees that throw their hair
Before them over their heads to dry in the sun.
But I was going to say when Truth broke in
With all her matter-of-fact about the ice-storm
(Now am I free to be poetical?)
I should prefer to have some boy bend them
As he went out and in to fetch the cows—
Some boy too far from town to learn baseball,
Whose only play was what he found himself,
Summer or winter, and could play alone.
One by one he subdued his father's trees
By riding them down over and over again
Until he took the stiffness out of them,
And not one but hung limp, not one was left
For him to conquer. He learned all there was
To learn about not launching out too soon
And so not carrying the tree away
Clear to the ground. He always kept his poise
To the top branches, climbing carefully
With the same pains you use to fill a cup
Up to the brim, and even above the brim.
Then he flung outward, feet first, with a swish,
Kicking his way down through the air to the ground.
So was I once myself a swinger of birches.
And so I dream of going back to be.
It's when I'm weary of considerations,
And life is too much like a pathless wood
Where your face burns and tickles with the cobwebs

Broken across it, and one eye is weeping
From a twig's having lashed across it open.
I'd like to get away from earth awhile
And then come back to it and begin over.
May no fate wilfully misunderstand me
And half grant what I wish and snatch me away
Not to return. Earth's the right place for love:
I don't know where it's likely to go better.
I'd like to go by climbing a birch tree,
And climb black branches up a snow-white trunk
Toward heaven, till the tree could bear no more,
But dipped its top and set me down again.
That would be good both going and coming back.
One could do worse than be a swinger of birches.

Stopping by Woods on a Snowy Evening

Whose woods these are I think I know.
His house is in the village though;
He will not see me stopping here
To watch his woods fill up with snow.

My little horse must think it queer
To stop without a farmhouse near
Between the woods and frozen lake
The darkest evening of the year.

He gives his harness bells a shake
To ask if there is some mistake.
The only other sound's the sweep
Of easy wind and downy flake.

The woods are lovely, dark and deep,
But I have promises to keep,
And miles to go before I sleep,
And miles to go before I sleep.

Brown's Descent
or The Willy-Nilly Slide

Brown lived at such a lofty farm
That everyone for miles could see

His lantern when he did his chores
　　In winter after half-past three.

And many must have seen him make
　　His wild descent from there one night,
'Cross lots, 'cross walls, 'cross everything,
　　Describing rings of lantern light.

Between the house and barn the gale
　　Got him by something he had on
And blew him out on the icy crust
　　That cased the world, and he was gone!

Walls were all buried, trees were few:
　　He saw no stay unless he stove
A hole in somewhere with his heel.
　　But though repeatedly he strove

And stamped and said things to himself,
　　And sometimes something seemed to yield,
He gained no foothold, but pursued
　　His journey down from field to field.

Sometimes he came with arms outspread
　　Like wings, revolving in the scene
Upon his longer axis, and
　　With no small dignity of mien.

Faster or slower as he chanced,
　　Sitting or standing as he chose,
According as he feared to risk
　　His neck, or thought to spare his clothes,

He never let the lantern drop.
　　And some exclaimed who saw afar
The figures he described with it,
　　"I wonder what those signals are

Brown makes at such an hour of night!
　　He's celebrating something strange.
I wonder if he's sold his farm,
　　Or been made Master of the Grange."

He reeled, he lurched, he bobbed, he checked;
　　He fell and made the lantern rattle
(But saved the light from going out.)
　　So halfway down he fought the battle,

Incredulous of his own bad luck.
　　And then becoming reconciled

To everything, he gave it up
    And came down coasting like a child.

"Well—I—be—" that was all he said,
    As standing in the river road,
He looked back up the slippery slope
    (Two miles it was) to his abode.

Sometimes as an authority
    On motor-cars, I'm asked if I
Should say our stock was petered out,
    And this is my sincere reply:

Yankees are what they always were.
    Don't think Brown ever gave up hope
Of getting home again because
    He couldn't climb that slippery slope;

Or even thought of standing there
    Until the January thaw
Should take the polish off the crust.
    He bowed with grace to natural law,

And then went round it on his feet,
    After the manner of our stock;
Not much concerned for those to whom,
    At that particular time o'clock,

It must have looked as if the course
    He steered was really straight away
From that which he was headed for—
    Not much concerned for them, I say;

No more so than became a man—
    And politician at odd seasons.
I've kept Brown standing in the cold
    While I invested him with reasons;

But now he snapped his eyes three times;
    Then shook his lantern, saying, "Ile's
'Bout out!" and took the long way home
    By road, a matter of several miles.

WILFRID W. GIBSON

1878–

Flannan Isle

"Though three men dwell on Flannan Isle
To keep the lamp alight,
As we steered under the lee, we caught
No glimmer through the night!"

A passing ship at dawn had brought
The news; and quickly we set sail,
To find out what strange thing might ail
The keepers of the deep-sea light.
The winter day broke blue and bright,
With glancing sun and glancing spray,
While o'er the swell our boat made way,
As gallant as a gull in flight.

But as we neared the lonely Isle,
And looked up at the naked height,
And saw the lighthouse towering white,
With blinded lantern that all night
Had never shot a spark
Of comfort through the dark,
So ghostly in the cold sunlight
It seemed that we were struck the while
With wonder all too dread for words.

And as into the tiny creek
We stole beneath the hanging crag,
We saw three queer, black, ugly birds—
Too big by far in my belief
For guillemot or shag—
Like seamen sitting bolt-upright
Upon a half-tide reef;
But as we neared, they plunged from sight
Without a sound or spurt of white.
And still too mazed to speak,

We landed, and made fast the boat,
And climbed the track in single file—

Each wishing he were safe afloat
On any sea, however far,
So be it far from Flannan Isle:
And still we seemed to climb and climb,
As though we'd lost all count of time,
And so must climb forevermore.
Yet all too soon we reached the door—
The black, sun-blistered lighthouse door,
That gaped for us ajar.

As on the threshold for a spell
We paused, we seemed to breathe the smell
Of limewash and of tar,
Familiar as our daily breath,
As though 'twere some strange scent of death:
And so, yet wondering, side by side
We stood a moment, still tongue-tied:
And each with black foreboding eyed
The door, ere we should fling it wide
To leave the sunlight for the gloom:
Till, plucking courage up, at last
Hard on each other's heels we passed
Into the living room.

Yet as we crowded through the door,
We only saw a table, spread
For dinner, meat and cheese and bread;
But all untouched; and no one there:
As though when they sat down to eat,
Ere they could even taste,
Alarm had come; and they in haste
Had risen and left the bread and meat:
For at the table-head a chair
Lay tumbled on the floor.
We listened; but we only heard
The feeble cheeping of a bird
That starved upon its perch:
And, listening still, without a word
We set about our hopeless search.

We hunted high, we hunted low;
And soon ransacked the empty house;
Then o'er the Island, to and fro,
We ranged, to listen and to look
In every cranny, cleft, or nook

That might have hid a bird or mouse.
But though we searched from shore to shore,
We found no sign in any place:
And soon again stood face to face
Before the gaping door:
And stole into the room once more
As frightened children steal.

Ay: though we hunted high and low,
And hunted everywhere,
Of the three men's fate we found no trace
Of any kind in any place,
But a door ajar, and an untouched meal,
And an overtoppled chair.

And so we listened in the gloom
Of that forsaken living room—
A chill clutch on our breath—
We thought how ill-chance came to all
Who kept the Flannan Light;
And how the rock had been the death
Of many a likely lad;
How six had come to a sudden end,
And three had gone stark mad:

And one whom we'd all known as friend
Had leapt from the lantern one still night,
And fallen dead by the lighthouse wall:
And long we thought
On the three we sought,
And of what might yet befall.

Like curs a glance has brought to heel,
We listened, flinching there:
And looked, and looked, on the untouched meal
And the overtoppled chair.

We seemed to stand for an endless while,
Though still no word was said,
Three men alive on Flannan Isle,
Who thought on three men dead.

OLIVER ST. JOHN GOGARTY
1878–

Verse

What should we know,
For better or worse,
Of the Long Ago,
Were it not for Verse:
What ships went down;
What walls were razed;
Who won the crown;
What lads were praised?
A fallen stone,
Or a waste of sands;
And all is known
Of Art-less lands.
But you need not delve
By the seaside hills
Where the Muse herself
All Time fulfils,
Who cuts with his scythe
All things but hers;
All but the blithe
Hexameters.

The Image-Maker

Hard is the stone, but harder still
The delicate preforming will
That guided by a dream alone,
Subdues and moulds the hardest stone,
Making the stubborn jade release
The emblem of eternal peace.

If but the will be firmly bent,
No stuff resists the mind's intent;

The adamant abets his skill
And sternly aids the artist's will,
To clothe in perdurable pride
Beauty his transient eyes descried.

The Plum Tree by the House

In morning light my damson showed
Its airy branches oversnowed
On all their quickening fronds,
That tingled where the early sun
Was flowing soft as silence on
Palm trees by coral ponds.
Out of the dark of sleep I come
To find the clay break into bloom,
The black boughs all in white!
I said, I must stand still and watch
This glory, strive no more to match
With similes things fair.
I am not fit to conjure up
A bird that's white enough to hop
Unstained in such a tree;
Nor crest him with the bloom to come
In purple glory on the plum.
Leave me alone with my delight
To store up joy against the night,
This moment leave to me!
Why should a poet strain his head
To make his mind a marriage bed;
Shall Beauty cease to bear?
There must be things which never shall
Be matched or made symmetrical
On earth or in the air;
Branches that Chinese draughtsmen drew,
Which none may find an equal to,
Unless he enter there
Where none may live—and more's the pity!—
The Perfect, the Forbidden City,
That's built—ah, God knows where!
Then leave me while I have the light
To fill my mind with growths of white,
Think of them longer than

Their budding hour, their springing day,
Until my mind is more than May;
And, may be, I shall plan
To make them yet break out like this
And blossom where their image is,
More lasting and more deep
Than coral boughs in light inurned,
When they are to the earth returned;
And I am turned to sleep.

After Galen

Only the Lion and the Cock,
As Galen says, withstand Love's shock.
So, dearest, do not think me rude
If I yield now to lassitude,
But sympathise with me. I know
You would not have me roar, or crow.

Death May Be Very Gentle

Death may be very gentle after all:
He turns his face away from arrogant knights
Who fling themselves against him in their fights;
But to the loveliest he loves to call.
And he has with him those whose ways were mild
And beautiful; and many a little child.

OLIVER GOLDSMITH

1730–1774

The Three Jolly Pigeons

Let schoolmasters puzzle their brain
    With grammar, and nonsense, and learning;

Good liquor, I stoutly maintain,
   Gives genius a better discerning.
Let them brag of their heathenish gods,
   Their Lethes, their Styxes, and Stygians,
Their *qui's*, and their *quae's*, and their *quod's*,
   They're all but a parcel of pigeons.
             Toroddle, toroddle, toroll!

When Methodist preachers come down,
   A-preaching that drinking is sinful,
I'll wager the rascals a crown,
   They always preach best with a skinful.
But when you come down with your pence,
   For a slice of their scurvy religion,
I'll leave it to all men of sense,
   But you, my good friend, are the pigeon.
             Toroddle, toroddle, toroll!

Then come, put the jorum about,
   And let us be merry and clever,
Our hearts and our liquors are stout,
   Here's the Three Jolly Pigeons forever.
Let some cry up woodcock or hare,
   Your bustards, your ducks, and your widgeons;
But of all of the birds in the air,
   Here's a health to the Three Jolly Pigeons.
             Toroddle, toroddle, toroll!

THOMAS GRAY

1716–1771

On the Death of a Favorite Cat, Drowned in a Tub of Gold Fishes

'Twas on a lofty vase's side,
Where China's gayest art had dyed
   The azure flowers that blow;
Demurest of the tabby kind,

134

The pensive Selima reclined,
   Gazed on the lake below.

Her conscious tail her joy declared;
The fair round face, the snowy beard,
   The velvet of her paws,
Her coat, that with the tortoise vies,
Her ears of jet, and emerald eyes,
   She saw; and purred applause.

Still had she gazed; but midst the tide
Two angel forms were seen to glide,
   The genii of the stream:
Their scaly armor's Tyrian hue
Through richest purple to the view
   Betrayed a golden gleam.

The hapless nymph with wonder saw:
A whisker first and then a claw,
   With many an ardent wish,
She stretched in vain to reach the prize.
What female heart can gold despise?
   What cat's averse to fish?

Presumptuous maid! with looks intent
Again she stretched, again she bent,
   Nor knew the gulf between.
(Malignant Fate sat by, and smiled.)
The slipp'ry verge her feet beguiled—
   She tumbled headlong in.

Eight times emerging from the flood
She mewed to ev'ry wat'ry god,
   Some speedy aid to send.
No dolphin came, no Nereid stirred:
Nor cruel Tom, nor Susan heard.
   A fav'rite has no friend!

From hence, ye beauties, undeceived,
Know, one false step is ne'er retrieved.
   And be with caution bold.
Not all that tempts your wand'ring eyes
And heedless hearts is lawful prize;
   Nor all that glisters, gold.

ARTHUR GUITERMAN

1871–1943

Bears

High up among the mountains, through a lovely grove of cedars
  They came on ferny forest ways and trails that lift and wind,
The bears of many ranges under celebrated leaders
  Assembling in a congress for the weal of all their kind.

  Black bears, brown bears,
  Sober bears and clown bears,
Chubby bears and tubby bears and bears austerely planned,
  Bears of mild benignity,
  Bears of simple dignity,
Coming to the Council of the Bruins of the Land.

A most tremendous Grizzly was Exalted Cockalorum;
  He didn't need a gavel for his paw was hard and square.
The meeting was conducted with unparalleled decorum,
  For no one ever questioned the decisions of the Chair.

  Fat bears, lean bears,
  Muddy bears and clean bears,
Tawny bears and brawny bears and bears in heavy coats,
  Bears of perspicacity,
  Bears of much loquacity,
Rumbling ghostly noises in their tummies and their throats.

They argued that their greatest need was more and better honey,
  That berries ought to propagate in every vacant space;
They voted that the Teddy Bear was anything but funny,
  Demanding his suppression as a Libel on the Race.

  Dark bears, light bears,
  Stupid bears and bright bears,
Gabby bears and flabby bears and bears of force and will,
  Bears of deep humility,
  Bears of marked ability,
Dealing with Conditions with extraordinary skill.

Their orators orated on the laxity of morals
    Contrasted with the beauty of the early forest den;
They favored arbitration for the settlement of quarrels
    And instant abolition of the armaments of men.

    Weak bears, strong bears,
      Proper bears and wrong bears,
  Eager bears and meager bears and bears morose and glum,
    Locally admired bears,
    Splendidly inspired bears,
Working for the Future and the Bear that Is to Come.

They settled mighty matters with miraculous discernment,
    They voted a Committee on the Stinginess of Bees,
They voted for a banquet and immediate adjournment
    And rolled away like shadows through the vistas of the trees.

    Red bears, grey bears,
      Gloomy bears and gay bears,
Ambling off in bevies down the boulder-bordered run,
    Bears in sweet amenity,
    Bears in calm serenity,
Sure that what is voted for is just as good as done.

THOMAS HARDY

1840–1928

Channel Firing

That night your great guns, unawares,
Shook all our coffins as we lay,
And broke the chancel window-squares,
We thought it was the Judgment-day

And sat upright. While drearisome
Arose the howl of wakened hounds:
The mouse let fall the altar-crumb,
The worms drew back into the mounds,

The glebe cow drooled. Till God called, "No;
It's gunnery practice out at sea
Just as before you went below;
The world is as it used to be:

"All nations striving strong to make
Red war yet redder. Mad as hatters
They do no more for Christés sake
Than you who are helpless in such matters.

"That this is not the judgment-hour
For some of them's a blessed thing,
For if it were they'd have to scour
Hell's floor for so much threatening. . . .

"Ha, ha! It will be warmer when
I blow the trumpet (if indeed
I ever do; for you are men,
And rest eternal sorely need)."

So down we lay again. "I wonder,
Will the world ever saner be,"
Said one, "than when He sent us under
In our indifferent century!"

And many a skeleton shook his head.
"Instead of preaching forty year,"
My neighbor Parson Thirdly said,
"I wish I had stuck to pipes and beer."

Again the guns disturbed the hour,
Roaring their readiness to avenge,
As far inland as Stourton Tower,
And Camelot, and starlit Stonehenge.

SARA HENDERSON HAY

1906–

Christmas, the Year One, A. D.

That year no wondering shepherds came,
Nor ever any more

The Magi from the glamorous East,
Crowding the narrow door.

There were no gifts of myrrh or gold,
Or jewels in glittering strands
Too heavy for a child to hold,
Too harsh for baby hands.

But Martha baked a barley cake,
Dorcas a spicy bun,
And goodman Joseph carved a toy
For Mary's little Son.

Timothy brought a woolly lamb,
Esther a fluted shell,
And all day long came friendly folk
To wish young Jesus well.

There was no sudden clash of steel
To make sweet Mary start,
Nor any dark, ambiguous words
Coiling about her heart.

Only the things of home, and peace,
With the calm stars above,
And little Jesus safe among
The holier gifts of love.

WILLIAM ERNEST HENLEY

1849–1903

A Late Lark

A late lark twitters from the quiet skies;
And from the west,
Where the sun, his day's work ended,
Lingers as in content,
There falls on the old, grey city
An influence luminous and serene,
A shining peace.

The smoke ascends
In a rosy-and-golden haze. The spires
Shine and are changed. In the valley
Shadows rise. The lark sings on. The sun,
Closing his benediction,
Sinks, and the darkening air
Thrills with a sense of the triumphing night—
Night with her train of stars
And her great gift of sleep.

So be my passing!
My task accomplished and the long day done,
My wages taken, and in my heart
Some late lark singing,
Let me be gathered to the quiet west,
The sundown splendid and serene,
Death.

GEORGE HERBERT

1593–1633

Virtue

Sweet day, so cool, so calm, so bright,
The bridal of the earth and sky,
The dew shall weep thy fall tonight,
   For thou must die.

Sweet rose, whose hue, angry and brave,
Bids the rash gazer wipe his eye,
Thy root is ever in its grave,
   And thou must die.

Sweet spring, full of sweet days and roses,
A box where sweets compacted lie,
My music shows ye have your closes,
   And all must die.

Only a sweet and virtuous soul,
Like seasoned timber, never gives;

But though the whole world turn to coal,
Then chiefly lives.

The Collar

I struck the board, and cried: "No more!
I will abroad.
What, shall I ever sigh and pine?
My lines and life are free—free as the road,
Loose as the wind, as large as store.
Shall I be still in suit?
Have I no harvest but a thorn
To let me blood, and not restore
What I have lost with cordial fruit?
Sure there was wine
Before my sighs did dry it; there was corn
Before my tears did drown it.
Is the year only lost to me?
Have I no bays to crown it?
No flowers, no garlands gay? all blasted,
All wasted?
Not so, my heart! But there is fruit,
And thou hast hands.
Recover all thy sigh-blown age
On double pleasures. Leave thy cold dispute
Of what is fit and not. Forsake thy cage,
Thy rope of sands,
Which petty thoughts have made (and made to thee
Good cable, to enforce and draw,
And be thy law,
While thou didst wink and wouldst not see.)
Away! take heed;
I will abroad!
Call in thy death's head there! Tie up thy fears!
He that forbears
To suit and serve his need
Deserves his load."
But as I raved, and grew more fierce and wild
At every word,
Methought I heard one calling, "Child!"
And I replied, "My Lord."

ROBERT HERRICK

1591–1674

The Argument of His Book

I sing of brooks, of blossoms, birds, and bowers,
Of April, May, of June, and July flowers.
I sing of Maypoles, hock-carts, wassails, wakes,
Of bridegrooms, brides, and of their bridal cakes.
I write of youth, of love, and have access
By these to sing of cleanly wantonness.
I sing of dews, of rains, and piece by piece
Of balm, of oil, of spice, and ambergris.
I sing of Time's trans-shifting; and I write
How roses first came red, and lilies white.
I write of groves, of twilights, and I sing
The court of Mab, and of the Fairy King.
I write of Hell; I sing (and ever shall)
Of heaven, and hope to have it after all.

To Daffodils

Fair daffodils, we weep to see
   You haste away so soon;
As yet the early-rising sun
   Has not attained his noon.
      Stay, stay
    Until the hasting day
      Has run
    But to the evensong;
And having prayed together, we
    Will go with you along.

We have short time to stay, as you;
   We have as short a spring;
As quick a growth to meet decay,
   As you, or any thing.

We die
As your hours do, and dry
Away
Like to the summer's rain,
Or as the pearls of morning's dew,
Ne'er to be found again.

Delight in Disorder

A sweet disorder in the dress
Kindles in clothes a wantonness:
A lawn about the shoulders thrown
Into a fine distractión,
An erring lace, which here and there
Enthralls the crimson stomacher,
A cuff neglectful, and thereby
Ribbands to flow confusedly,
A winning wave, deserving note,
In the tempestuous petticoat,
A careless shoestring, in whose tie
I see a wild civility—
Do more bewitch me than when art
Is too precise in every part.

The Night-Piece, to Julia

Her eyes the glowworm lend thee;
The shooting stars attend thee;
    And the elves also,
    Whose little eyes glow
Like the sparks of fire, befriend thee.

No will-o'-the-wisp mislight thee,
Nor snake or slowworm bite thee;
    But on, on thy way
    Not making a stay,
Since ghosts there's none to affright thee.

Let not the dark thee cumber;
What though the moon does slumber?
    The stars of the night

Will lend thee their light,
Like tapers clear without number.

Then, Julia, let me woo thee,
Thus, thus to come unto me;
    And when I shall meet
    Thy silv'ry feet,
My soul I'll pour into thee.

A Ternary of Littles, upon a Pipkin of Jelly Sent to a Lady

A little saint best fits a little shrine,
A little prop best fits a little vine,
As my small cruse best fits my little wine.

A little seed best fits a little soil,
A little trade best fits a little toil,
As my small jar best fits my little oil.

A little bin best fits a little bread,
A little garland fits a little head,
As my small stuff best fits my little shed.

A little hearth best fits a little fire,
A little chapel fits a little choir,
As my small bell best fits my little spire.

A little stream best fits a little boat,
A little lead best fits a little float,
As my small pipe best fits my little note.

A little meat best fits a little belly,
As sweetly, lady, give me leave to tell ye,
This little pipkin fits this little jelly.

Not Every Day Fit for Verse

'Tis not ev'ry day that I
Fitted am to prophesy.
No, but when the spirit fills
The fantastic pannicles
Full of fire, then I write

144

As the godhead doth indite.
Thus enraged, my lines are hurled
Like the Sibyl's through the world.
Look how next the holy fire
Either slakes or doth retire;
So the fancy cools, till when
That brave spirit comes again.

A *Thanksgiving to God for His House*

Lord, thou hast given me a cell
    Wherein to dwell,
A little house, whose humble roof
    Is weatherproof,
Under the spars of which I lie
    Both soft and dry;
Where thou, my chamber for to ward,
    Hast set a guard
Of harmless thoughts to watch and keep
    Me while I sleep.
Low is my porch, as is my fate,
    Both void of state;
And yet the threshold of my door
    Is worn by the poor,
Who thither come and freely get
    Good words or meat.
Like as my parlor, so my hall
    And kitchen's small:
A little buttery and therein
    A little bin,
Which keeps my little loaf of bread
    Unchipped, unflead;
Some brittle sticks of thorn or briar
    Make me a fire,
Close by whose living coal I sit
    And glow like it.
Lord, I confess too, when I dine,
    The pulse is thine,
And all those other bits that be
    There placed by thee—
The worts, the purslain, and the mess
    Of water cress,

Which of thy kindness thou hast sent;
    And my content
Makes those and my belovéd beet
    To be more sweet.
'Tis thou that crown'st my glittering hearth
    With guiltless mirth,
And giv'st me wassail bowls to drink,
    Spiced to the brink.
Lord, 'tis thy plenty-dropping hand
    That soils my land,
And giv'st me, for my bushel sown,
    Twice ten for one.
Thou mak'st my teeming hen to lay
    Her egg each day,
Besides my healthful ewes to bear
    Me twins each year,
The while the conduits of my kine
    Run cream, for wine.
All these, and better, thou dost send
    Me, to this end,
That I should render for my part
    A thankful heart,
Which, fired with incense, I resign
    As wholly thine;
But the acceptance—that must be,
    My Christ, by thee.

A Grace for a Child

Here a little child I stand,
Heaving up my either hand;
Cold as paddocks though they be,
Here I lift them up to Thee,
For a benison to fall
On our meat, and on us all. Amen.

OLIVER WENDELL HOLMES

1809–1894

The Deacon's Masterpiece
or, The Wonderful "One-Hoss Shay"

A Logical Story

Have you heard of the wonderful one-hoss shay,
That was built in such a logical way
It ran a hundred years to a day,
And then, of a sudden, it—ah, but stay,
I'll tell you what happened without delay,
Scaring the parson into fits,
Frightening people out of their wits—
Have you ever heard of that, I say?

Seventeen hundred and fifty-five.
Georgius Secundus was then alive—
Snuffy old drone from the German hive.
That was the year when Lisbon-town
Saw the earth open and gulp her down,
And Braddock's army was done so brown,
Left without a scalp to its crown.
It was on the terrible Earthquake-day
That the Deacon finished the one-hoss shay.

Now in building of chaises, I tell you what,
There is always *somewhere* a weakest spot—
In hub, tire, felloe, in spring or thill,
In panel, or crossbar, or floor, or sill,
In screw, bolt, thoroughbrace—lurking still,
Find it somewhere you must and will—
Above or below, or within or without—
And that's the reason, beyond a doubt,
That a chaise *breaks down* but doesn't *wear out*.

But the Deacon swore (as Deacons do,
With an "I dew vum," or an "I tell *yeou*")
He would build one shay to beat the taown
'N' the keounty 'n' all the kentry raoun';

It should be so built that it *couldn'* break daown:
"Fur," said the Deacon " 't's mighty plain
Thut the weakes' place mus' stan' the strain;
'N' the way t' fix it, uz I maintain, is only jest
T' make that place uz strong uz the rest."

So the Deacon inquired of the village folk
Where he could find the strongest oak,
That couldn't be split nor bent nor broke—
That was for spokes and floor and sills;
He sent for lancewood to make the thills;
The crossbars were ash from the straightest trees,
The panels of whitewood, that cuts like cheese
But lasts like iron for things like these;
The hubs of logs from the "Settler's ellum"—
Last of its timber—they couldn't sell 'em,
Never an axe had seen their chips,
And the wedges flew from between their lips,
Their blunt ends frizzled like celery-tips;
Step and prop-iron, bolt and screw,
Spring, tire, axle, and linchpin too,
Steel of the finest, bright and blue;
Thoroughbrace bison-skin, thick and wide;
Boot, top, dasher, from tough old hide
Found in the pit when the tanner died.
That was the way he "put her through."
"There!" said the Deacon, "naow she'll dew!"

Do! I tell you, I rather guess
She was a wonder, and nothing less!
Colts grew horses, beards turned grey,
Deacon and deaconess dropped away,
Children and grandchildren—where were they?
But there stood the stout old one-hoss shay
As fresh as on Lisbon-earthquake-day!

EIGHTEEN HUNDRED—it came and found
The Deacon's masterpiece strong and sound.
Eighteen hundred increased by ten—
"Hahnsum kerridge" they called it then.
Eighteen hundred and twenty came—
Running as usual; much the same.
Thirty and forty at last arrive,
And then come fifty, and FIFTY-FIVE.

Little of all we value here
Wakes on the morn of its hundredth year

148

Without both feeling and looking queer.
In fact, there's nothing that keeps its youth,
So far as I know, but a tree and truth.
(This is a moral that runs at large;
Take it.—You're welcome.—No extra charge.)

FIRST OF NOVEMBER—the Earthquake-day—
There are traces of age in the one-hoss shay,
A general flavor of mild decay,
But nothing local, as one may say.
There couldn't be—for the Deacon's art
Had made it so like in every part
That there wasn't a chance for one to start,
For the wheels were just as strong as the thills,
And the floor was just as strong as the sills,
And the panels just as strong as the floor,
And the whipple-tree neither less nor more,
And the back-crossbar as strong as the fore,
And spring and axle and hub *encore*.
And yet, *as a whole*, it is past a doubt
In another hour it will be *worn out!*

First of November, fifty-five!
This morning the parson takes a drive.
Now, small boys, get out of the way!
Here comes the wonderful one-hoss shay,
Drawn by a rat-tailed, ewe-necked bay.
"Huddup!" said the parson.—Off went they.
The parson was working his Sunday's text—
Had got to *fifthly*, and stopped perplexed
At what the—Moses—was coming next.
All at once the horse stood still,
Close by the meet'n'-house on the hill.
First a shiver, and then a thrill,
Then something decidedly like a spill—
And the parson was sitting upon a rock,
At half past nine by the meet'n'-house clock—
Just the hour of the Earthquake shock!
What do you think the parson found,
When he got up and stared around?
The poor old chaise in a heap or mound,
As if it had been to the mill and ground!
You see, of course, if you're not a dunce,
How it went to pieces all at once—
All at once, and nothing first—
Just as bubbles do when they burst.

End of the wonderful one-hoss shay.
Logic is logic. That's all I say.

GERARD MANLEY HOPKINS

1844–1889

The Habit of Perfection

Elected Silence, sing to me
And beat upon my whorléd ear,
Pipe me to pastures still and be
The music that I care to hear.

Shape nothing, lips; be lovely-dumb:
It is the shut, the curfew sent
From there where all surrenders come
Which only makes you eloquent.

Be shelléd, eyes, with double dark
And find the uncreated light:
This ruck and reel which you remark
Coils, keeps, and teases simple sight.

Palate, the hutch of tasty lust,
Desire not to be rinsed with wine:
The can must be so sweet, the crust
So fresh that come in fasts divine!

Nostrils, your careless breath that spend
Upon the stir and keep of pride,
What relish shall the censers send
Along the sanctuary side!

O feel-of-primrose hands, O feet
That want the yield of plushy sward,
But you shall walk the golden street
And you unhouse and house the Lord.

And, Poverty, be thou the bride
And now the marriage feast begun,
And lily-colored clothes provide
Your spouse not labored-at nor spun.

150

The Windhover

To Christ our Lord

I caught this morning morning's minion, king-
    dom of daylight's dauphin, dapple-dawn-drawn Falcon, in his
      riding
Of the rolling level underneath him steady air, and striding
High there, how he rung upon the rein of a wimpling wing
In his ecstasy! then off, off forth on swing,
    As a skate's heel sweeps smooth on a bow-bend: the hurl and
      gliding
Rebuffed the big wind. My heart in hiding
Stirred for a bird—the achieve of, the mastery of the thing!

Brute beauty and valor and act, oh air, pride, plume, here
    Buckle! AND the fire that breaks from thee then, a billion
Times told lovelier, more dangerous, O my chevalier!

    No wonder of it: sheer plod makes plough down sillion
Shine, and blue-bleak embers, ah my dear,
    Fall, gall themselves, and gash gold-vermilion.

Pied Beauty

Glory be to God for dappled things—
    For skies of couple-color as a brinded cow;
      For rose-moles all in stipple upon trout that swim;
Fresh-firecoal chestnut-falls; finches' wings;
    Landscape plotted and pieced—fold, fallow, and plough;
    And all trades, their gear and tackle and trim.

All things counter, original, spare, strange;
    Whatever is fickle, freckled (who knows how?)
    With swift, slow; sweet, sour; adazzle, dim;
He fathers-forth whose beauty is past change:
        Praise him.

Felix Randal

Felix Randal the farrier, oh he is dead then? my duty all ended,
Who have watched his mould of man, big-boned and hardy-hand-
    some

Pining, pining, till time when reason rambled in it and some
Fatal four disorders, fleshed there, all contended?

Sickness broke him. Impatient he cursed at first, but mended
Being anointed and all; though a heavenlier heart began some
Months earlier, since I had our sweet reprieve and ransom
Tendered to him. Ah well, God rest him all road ever he offended!

This seeing the sick endears them to us, us too it endears.
My tongue had taught thee comfort, touch had quenched thy tears,
Thy tears that touched my heart, child, Felix, poor Felix Randal;

How far from then forethought of, all thy more boisterous years,
When thou at the random grim forge, powerful amidst peers,
Didst fettle for the great grey drayhorse his bright and battering
   sandal!

Spring and Fall: To a Young Child

Margaret, are you grieving
Over Goldengrove unleaving?
Leaves, like the things of man, you
With your fresh thoughts care for, can you?
Ah! as the heart grows older
It will come to such sights colder
By and by, nor spare a sigh
Though worlds of wanwood leafmeal lie;
And yet you will weep and know why.
Now no matter, child, the name:
Sorrow's springs are the same.
Nor mouth had, no nor mind, expressed
What heart heard of, ghost guessed:
It is the blight man was born for,
It is Margaret you mourn for.

Inversnaid

This darksome burn, horseback brown,
His rollrock highroad roaring down,
In coop and in comb the fleece of his foam
Flutes and low to the lake falls home.

A windpuff-bonnet of fawn-froth
Turns and twindles over the broth
Of a pool so pitchblack, fell-frowning,
It rounds and rounds despair to drowning.

Degged with dew, dappled with dew
Are the groins of the braes that the brook treads **through,**
Wiry heathpacks, flitches of fern,
And the beadbonny ash that sits over the burn.

What would the world be, once bereft
Of wet and of wildness? Let them be left,
Oh let them be left, wildness and wet;
Long live the weeds and the wilderness yet.

A. E. HOUSMAN

1859–1936

To an Athlete Dying Young

The time you won your town the race
We chaired you through the marketplace;
Man and boy stood cheering by,
And home we brought you shoulder-high.

Today, the road all runners come,
Shoulder-high we bring you home.
And set you at your threshold down,
Townsman of a stiller town.

Smart lad, to slip betimes away
From fields where glory does not stay,
And early though the laurel grows
It withers quicker than the rose.

Eyes the shady night has shut
Cannot see the record cut,
And silence sounds no worse than cheers
After earth has stopped the ears:

Now you will not swell the rout
Of lads that wore their honors out,

Runners whom renown outran
And the name died before the man.

So set, before its echoes fade,
The fleet foot on the sill of shade,
And hold to the low lintel up
The still-defended challenge-cup.

And round that early-laureled head
Will flock to gaze the strengthless dead,
And find unwithered on its curls
The garland briefer than a girl's.

On Wenlock Edge

On Wenlock Edge the wood's in trouble;
    His forest fleece the Wrekin heaves;
The gale, it plies the saplings double,
    And thick on Severn snow the leaves.

'Twould blow like this through holt and hanger
    When Uricon the city stood:
'Tis the old wind in the old anger,
    But then it threshed another wood.

Then—'twas before my time—the Roman
    At yonder heaving hill would stare:
The blood that warms an English yeoman,
    The thoughts that hurt him, they were there.

There, like the wind through woods in riot,
    Through him the gale of life blew high;
The tree of man was never quiet:
    Then 'twas the Roman, now 'tis I.

The gale, it plies the saplings double,
    It blows so hard, 'twill soon be gone:
Today the Roman and his trouble
    Are ashes under Uricon.

Fancy's Knell

When lads were home from labor
    At Abdon under Clee,
A man would call his neighbor
    And both would send for me.
And where the light in lances
    Across the mead was laid,
There to the dances
    I fetched my flute and played.

Ours were idle pleasures,
    Yet oh content we were,
The young to wind the measures,
    The old to heed the air;
And I to lift with playing
    From tree and tower and steep
The light delaying,
    And flute the sun to sleep.

The youth toward his fancy
    Would turn his brow of tan,
And Tom would pair with Nancy
    And Dick step off with Fan;
The girl would lift her glances
    To his, and both be mute:
Well went the dances
    At evening to the flute.

Wenlock Edge was umbered,
    And bright was Abdon Burf,
And warm between them slumbered
    The smooth green miles of turf;
Until from grass and clover
    The upshot beam would fade,
And England over
    Advanced the lofty shade.

The lofty shade advances,
    I fetch my flute and play:
Come, lads, and learn the dances
    And praise the tune today.
Tomorrow, more's the pity,
    Away we both must hie,
To air the ditty,
    And to earth I.

We'll to the Woods No More

We'll to the woods no more,
The laurels all are cut,
The bowers are bare of bay
That once the Muses wore;
The year draws in the day
And soon will evening shut:
The laurels all are cut,
We'll to the woods no more.
Oh we'll no more, no more
To the leafy woods away,
To the high wild woods of laurel
And the bowers of bay no more.

LEIGH HUNT

1784–1859

Jenny Kissed Me

Jenny kissed me when we met,
　　Jumping from the chair she sat in;
Time, you thief, who love to get
　　Sweets into your list, put that in!
Say I'm weary, say I'm sad,
　　Say that health and wealth have missed me.
Say I'm growing old, but add,
　　　　　Jenny kissed me.

BEN JONSON

1572–1637

Hymn to Diana

Queen and Huntress, chaste and fair,
    Now the sun is laid to sleep,
Seated in thy silver chair
    State in wonted manner keep:
        Hesperus entreats thy light,
        Goddess excellently bright.

Earth, let not thy envious shade
    Dare itself to interpose;
Cynthia's shining orb was made
    Heaven to clear when day did close:
        Bless us then with wishéd sight,
        Goddess excellently bright.

Lay thy bow of pearl apart
    And thy crystal-shining quiver;
Give unto the flying hart
    Space to breathe, how short soever:
        Thou that mak'st a day of night,
        Goddess excellently bright!

JAMES JOYCE

1882–1941

I Hear an Army

I hear an army charging upon the land,
    And the thunder of horses plunging, foam about their knees:

Arrogant in black armor behind them stand,
   Disdaining the reins, with fluttering whips the charioteers.

They cry unto the night their battle-name:
   I moan in sleep when I hear afar their whirling laughter.
They cleave the gloom of dreams, a blinding flame,
   Clanging, clanging upon the heart as upon an anvil.

They come shaking in triumph their long, green hair:
   They come out of the sea and run shouting by the shore.
My heart, have you no wisdom thus to despair?
   My love, my love, my love, why have you left me alone?

All Day I Hear the Noise of Waters

All day I hear the noise of waters
    Making moan,
Sad as the seabird is when going
    Forth alone
He hears the winds cry to the waters'
    Monotone.

The grey winds, the cold winds are blowing
    Where I go;
I hear the noise of many waters
    Far below;
All day, all night, I hear them flowing
    To and fro.

JOHN KEATS

1795–1821

Lines on the Mermaid Tavern

Souls of poets dead and gone,
What Elysium have ye known,
Happy field or mossy cavern,

Choicer than the Mermaid Tavern?
Have ye tippled drink more fine
Than mine host's Canary wine?
Or are fruits of Paradise
Sweeter than those dainty pies
Of venison? O generous food!
Dressed as though bold Robin Hood
Would, with his maid Marian,
Sup and bowse from horn and can.

I have heard that on a day
Mine host's signboard flew away,
Nobody knew whither, till
An astrologer's old quill
To a sheepskin gave the story—
Said he saw you in your glory,
Underneath a new-old sign
Sipping beverage divine,
And pledging with contented smack
The Mermaid in the Zodiac.

Souls of poets dead and gone,
What Elysium have ye known,
Happy field or mossy cavern,
Choicer than the Mermaid Tavern?

La Belle Dame Sans Merci *

"Oh, what can ail thee, knight-at-arms,
    Alone and palely loitering?
The sedge has withered from the lake,
    And no birds sing.

"Oh, what can ail thee, knight-at-arms,
    So haggard and so woebegone?
The squirrel's granary is full,
    And the harvest's done.

I see a lily on thy brow
    With anguish moist and fever dew,
And on thy cheek a fading rose
    Fast withereth too.

* The beautiful lady without pity.

I met a lady in the meads
    Full beautiful, a faery's child;
Her hair was long, her foot was light
    And her eyes were wild.

I set her on my pacing steed,
    And nothing else saw all day long,
For sidelong would she bend and sing
    A faery's song.

I made a garland for her head,
    And bracelets too, and fragrant zone;
She looked at me as she did love,
    And made sweet moan.

She found me roots of relish sweet,
    And honey wild, and manna dew,
And sure in language strange she said,
    "I love thee true."

She took me to her elfin grot,
    And there she wept and sighed full sore,
And there I shut her wild, wild eyes
    With kisses four.

And there she lullèd me asleep
    And there I dreamed—ah woe betide!—
The latest dream I ever dreamed
    On the cold hill side.

I saw pale kings and princes too,
    Pale warriors death-pale were they all;
They cried, "La belle Dame sans Merci
    Thee hath in thrall."

I saw their starved lips in the gloam
    With horrid warning gapèd wide;
And I awoke and found me here
    On the cold hill's side.

And this is why I sojourn here,
    Alone and palely loitering;
Though the sedge has withered from the lake,
    And no birds sing.

Ode to a Nightingale

My heart aches, and a drowsy numbness pains
  My sense, as though of hemlock I had drunk,
Or emptied some dull opiate to the drains
  One minute past, and Lethe-wards had sunk:
'Tis not through envy of thy happy lot,
  But being too happy in thine happiness—
    That thou, light wingéd dryad of the trees,
      In some melodious plot
Of beechen green and shadows numberless
  Singest of summer in full-throated ease.

Oh for a draught of vintage that hath been
  Cooled a long age in the deep-delved earth,
Tasting of Flora and the country green,
  Dance, and Provençal song, and sunburnt mirth!
Oh for a beaker full of the warm South,
  Full of the true, the blushful Hippocrene,
    With beaded bubbles winking at the brim,
      And purple-stainéd mouth;
    That I might drink, and leave the world unseen,
    And with thee fade away into the forest dim:

Fade far away, dissolve, and quite forget
  What thou among the leaves hast never known—
The weariness, the fever, and the fret
  Here, where men sit and hear each other groan;
Where palsy shakes a few, sad, last grey hairs;
  Where youth grows pale, and specter-thin, and dies;
    Where but to think is to be full of sorrow
      And leaden-eyed despairs;
    Where beauty cannot keep her lustrous eyes,
    Or new love pine at them beyond tomorrow.

Away! away! for I will fly to thee,
  Not charioted by Bacchus and his pards,
But on the viewless wings of poesy,
  Though the dull brain perplexes and retards:
Already with thee! tender is the night,
  And haply the Queen-Moon is on her throne,
    Clustered around by all her starry fays;
      But here there is no light,
Save what from heaven is with the breezes blown
    Through verdurous glooms and winding, mossy
        ways.

I cannot see what flowers are at my feet,
  Nor what soft incense hangs upon the boughs,
But in embalmed darkness guess each sweet
  Wherewith the seasonable month endows
The grass, the thicket, and the fruit-tree wild;
  White hawthorn, and the pastoral eglantine;
    Fast fading violets covered up in leaves;
      And mid-May's eldest child,
  The coming musk-rose, full of dewy wine,
    The murmurous haunt of flies on summer eves.

Darkling I listen; and for many a time
  I have been half in love with easeful death,
Called him soft names in many a muséd rime,
  To take into the air my quiet breath;
Now more than ever seems it rich to die,
  To cease upon the midnight with no pain,
    While thou art pouring forth thy soul abroad
      In such an ecstasy!
  Still wouldst thou sing, and I have ears in vain—
    To thy high requiem become a sod.

Thou wast not born for death, immortal bird!
  No hungry generations tread thee down;
The voice I hear this passing night was heard
  In ancient days by emperor and clown:
Perhaps the self-same song that found a path
  Through the sad heart of Ruth, when, sick for home,
    She stood in tears amid the alien corn—
      The same that ofttimes hath
  Charmed magic casements, opening on the foam
    Of perilous seas, in faery lands forlorn.

Forlorn! the very word is like a bell
  To toll me back from thee to my sole self!
Adieu! the fancy cannot cheat so well
  As she is famed to do, deceiving elf.
Adieu! adieu! thy plaintive anthem fades
  Past the near meadows, over the still stream,
    Up the hillside; and now 'tis buried deep
      In the next valley-glades:
  Was it a vision or a waking dream?
    Fled is that music.—Do I wake or sleep?

162

Ode on Melancholy

No, no, go not to Lethe, neither twist
 Wolfsbane, tight-rooted, for its poisonous wine;
Nor suffer thy pale forehead to be kissed
 By nightshade, ruby grape of Proserpine;
Make not your rosary of yew-berries,
  Nor let the beetle, nor the death-moth be
   Your mournful Psyche, nor the downy owl
A partner in your sorrow's mysteries;
  For shade to shade will come too drowsily,
   And drown the wakeful anguish of the soul.

But when the melancholy fit shall fall
 Sudden from heaven like a weeping cloud,
That fosters the droop-headed flowers all,
 And hides the green hill in an April shroud;
Then glut thy sorrow on a morning rose,
  Or on the rainbow of the salt sand-wave,
   Or on the wealth of globéd peonies;
Or if thy mistress some rich anger shows,
  Emprison her soft hand and let her rave,
   And feed deep, deep upon her peerless eyes.

She dwells with beauty—beauty that must die;
 And joy, whose hand is ever at his lips
Bidding adieu; and aching pleasure nigh,
 Turning to poison while the bee-mouth sips:
Ay, in the very temple of delight
 Veiled melancholy has her sovran shrine,
  Though seen of none save him whose strenuous tongue
 Can burst joy's grape against his palate fine;
His soul shall taste the sadness of her might
 And be among her cloudy trophies hung.

When I Have Fears

When I have fears that I may cease to be
 Before my pen has gleaned my teeming brain,
Before high piléd books, in charactry,
 Hold like rich garners the full-ripened grain;
When I behold, upon the night's starred face,
 Huge cloudy symbols of a high romance,

And think that I may never live to trace
   Their shadows, with the magic hand of chance;
And when I feel, fair creature of an hour,
   That I shall never look upon thee more,
Never have relish in the faery power
   Of unreflecting love!—then on the shore
Of the wide world I stand alone and think,
Till love and fame to nothingness do sink.

SIDNEY KEYES

1922–1943

Plowman

Time was I was a plowman driving
Hard furrows, never resting, under the moon
Or in the frostbound bright-eyed morning
Laboring still; my team sleek-hided
As mulberry leaves, my team my best delight
After the sidelong blade my hero.
My iron-shod horses, my heroic walkers.
Now all that's finished. Rain's fallen now
Smudging my furrows, the comfortable
Elms are windpicked and harbor now no singer
Or southward homing bird; my horses grazing
Impossible mountainsides, long-frogged and lonely.
And I'm gone on the roads, a peevish man
Contending with the landscape, arguing
With shrike and shrewmouse and my face in puddles;
A tiresome man not listened to nor housed
By the wise housewife, not kissed nor handled
By any but wild weeds and summer winds.
Time was I was a fine strong fellow
Followed by girls. Now I keep company
Only with seasons and the cold crazy moon.

HENRY KINGSLEY
1830–1876

At Glastonbury

Magdalen at Michael's gate
   Tirléd at the pin;
On Joseph's thorn sang the blackbird,
   "Let her in! Let her in!"

"Hast thou seen the wounds?" said Michael,
   "Knowest thou thy sin?"
"It is evening, evening," sang the blackbird;
   "Let her in! Let her in!"

"Yes, I have seen the wounds,
   And I know my sin."
"She knows it well, well, well," sang the blackbird;
   "Let her in! Let her in!"

"Thou bringest no offerings," said Michael,
   "Nought save sin."
And the blackbird sang: "She is sorry, sorry, sorry.
   Let her in! Let her in!"

When he had sung himself to sleep,
   And night did begin,
One came and opened Michael's gate,
   And Magdalen went in.

RUDYARD KIPLING

1865–1936

The Gipsy Trail

The white moth to the closing bine,
  The bee to the opened clover,
And the gipsy blood to the gipsy blood
  Ever the wide world over.

Ever the wide world over, lass,
  Ever the trail held true,
Over the world and under the world,
  And back at the last to you.

Out of the dark of the gorgio camp,
  Out of the grime and the grey,
(Morning waits at the end of the world)
  Gipsy, come away!

The wild boar to the sun-dried swamp,
  The red crane to her reed,
And the Romany lass to the Romany lad
  By the tie of a roving breed.

The pied snake to the rifted rock,
  The buck to the stony plain,
And the Romany lass to the Romany lad,
  And both to the road again.

Both to the road again, again!
  Out on a clean sea-track—
Follow the cross of the gipsy trail
  Over the world and back!

Follow the Romany patteran
  North where the blue bergs sail,
And the bows are grey with the frozen spray,
  And the masts are shod with mail.

Follow the Romany patteran
  Sheer to the Austral Light,

Where the besom of God is the wild South wind,
   Sweeping the sea-floors white.

Follow the Romany patteran
   West to the sinking sun,
Till the junk-sails lift through the houseless drift,
   And the east and west are one.

Follow the Romany patteran
   East where the silence broods
By a purple wave on an opal beach
   In the hush of the Mahim woods.

"The wild hawk to the windswept sky,
   The deer to the wholesome wold,
And the heart of a man to the heart of a maid,
   As it was in the days of old."

The heart of a man to the heart of a maid—
   Light of my tents, be fleet.
Morning waits at the end of the world,
   And the world is all at our feet!

The Ballad of Fisher's Boardinghouse

(That night, when through the mooring-chains
   The wide-eyed corpse rolled free,
To blunder down by Garden Reach
   And rot at Kedgeree,
The tale the Hughli told the shoal
   The lean shoal told to me.)

     . . . . .

'Twas Fultah Fisher's boardinghouse,
   Where sailormen reside,
And there were men of all the ports
   From Mississip' to Clyde,
And regally they spat and smoked,
   And fearsomely they lied.

They lied about the purple sea
   That gave them scanty bread,
They lied about the earth beneath,
   The Heavens overhead,
For they had looked too often on
   Black rum when that was red.

They told their tales of wreck and wrong,
    Of shame and lust and fraud,
They backed their toughest statements with
    The brimstone of the Lord,
And crackling oaths went to and fro
    Across the fist-banged board.

And there was Hans the blue-eyed Dane,
    Bull-throated, bare of arm,
Who carried on his hairy chest
    The maid Ultruda's charm—
The little silver crucifix
    That keeps a man from harm.

And there was Jake Without-the-Ears,
    And Pamba the Malay,
And Carboy Gin the Guinea cook,
    And Luz from Vigo Bay,
And Honest Jack who sold them slops
    And harvested their pay.

And there was Salem Hardieker,
    A lean Bostonian he—
Russ, German, English, Halfbreed, Finn,
    Yank, Dane, and Portugee,
At Fultah Fisher's boardinghouse
    They rested from the sea.

Now Anne of Austria shared their drinks,
    Collinga knew her fame,
From Tarnau in Galicia
    To Jaun Bazar she came,
To eat the bread of infamy
    And take the wage of shame.

She held a dozen men to heel—
    Rich spoil of war was hers,
In hose and gown and ring and chain,
    From twenty mariners,
And by Port Law, that week men called
    Her Salem Hardieker's.

But seamen learnt—what landsmen know—
    That neither gifts nor gain
Can hold a winking light o' love
    Or fancy's flight restrain,

When Anne of Austria rolled her eyes
　　On Hans the blue-eyed Dane.

Since life is strife, and strife means knife
　　From Howrah to the Bay,
And he may die before the dawn
　　Who liquored out the day,
In Fultah Fisher's boardinghouse
　　We woo while yet we may.

But cold was Hans the blue-eyed Dane,
　　Bull-throated, bare of arm,
And laughter shook the chest beneath
　　The maid Ultruda's charm—
The little silver crucifix
　　That keeps a man from harm.

"You speak to Salem Hardieker;
　　You was his girl, I know.
I ship mineselfs tomorrow, see,
　　Und round the Skaw we go,
South, down the Cattegat, by Hjelm,
　　To Besser in Saro."

When love rejected turns to hate,
　　All ill betide the man.
"You speak to Salem Hardieker"—
　　She spoke as woman can.
A scream—a sob—"He called me—names!"
　　And then the fray began.

An oath from Salem Hardieker,
　　A shriek upon the stairs,
A dance of shadows on the wall,
　　A knife-thrust unawares—
And Hans came down, as cattle drop,
　　Across the broken chairs.

·　·　·　·　·

In Anne of Austria's trembling hands
　　The weary head fell low—
"I ship mineselfs tomorrow, straight
　　For Besser in Saro;
Und there Ultruda comes to me
　　At Easter, und I go

"South, down the Cattegat.—What's here?
　　There—are—no—lights—to—guide!"

The mutter ceased, the spirit passed.
    And Anne of Austria cried
In Fultah Fisher's boardinghouse
    When Hans the mighty died.

Thus slew they Hans the blue-eyed Dane,
    Bull-throated, bare of arm,
But Anne of Austria looted first
    The maid Ultruda's charm—
The little silver crucifix
    That keeps a man from harm.

Heriot's Ford

"What's that that hirples at my side?"
The foe that you must fight, my lord.
"That rides as fast as I can ride?"
The shadow of your might, my lord.

"Then wheel my horse against the foe!"
He's down and overpast, my lord.
You war against the sunset-glow,
The judgment follows fast, my lord!

"Oh who will stay the sun's descent?"
King Joshua he is dead, my lord.
"I need an hour to repent!"
'Tis what our sister said, my lord.

"Oh do not slay me in my sins!"
You're safe awhile with us, my lord.
"Nay, kill me ere my fear begins!"
We would not serve you thus, my lord.

"Where is the doom that I must face?"
Three little leagues away, my lord.
"Then mend the horses' laggard pace!"
We need them for next day, my lord.

"Next day—next day! Unloose my cords!"
Our sister needed none, my lord.
You had no mind to face our swords,
And—where can cowards run, my lord?

"You would not kill the soul alive?"
'Twas thus our sister cried, my lord.

"I dare not die with none to shrive."
But so our sister died, my lord.

"Then wipe the sweat from brow and cheek."
It runnels forth afresh, my lord.
"Uphold me—for the flesh is weak."
You've finished with the Flesh, my lord!

Harp Song of the Dane Women

What is a woman that you forsake her,
And the hearth-fire and the home-acre,
To go with the old grey Widow-maker?

She has no house to lay a guest in—
But one chill bed for all to rest in,
That the pale suns and the stray bergs nest in.

She has no strong white arms to fold you,
But the ten-times-fingering weed to hold you—
Out on the rocks where the tide has rolled you.

Yet when the signs of summer thicken,
And the ice breaks, and the birch-buds quicken,
Yearly you turn from our side, and sicken—

Sicken again for the shouts and the slaughters.
You steal away to the lapping waters,
And look at your ship in her winter-quarters.

You forget our mirth and talk at the tables,
The kine in the shed and the horse in the stables—
To pitch her sides and go over her cables.

Then you drive out where the storm-clouds swallow,
And the sound of your oar-blades, falling hollow,
Is all we have left through the months to follow.

Ah what is Woman that you forsake her,
And the hearth-fire and the home-acre,
To go with the old grey Widow-maker?

The Seal's Lullaby

Oh hush thee, my baby, the night is behind us,
And black are the waters that sparkled so green.

The moon, o'er the combers, looks downward to find us
  At rest in the hollows that rustle between.
Where billow meets billow, there soft be thy pillow;
  Ah, weary wee flipperling, curl at thy ease!
The storm shall not wake thee, nor shark overtake thee,
  Asleep in the arms of the slow-swinging seas.

WALTER SAVAGE LANDOR
1775–1864

Dirce

Stand close around, ye Stygian set,
With Dirce in one boat conveyed!
Or Charon, seeing, may forget
That he is old and she a shade.

ANDREW LANG
1844–1912

The Odyssey

As one that for a weary space has lain
  Lulled by the song of Circe and her wine
  In gardens near the pale of Proserpine,
Where that Aeaean isle forgets the main,
And only the low lutes of love complain,
  And only shadows of wan lovers pine—
  As such an one were glad to know the brine
Salt on his lips, and the large air again—
So gladly, from the songs of modern speech
  Men turn, and see the stars, and feel the free

Shrill wind beyond the close of heavy flowers,
And through the music of the languid hours
They hear like ocean on a western beach
The surge and thunder of the Odyssey.

EDWARD LEAR

1812–1888

The Owl and the Pussy-Cat

The Owl and the Pussy-cat went to sea
    In a beautiful pea-green boat:
They took some honey, and plenty of money
    Wrapped up in a five-pound note.
The Owl looked up to the stars above
    And sang to a small guitar,
"O lovely Pussy, O Pussy, my love,
    What a beautiful Pussy you are,
            You are, you are!
    What a beautiful Pussy you are!"

Pussy said to the Owl: "You elegant fowl,
    How charmingly sweet you sing!
Oh let us be married; too long we have tarried—
    But what shall we do for a ring?"
They sailed away for a year and a day
    To the land where the bong-tree grows;
And there in a wood a Piggy-wig stood
    With a ring at the end of his nose,
            His nose, his nose,
    With a ring at the end of his nose.

"Dear Pig, are you willing to sell for one shilling
    Your ring?" Said the Piggy, "I will."
So they took it away and were married next day
    By the turkey who lives on the hill.
They dined on mince and slices of quince,
    Which they ate with a runcible spoon;
And hand in hand on the edge of the sand

They danced by the light of the moon,
The moon, the moon,
They danced by the light of the moon.

The Jumblies

They went to sea in a sieve, they did;
   In a sieve they went to sea;
In spite of all their friends could say,
On a winter's morn, on a stormy day,
   In a sieve they went to sea.
And when the sieve turned round and round,
And everyone cried, "You'll all be drowned!"
They called aloud: "Our sieve ain't big.
But we don't care a button; we don't care a fig:
   In a sieve we'll go to sea!"
      Far and few, far and few,
         Are the lands where the Jumblies live;
         Their heads are green, and their hands are blue;
         And they went to sea in a sieve.

They sailed away in a sieve, they did,
   In a sieve they sailed so fast,
With only a beautiful pea-green veil
Tied with a ribbon, by way of a sail,
   To a small tobacco-pipe mast.
And everyone said who saw them go:
"Oh won't they be soon upset, you know!
For the sky is dark, and the voyage is long;
And happen what may, it's extremely wrong
   In a sieve to sail so fast."

The water it soon came in, it did;
   The water it soon came in:
So, to keep them dry, they wrapped their feet
In a pinky paper all folded neat:
   And they fastened it down with a pin.
And they passed the night in a crockery-jar;
And each of them said: "How wise we are!
Though the sky be dark, and the voyage be long,
Yet we never can think we were rash or wrong,
   While around in our sieve we spin."

And all night long they sailed away;
   And when the sun went down,
They whistled and warbled a moony song
To the echoing sound of a coppery gong,
   In the shade of the mountains brown:
"Oh Timballoo! how happy we are
When we live in a sieve and a crockery-jar!
And all night long in the moonlight pale
We sail away with a pea-green sail
   In the shade of the mountains brown."

They sailed to the Western Sea, they did—
   To a land all covered with trees:
And they bought an owl, and a useful cart,
And a pound of rice, and a cranberry-tart,
   And a hive of silvery bees;
And they bought a pig, and some green jackdaws,
And a lovely monkey with lollipop paws,
And forty bottles of ring-bo-ree,
   And no end of Stilton cheese.

And in twenty years they all came back—
   In twenty years or more;
And everyone said, "How tall they've grown!
For they've been to the Lakes, and the Terrible Zone,
   And the hills of Chankly Bore."
And they drank their health and gave them a feast
Of dumplings made of beautiful yeast;
And everyone said, "If we only live,
We too will go to sea in a sieve,
   To the hills of the Chankly Bore."
      Far and few, far and few,
        Are the lands where the Jumblies live.
      Their heads are green, and their hands are blue;
        And they went to sea in a sieve.

WINIFRED M. LETTS
1882–

The Spires of Oxford

I saw the spires of Oxford
   As I was passing by,
The grey spires of Oxford
   Against a pearl-grey sky;
My heart was with the Oxford men
   Who went abroad to die.

The years go fast in Oxford,
   The golden years and gay;
The hoary colleges look down
   On careless boys at play,
But when the bugles sounded—War!
   They put their games away.

They left the peaceful river,
   The cricket field, the quad,
The shaven lawns of Oxford
   To seek a bloody sod.
They gave their merry youth away
   For country and for God.

God rest you, happy gentlemen,
   Who laid your good lives down,
Who took the khaki and the gun
   Instead of cap and gown.
God bring you to a fairer place
   Than even Oxford town.

VACHEL LINDSAY

1879–1931

The Congo

(A study of the Negro Race)

I—THEIR BASIC SAVAGERY

A deep roll-
ing bass
Fat black bucks in a wine-barrel room,
Barrel-house kings, with feet unstable,
Sagged and reeled and pounded on the table,
Pounded on the table,
Beat an empty barrel with the handle of a broom,
Hard as they were able,
Boom, boom, BOOM,
With a silk umbrella and the handle of a broom,
Boomlay, boomlay, boomlay, BOOM.

More deliber-
ate.
Solemnly
chanted
THEN I had religion, THEN I had a vision.
I could not turn from their revel in derision.
THEN I SAW THE CONGO, CREEPING THROUGH THE BLACK,
CUTTING THROUGH THE JUNGLE WITH A GOLDEN TRACK.
Then along that riverbank
A thousand miles
Tattooed cannibals danced in files;
Then I heard the boom of the blood-lust song
And a thigh-bone beating on a tin-pan gong.
And "BLOOD!" screamed the whistles and the fifes of the
warriors,

A rapidly
piling climax
of speed and
racket
"BLOOD!" screamed the skull-faced, lean witch-doctors;
"Whirl ye the deadly voodoo rattle,
Harry the uplands,
Steal all the cattle,
Rattle-rattle, rattle-rattle, BING!
Boomlay, boomlay, boomlay, BOOM!"

With a
philosophic
pause
A roaring, epic, ragtime tune
From the mouth of the Congo
To the Mountains of the Moon.
Death is an elephant,
Torch-eyed and horrible,

Foam-flanked and terrible.

Shrilly and with a heavily accented metre

Boom, steal the pygmies,
Boom, kill the Arabs,
Boom, kill the white men,

Like the wind in the chimney

Hoo, hoo, hoo.
Listen to the yell of Leopold's ghost
Burning in Hell for his hand-maimed host.
Hear how the demons chuckle and yell
Cutting his hands off down in Hell.
Listen to the creepy proclamation,
Blown through the lairs of the forest-nation,
Blown past the white-ants' hill of clay,
Blown past the marsh where the butterflies play:

All the O sounds very golden. Heavy accents very heavy. Light accents very light. Last line whispered

"Be careful what you do,
Or Mumbo Jumbo, god of the Congo,
And all of the other
Gods of the Congo,
Mumbo Jumbo will hoodoo you,
Mumbo Jumbo will hoodoo you,
Mumbo Jumbo will hoodoo you."

II—THEIR IRREPRESSIBLE HIGH SPIRITS

Rather shrill and high

Wild crap-shooters with a whoop and a call
Danced the juba in their gambling-hall,
And laughed fit to kill, and shook the town,
And guyed the policemen and laughed them down
With a boomlay, boomlay, boomlay, boom. . . .

Read exactly as in first section.

Then I saw the Congo, creeping through the black,
Cutting through the jungle with a golden track.

Lay emphasis on the delicate ideas. Keep as light-footed as possible

A Negro fairyland swung into view,
A minstrel river
Where dreams come true.
The ebony palace soared on high
Through the blossoming trees to the evening sky.
The inlaid porches and casements shone
With gold and ivory and elephant-bone.
And the black crowd laughed till their sides were sore
At the baboon butler in the agate door,
And the well-known tunes of the parrot band
That trilled on the bushes of that magic land.

With pomposity

A troupe of skull-faced witch-men came
Through the agate doorway in suits of flame—
Yea, long-tailed coats with a gold-leaf crust
And hats that were covered with diamond dust.

And the crowd in the court gave a whoop and a call
And danced the juba from wall to wall.

With a great deliberation and ghostliness

But the witch-men suddenly stilled the throng
With a stern cold glare, and a stern old song:
"Mumbo Jumbo will hoodoo you." . . .

With overwhelming assurance, good cheer, and pomp

Just then from the doorway, as fat as shotes
Came the cake-walk princes in the long red coats,
Canes with a brilliant lacquer shine,
And tall silk hats that were red as wine.

With growing speed and sharply marked dance-rhythm

And they pranced with their butterfly partners there,
Coal-black maidens with pearls in their hair,
Knee-skirts trimmed with the jessamine sweet,
And bells on their ankles and little black feet.
And the couples railed at the chant and the frown
Of the witch-men lean, and laughed them down.
(Oh rare was the revel, and well worth while
That made those glowering witch-men smile.)

With a touch of Negro dialect, and as rapidly as possible toward the end

The cake-walk royalty then began
To walk for a cake that was tall as a man
To the tune of "Boomlay, boomlay, BOOM,"
While the witch-men laughed, with a sinister air,
And sang with the scalawags prancing there:
"Walk with care, walk with care,
Or Mumbo-Jumbo, god of the Congo,
And all of the other
Gods of the Congo,
Mumbo Jumbo will hoodoo you.
Beware, beware, walk with care,
Boomlay, boomlay, boomlay, boom,
Boomlay, boomlay, boomlay, boom,
Boomlay, boomlay, boomlay, boom,
Boomlay, boomlay, boomlay,
BOOM!"

Slow philosophic calm

Oh rare was the revel, and well worth while
That made those glowering witch-men smile.

III—THE HOPE OF THEIR RELIGION

Heavy bass. With a literal imitation of camp-meeting racket and trance

A good old Negro in the slums of the town
Preached at a sister for her velvet gown.
Howled at a brother for his low-down ways,
His prowling, guzzling, sneak-thief days.
Beat on the Bible till he wore it out

Starting the jubilee revival shout.
And some had visions, as they stood on chairs,
And sang of Jacob and the golden stairs.
And they all repented, a thousand strong,
From their stupor and savagery and sin and wrong,
And slammed with their hymn-books till they shook the
    room
With "Glory, glory, glory,"
And "Boom, boom, BOOM."

Exactly as in the first section. THEN I SAW THE CONGO, CREEPING THROUGH THE BLACK,
CUTTING THROUGH THE JUNGLE WITH A GOLDEN TRACK.
Begin with terror and power, end with joy. And the grey sky opened like a new-rent veil
And showed the Apostles with their coats of mail.
In bright white steel they were seated round
And their fire-eyes watched where the Congo wound.
And the twelve Apostles, from their throne on high,
Thrilled all the forest with their heavenly cry:
Sung to the tune of "Hark, ten thousand harps and voices" "Mumbo Jumbo will die in the jungle;
Never again will he hoodoo you,
Never again will he hoodoo you."

With growing deliberation and joy Then along that river, a thousand miles,
The vine-snared trees fell down in files.
Pioneer angels cleared the way
For a Congo paradise, for babes at play
For sacred capitals, for temples clean.
Gone were the skull-faced witch-men lean;
In a rather high key—as delicately as possible There, where the wild ghost-gods had wailed,
A million boats of the angels sailed
With oars of silver, and prows of blue,
And silken pennants that the sun shone through—
'Twas a land transfigured, 'twas a new creation.
Oh a singing wind swept the Negro nation,
And on through the backwoods clearing flew:
To the tune of "Hark, ten thousand harps and voices" "Mumbo Jumbo is dead in the jungle.
Never again will he hoodoo you,
Never again will he hoodoo you."

Redeemed were the forests, the beasts and the men,
And only the vulture dared again
By the far lone mountains of the moon
Dying down into a penetrating, terrified whisper To cry, in the silence, the Congo tune:
"Mumbo Jumbo will hoodoo you,
Mumbo Jumbo will hoodoo you.
Mumbo . . . Jumbo . . . will . . . hoodoo . . . you."

HENRY WADSWORTH LONGFELLOW
1807–1882

My Lost Youth

Often I think of the beautiful town
   That is seated by the sea;
Often in thought go up and down
The pleasant streets of that dear old town,
    And my youth comes back to me.
      And a verse of a Lapland song
      Is haunting my memory still:
      "A boy's will is the wind's will,
And the thoughts of youth are long, long thoughts."

I can see the shadowy lines of its trees,
   And catch in sudden gleams
The sheen of the far-surrounding seas,
And islands that were the Hesperides
    Of all my boyish dreams.
      And the burden of that old song,
      It murmurs and whispers still:
      "A boy's will is the wind's will,
And the thoughts of youth are long, long thoughts."

I remember the black wharves and the slips,
   And the sea-tides tossing free;
And Spanish sailors with bearded lips,
And the beauty and mystery of the ships,
    And the magic of the sea.
      And the voice of that wayward song
      Is singing and saying still:
      "A boy's will is the wind's will,
And the thoughts of youth are long, long thoughts."

I remember the bulwarks by the shore,
   And the fort upon the hill;
The sunrise gun, with its hollow roar,
The drum-beat repeated o'er and o'er,
    And the bugle wild and shrill.
      And the music of that old song
      Throbs in my memory still:

"A boy's will is the wind's will,
And the thoughts of youth are long, long thoughts."

I remember the sea-fight far away,
  How it thundered o'er the tide!
And the dead captains, as they lay
In their graves, o'erlooking the tranquil bay
  Where they in battle died.
    And the sound of that mournful song
    Goes through me with a thrill:
    "A boy's will is the wind's will,
And the thoughts of youth are long, long thoughts."

I can see the breezy dome of groves,
  The shadows of Deering's Woods;
And the friendships old and the early loves
Come back with a Sabbath sound, as of doves
  In quiet neighborhoods.
    And the verse of that sweet old song,
    It flutters and murmurs still:
    "A boy's will is the wind's will,
And the thoughts of youth are long, long thoughts."

I remember the gleams and glooms that dart
  Across the schoolboy's brain;
The song and the silence in the heart,
That in part are prophecies, and in part
  Are longings wild and vain.
    And the voice of that fitful song
    Sings on, and is never still:
    "A boy's will is the wind's will,
And the thoughts of youth are long, long thoughts."

There are things of which I may not speak;
  There are dreams that cannot die;
There are thoughts that make the strong heart weak,
And bring a pallor into the cheek,
  And a mist before the eye.
    And the words of that fatal song
    Come over me like a chill:
    "A boy's will is the wind's will,
And the thoughts of youth are long, long thoughts."

Strange to me now are the forms I meet
  When I visit the dear old town;
But the native air is pure and sweet,

And the trees that o'ershadow each well-known street,
  As they balance up and down,
    Are singing the beautiful song,
    Are sighing and whispering still:
    "A boy's will is the wind's will,
And the thoughts of youth are long, long thoughts."

And Deering's Woods are fresh and fair,
  And with joy that is almost pain
My heart goes back to wander there,
And among the dreams of the days that were,
  I find my lost youth again.
    And the strange and beautiful song,
    The groves are repeating it still:
    "A boy's will is the wind's will,
And the thoughts of youth are long, long thoughts."

Chaucer

An old man in a lodge within a park;
  The chamber walls depicted all around
  With portraitures of huntsman, hawk, and hound,
  And the hurt deer. He listeneth to the lark,
Whose song comes with the sunshine through the dark
  Of painted glass in leaden lattice bound;
  He listeneth and he laugheth at the sound,
  Then writeth in a book like any clerk.
He is the poet of the dawn, who wrote
  The Canterbury Tales, and his old age
  Made beautiful with song; and as I read
I hear the crowing cock, I hear the note
  Of lark and linnet, and from every page
  Rise odors of ploughed field or flowery mead.

The Tide Rises, The Tide Falls

The tide rises, the tide falls,
The twilight darkens, the curlew calls;
Along the sea-sands damp and brown
The traveler hastens toward the town,
  And the tide rises, the tide falls.

Darkness settles on roofs and walls,
But the sea, the sea in the darkness calls;
The little waves, with their soft, white hands,
Efface the footprints in the sands,
    And the tide rises, the tide falls.

The morning breaks; the steeds in their stalls
Stamp and neigh, as the hostler calls;
The day returns, but nevermore
Returns the traveler to the shore,
    And the tide rises, the tide falls.

The Day Is Done

The day is done, and the darkness
    Falls from the wings of night,
As a feather is wafted downward
    From an eagle in his flight.

I see the lights of the village
    Gleam through the rain and the mist,
And a feeling of sadness comes o'er me
    That my soul cannot resist:

A feeling of sadness and longing,
    That is not akin to pain,
And resembles sorrow only
    As the mist resembles rain.

Come, read to me some poem,
    Some simple and heartfelt lay,
That shall soothe this restless feeling,
    And banish the thoughts of day.

Not from the grand old masters,
    Not from the bards sublime,
Whose distant footsteps echo
    Through the corridors of Time.

For, like strains of martial music,
    Their mighty thoughts suggest
Life's endless toil and endeavor;
    And tonight I long for rest.

Read from some humbler poet,
   Whose songs gushed from his heart,
As showers from the clouds of summer,
   Or tears from the eyelids start;

Who through long days of labor,
   And nights devoid of ease,
Still heard in his soul the music
   Of wonderful melodies.

Such songs have power to quiet
   The restless pulse of care,
And come like the benediction
   That follows after prayer.

Then read from the treasured volume
   The poem of thy choice,
And lend to the rime of the poet
   The beauty of thy voice.

And the night shall be filled with music,
   And the cares that infest the day
Shall fold their tents like the Arabs,
   And as silently steal away.

RICHARD LOVELACE

1618–1657?

To Althea, from Prison

When Love with unconfinéd wings
   Hovers within my gates,
And my divine Althea brings
   To whisper at the grates;
When I lie tangled in her hair
   And fettered to her eye—
The gods that wanton in the air
   Know no such liberty.

When flowing cups run swiftly round
   With no allaying Thames,

Our careless heads with roses bound,
    Our hearts with loyal flames;
When thirsty grief in wine we steep,
    When healths and drafts go free—
Fishes that tipple in the deep
    Know no such liberty.

When, like committed linnets, I
    With shriller throat shall sing
The sweetness, mercy, majesty,
    And glories of my King;
When I shall voice aloud how good
    He is, how great should be—
Enlargéd winds, that curl the flood,
    Know no such liberty.

Stone walls do not a prison make,
    Nor iron bars a cage;
Minds innocent and quiet take
    That for an hermitage;
If I have freedom in my love
    And in my soul am free,
Angels alone, that soar above,
    Enjoy such liberty.

To Lucasta, Going to the Wars

Tell me not, sweet, I am unkind,
    That from the nunnery
Of thy chaste breast and quiet mind
    To war and arms I fly.

True, a new mistress now I chase,
    The first foe in the field;
And with a stronger faith embrace
    A sword, a horse, a shield.

Yet this inconstancy is such
    As thou too shalt adore;
I could not love thee, dear, so much,
    Loved I not honor more.

AMY LOWELL

1874–1925

Four Sides to a House

Peter, Peter, along the ground,
Is it wind I hear, or your shoes' sound?
Peter, Peter, across the air,
Do dead leaves fall, or is it your hair?
Peter, Peter, north and south,
They have stopped your mouth
With water, Peter.

The long road runs, and the long road runs,
  Who comes over the long road, Peter?
Who knocks at the door in the cold twilight
And begs a heap of straw for the night,
And a bit of a sup, and a bit of bite—
  Do you know the face, Peter?

He lays him down on the floor and sleeps.
  Must you wind the clock, Peter?
It will strike and strike the dark night through.
He will sleep past one, he will sleep past two,
But when it strikes three what will he do?
  He will rise and kill you, Peter.

He will open the door to one without.
  Do you hear that voice, Peter?
Two men prying and poking about,
Is it here, is it there, is it in, is it out?
Cover his staring eyes with a clout.
  But you're dead, dead, Peter.

They have ripped up the boards, they have pried up the
      stones,
  They have found your gold, dead Peter.
Ripe, red coins to itch a thief's hand,
But you drip ripe red on the floor's white sand,
You burn their eyes like a firebrand.
  They must quench you, Peter.

It is dark in the north, it is dark in the south.
    The wind blows your white hair, Peter.
One at your feet and one at your head.
A soft bed, a smooth bed,
Scarcely a splash, you sink like lead.
    Sweet water in your well, Peter.

Along the road and along the road,
    The next house, Peter.
Foursquare to the bright and the shade of the moon.
The north winds shuffle, the south winds croon,
Water with white hair overstrewn.
    The door, the door, Peter!
Water seeps under the door.

They have risen up in the morning grey.
    What will they give to Peter?
The sorrel horse with the tail of gold,
Fastest pacer ever was foaled.
Shoot him, skin him, blanch his bones,
Nail up his skull with a silver nail
Over the door; it will not fail.
No ghostly thing can ever prevail
    Against a horse's skull, Peter.

Over the lilacs, gazing down,
    Is a window, Peter.
The north winds call, and the south winds cry.
Silver white hair in a bitter blowing,
Eel-green water washing by,
A red mouth floating and flowing.
    Do you come, Peter?

They rose as the last star sank and set.
    One more for Peter.
They slew the black mare at the flush of the sun,
And nailed her skull to the window-stone.
In the light of the moon how white it shone—
    And your breathing mouth, Peter!

Around the house, and around the house,
With a wind that is north, and a wind that is south,
    Peter, Peter.
Mud and ooze and a dead man's wrist
Wrenching the shutters apart, like mist
The mud and the ooze and the dead man twist.
    They are praying, Peter.

Three in stable a week ago.
    This is the last, Peter.
"My strawberry roan in the morning clear,
Lady heart and attentive ear,
Foot like a kitten, nose like a deer,
But the fear! The fear!"
    Three skulls, Peter.

The sun goes down, and the night draws in.
    Toward the hills, Peter.
What lies so stiff on the hill-room floor,
When the gusty wind claps to the door?
They have paid three horses and two men more.
    Gather your gold, Peter.

Softly, softly, along the ground
Lest your shoes sound,
Gently, gently, across the air
Lest it stream, your hair.
North and south
For your aching mouth.
But the moon is old, Peter,
And death is long, and the well is deep.
Can you sleep, sleep, Peter?

JOHN LYLY

1554?–1606

Cupid and My Campaspe

Cupid and my Campaspe played
At cards for kisses; Cupid paid.
He stakes his quiver, bow, and arrows,
His mother's doves and team of sparrows:
Loses them too; then down he throws
The coral of his lip, the rose
Growing on's cheek (but none knows how);
With these the crystal of his brow,
And then the dimple of his chin—

All these did my Campaspe win.
At last he set her both his eyes;
She won, and Cupid blind did rise.
   O Love, has she done this to thee?
   What shall, alas! become of me?

PHYLLIS McGINLEY

1905–

The Giveaway

Saint Bridget was
A problem child.
Although a lass
Demure and mild,
And one who strove
To please her dad,
Saint Bridget drove
The family mad.
For here's the fault in Bridget lay:
She *would* give everything away.

To any soul
Whose luck was out
She'd give her bowl
Of stirabout;
She'd give her shawl,
Divide her purse
With one or all.
And what was worse,
When she ran out of things to give
She'd borrow from a relative.

Her father's gold,
Her grandsire's dinner,
She'd hand to cold
And hungry sinner;
Give wine, give meat,
No matter whose;

Take from her feet
The very shoes,
And when her shoes had gone to others,
Fetch forth her sister's and her mother's.

She could not quit.
She had to share;
Gave bit by bit
The silverware
The barnyard geese,
The parlor rug,
Her little niece-
'S christening mug,
Even her bed to those in want,
And then the mattress of her aunt.

An easy touch
For poor and lowly,
She gave so much
And grew so holy
That when she died
Of years and fame,
The countryside
Put on her name,
And still the Isles of Erin fidget
With generous girls named Bride or Bridget.

Well, one must love her.
Nonetheless,
In thinking of her
Givingness,
There's no denial
She must have been
A sort of trial
To her kin.
The moral, too, seems rather quaint.
Who had the patience of a saint,
From evidence presented here?
Saint Bridget? Or her near and dear?

ARCHIBALD MacLEISH

1892–

"Not Marble, nor the Gilded Monuments"

The praisers of women in their proud and beautiful poems,
Naming the grave mouth and the hair and the eyes,
Boasted those they loved should be forever remembered:
These were lies.

The words sound but the face in the Istrian sun is forgotten.
The poet speaks but to her dead ears no more.
The sleek throat is gone—and the breast that was troubled to
    listen:
Shadow from door.

Therefore I will not praise your knees nor your fine walking
Telling you men shall remember your name as long
As lips move or breath is spent or the iron of English
Rings from a tongue.

I shall say you were young, and your arms straight, and your mouth
    scarlet:
I shall say you will die and none will remember you:
Your arms change, and none remember the swish of your garments,
Nor the click of your shoe.

Not with my hand's strength, not with difficult labor
Springing the obstinate words to the bones of your breast
And the stubborn line to your young stride and the breath to your
    breathing
And the beat to your haste
Shall I prevail on the hearts of unborn men to remember.

(What is a dead girl but a shadowy ghost
Or a dead man's voice but a distant and vain affirmation
Like dream words most)

Therefore I will not speak of the undying glory of women.
I will say you were young and straight and your skin fair
And you stood in the door and the sun was a shadow of leaves on
    your shoulders
And a leaf on your hair—

I will not speak of the famous beauty of dead women:
I will say the shape of a leaf lay once on your hair.
Till the world ends and the eyes are out and the mouths broken
Look! It is there!

You, Andrew Marvell

And here face down beneath the sun
And here upon earth's noonward height
To feel the always coming on
The always rising of the night

To feel creep up the curving east
The earthly chill of dusk and slow
Upon those under lands the vast
And ever-climbing shadow grow

And strange at Ecbatan the trees
Take leaf by leaf the evening strange
The flooding dark about their knees
The mountains over Persia change

And now at Kermanshah the gate
Dark empty and the withered grass
And through the twilight now the late
Few travelers in the westward pass

And Baghdad darken and the bridge
Across the silent river gone
And through Arabia the edge
Of evening widen and steal on

And deepen on Palmyra's street
The wheel rut in the ruined stone
And Lebanon fade out and Crete
High through the clouds and overblown

And over Sicily the air
Still flashing with the landward gulls
And loom and slowly disappear
The sails above the shadowy hulls

And Spain go under and the shore
Of Africa the gilded sand
And evening vanish and no more
The low pale light across that land

Nor now the long light on the sea—

And here face downward in the sun
To feel how swift how secretly
The shadow of the night comes on . . .

Words in Time

Bewildered with the broken tongue
Of wakened angels in our sleep—
Then, lost the music that was sung
And lost the light time cannot keep!

There is a moment when we lie
Bewildered, wakened out of sleep,
When light and sound and all reply:
That moment time must tame and keep.

That moment, like a flight of birds
Flung from the branches where they sleep,
The poet with a beat of words
Flings into time for time to keep.

CHRISTOPHER MARLOWE

1564–1593

The Passionate Shepherd to His Love

Come live with me and be my love,
And we will all the pleasures prove
That hills and valleys, dales and fields,
And all the craggy mountains yields.

And we will sit upon the rocks
And see the shepherds feed their flocks
By shallow rivers, to whose falls
Melodious birds sing madrigals.

And I will make thee beds of roses
And a thousand fragrant posies,
A cap of flowers, and a kirtle
Embroidered all with leaves of myrtle,

A gown made of the finest wool,
Which from our pretty lambs we pull,
Fair-linéd slippers for the cold,
With buckles of the purest gold,

A belt of straw and ivy-buds
With coral clasps and amber studs.
And if these pleasures may thee move,
Come live with me and be my love.

Thy silver dishes for thy meat,
As precious as the gods do eat,
Shall on an ivory table be
Prepared each day for thee and me.

The shepherd swains shall dance and sing
For thy delight each May morning.
If these delights thy mind may move,
Then live with me and be my love.

DON MARQUIS

1878–1937

The Tom-Cat

At midnight in the alley
  A Tom-Cat comes to wail,
And he chants the hate of a million years
  As he swings his snaky tail.

Malevolent, bony, brindled,
  Tiger and devil and bard,
His eyes are coals from the middle of Hell
  And his heart is black and hard.

He twists and crouches and capers
   And bares his curved sharp claws,
And he sings to the stars of the jungle nights
   Ere cities were, or laws.

Beast from a world primeval,
   He and his leaping clan,
When the blotched red moon leers over the roofs,
   Give voice to their scorn of man.

He will lie on a rug tomorrow
   And lick his silky fur,
And veil the brute in his yellow eyes
   And play he's tame, and purr.

But at midnight in the alley
   He will crouch again and wail,
And beat the time for his demon's song
   With the swing of his demon's tail.

ANDREW MARVELL

1621–1678

To His Coy Mistress

Had we but world enough and time,
This coyness, lady, were no crime.
We would sit down and think which way
To walk and pass our long love's day.
Thou by the Indian Ganges' side
Shouldst rubies find; I by the tide
Of Humber would complain. I would
Love you ten years before the flood,
And you should, if you please, refuse
Till the conversion of the Jews.
My vegetable love should grow
Vaster than empires, and more slow;
An hundred years should go to praise
Thine eyes and on thy forehead gaze;

Two hundred to adore each breast,
But thirty thousand to the rest:
An age at least to every part,
And the last age should show your heart.
For, lady, you deserve this state,
Nor would I love at lower rate.

   But at my back I always hear
Time's wingèd chariot hurrying near;
And yonder all before us lie
Deserts of vast eternity.
Thy beauty shall no more be found,
Nor in thy marble vault shall sound
My echoing song; then worms shall try
That long-preserved virginity,
And your quaint honor turn to dust,
And into ashes all my lust.
The grave's a fine and private place,
But none, I think, do there embrace.

   Now, therefore, while the youthful hue
Sits on thy skin like morning dew,
And while thy willing soul transpires
At every pore with instant fires,
Now let us sport us while we may,
And now, like am'rous birds of prey,
Rather at once our time devour
Than languish in his slow-chapped power.
Let us roll all our strength and all
Our sweetness up into one ball,
And tear our pleasures with rough strife
Thorough the iron gates of life.
Thus, though we cannot make our sun
Stand still, yet we will make him run.

The Execution of King Charles

While round the armèd bands
  Did clap their bloody hands:
He nothing common did, or mean,
Upon that memorable scene,
  But with his keener eye
  The axe's edge did try;
Nor called the gods with vulgar spite

To vindicate his helpless right,
But bowed his comely head
Down, as upon a bed.

The Garden

How vainly men themselves amaze
To win the palm, the oak, or bays,
And their incessant labors see
Crowned from some single herb or tree,
Whose short and narrow-vergéd shade
Does prudently their toils upbraid;
While all flowers and all trees do close
To weave the garlands of repose!

Fair quiet, have I found thee here,
And innocence, thy sister dear!
Mistaken long, I sought you then
In busy companies of men.
Your sacred plants, if here below,
Only among the plants will grow.
Society is all but rude,
To this delicious solitude.

No white nor red was ever seen
So am'rous as this lovely green.
Fond lovers, cruel as their flame,
Cut in these trees their mistress' name:
Little, alas, they know or heed
How far these beauties hers exceed!
Fair trees! wheres'e'er your barks I wound,
No name shall but your own be found.

When we have run our passions' heat
Love hither makes his best retreat.
The gods, that mortal beauty chase,
Still in a tree did end their race.
Apollo hunted Daphne so,
Only that she might laurel grow;
And Pan did after Syrinx speed,
Not as a nymph, but for a reed.

What wondrous life is this I lead!
Ripe apples drop about my head;

And luscious clusters of the vine
Upon my mouth do crush their wine;
The nectarine and curious peach
Into my hands themselves do reach;
Stumbling on melons, as I pass,
Ensnared with flowers, I fall on grass.

Meanwhile the mind, from pleasure less,
Withdraws into its happiness:
The mind, that ocean where each kind
Does straight its own resemblance find;
Yet it creates, transcending these,
Far other worlds and other seas;
Annihilating all that's made
To a green thought in a green shade.

Here at the fountain's sliding foot,
Or at some fruit tree's mossy root,
Casting the body's vest aside,
My soul into the boughs does glide:
There like a bird it sits and sings,
Then whets, and combs its silver wings;
And, till prepared for longer flight,
Waves in its plumes the various light.

Such was that happy garden state
While man there walked without a mate:
After a place so pure and sweet,
What other help could yet be meet!
But 'twas beyond a mortal's share
To wander solitary there:
Two paradises 'twere in one,
To live in paradise alone.

How well the skilful gard'ner drew
Of flowers and herbs this dial new;
Where from above the milder sun
Does through a fragrant zodiac run;
And, as it works, the industrious bee
Computes its time as well as we.
How could such sweet and wholesome hours
Be reckoned but with herbs and flowers!

JOHN MASEFIELD
1878–

Cargoes

Quinquireme of Nineveh from distant Ophir,
Rowing home to haven in sunny Palestine,
With a cargo of ivory,
And apes and peacocks,
Sandalwood, cedarwood, and sweet white wine.

Stately Spanish galleon coming from the Isthmus,
Dipping through the Tropics by the palm-green shores,
With a cargo of diamonds,
Emeralds, amethysts,
Topazes, and cinnamon, and gold moidores.

Dirty British coaster with a salt-caked smokestack,
Butting through the Channel in the mad March days,
With a cargo of Tyne coal,
Road-rails, pig-lead,
Firewood, ironware, and cheap tin trays.

On Growing Old

Be with me, Beauty, for the fire is dying;
My dog and I are old, too old for roving.
Man, whose young passion sets the spindrift flying,
Is soon too lame to march, too cold for loving.
I take the book and gather to the fire,
Turning old yellow leaves; minute by minute
The clock ticks to my heart; a withered wire
Moves a thin ghost of music in the spinet.
I cannot sail your seas, I cannot wander
Your corn-land nor your hill-land nor your valleys
Ever again, nor share the battle yonder
Where the young knight the broken squadron rallies.
Only stay quiet while my mind remembers
The beauty of fire from the beauty of embers.

200

Beauty, have pity, for the strong have power,
The rich their wealth, the beautiful their grace,
Summer of man its sunlight and its flower,
Springtime of man all April in a face.
Only, as in the jostling in the Strand,
Where the mob thrusts or loiters or is loud,
The beggar with the saucer in his hand
Asks only a penny from the passing crowd,
So, from this glittering world with all its fashion,
Its fire and play of men, its stir, its march,
Let me have wisdom, Beauty, wisdom and passion,
Bread to the soul, rain where the summers parch.
Give me but these, and though the darkness close
Even the night will blossom as the rose.

The Rose of the World

Dark Eleanor and Henry sat at meat
At Woodstock in the royal hunting-seat.

Eleanor said: "The wind blows bitter chill . . .
Will you go out?" King Henry said, "I will."

Eleanor said: "But on so black a night . . .
Will you still go?" He said, "I take delight . . .

"In these wild windy nights with branches swaying
And the wolves howling and the nightmare neighing."

She said, "May I come, too?" "But no," said he;
"No, for at night, if robbers set on me

"I can defend myself . . . I could not you
In the pitch darkness without retinue."

Eleanor said, "Why is it that you go
Thus, and alone?" He said: "You cannot know.

"Leave the King's secrets: let the fact suffice;
Duty demands it and I pay the price."

While Henry reached his sword-belt from the ledge
She pinned a tassel in his mantle's edge,

A clue of white silk that would glimmer pale
About his ankles as he trod the gale.

*   *   *

Henry went swiftly in the roaring night,
Eleanor saw her token glimmer white.

She followed down the hill, along the brook,
Just seeing by the clue the way he took.

He reached the forest where the hazels swayed . . .
Her soul was too intent to be afraid.

He pushed within the forest and was gone
But still among the scrub her token shone.

In the blind forest many trackways led,
The hazels swayed, the token showed ahead.

And as she followed she untwined a skein
Of silken floss to lead her out again.

The gale roared in the branches: the beasts shook
Not knowing which direction the step took.

Eleanor knew: she followed through the night
King Henry's mantle with its patch of white.

A long, long way she followed: but at last . . .
A clearing in the forest sweetly-grassed

With apple-trees in blossom that the gale
Tore and flung forth; the token glimmered pale.

Beyond the apple-garth a little house
Stood, shuttered close among the tossing boughs.

Light shone from out the bower window-chinks;
Eleanor crept as cat-like as the lynx.

The white patch lingered at the door: she heard
A signal knock: within doors someone stirred.

All stealthily and still as though for sin
The door undid and Henry passed within.

Then the lock turned and Eleanor crept near.
In the gale's roaring she could nothing hear.

Yet near the door a fragrance in the air
Told that a red rose had been crumpled there.

Then in the breaking storm a wild moon showed
The fashion of that secret wood abode.

The windows high: each crevice tightly shut.
Over the lintel-piece a rose was cut . . .

Eleanor crept about as a cat creeps
In evil midnights when the master sleeps.

No dog was there: no sign of life was there,
Save the faint smell of roses in the air;

And hours passed and hurrying showers passed.
Eleanor watched what fish would come to cast.

Then suddenly, before the east grew grey,
The bolt withdrew to let the King away . . .

Eleanor had but time to crouch and hush
Close in the green of a sweet-briar bush.

She heard no word, but someone whispered close
In the King's ear, a someone like a rose.

And white arms, with their clinking bangles, drew
The King's head downward in a long adieu.

Then the King turned and quietly the door
Closed, and the house was silent as before.

* * *

Eleanor watched, but, lo, the patch of white
Was gone, that should have led her through the night.

Yet following on his steps she saw his frame
Retread in front of her the way he came.

And suddenly she saw him halting dead:
His scabbard's end had caught her guiding thread.

She heard him snap it, but she inly knew
He had not guessed the thread to be a clue.

Afterwards Henry hurried, for the day
Came swiftly, now the storm had blown away.

And lo, the beanfield sweet and blackbirds waking
Leaping from hedge and setting brambles shaking,

And Woodstock dim in trees with nothing stirring
Save the cats homing after nights of erring.

* * *

Eleanor decked herself in all her pride,
All that had graced her as King Henry's bride.

"Were you out late?" she asked. He answered, "No . . .
It was not midnight when we rose to go.

"These midnight councils seldom sit for long."
Eleanor hummed a merry scrap of song.

She went into her turret and undid
Her chest with iron bandings on the lid.

She took a drowsy and a biting draught
And mixed them both and as she mixed she laughed . . .

"This is as heavy sleep upon the life . . .
And this is cutting as an Eastern knife,

"Together they will still the April grace
Of Mistress White-Arms in the rosy place."

She put the potion in a golden flask,
King Henry's gift, and went upon her task.

King Henry asked her, "Whither are you bound?"
"On charity," she said, "my daily round . . .

"The Christian charity I must not spare
To those poor women lying suffering there."

He said, "God bless your charity." And she
Replied "Amen," and went forth quietly.

She visited her sick with bread and wine,
Then searched the forest for her silken sign.

She found the floss still clinging, leading in.
"The hunt is up," she said. "The hounds begin."

The forest was all thicket, but the lane
To tread was blazoned by the silken skein.

Though it was dark in covert, her delight
In what her spirit purposed gave her light.

Then lo, the clearing, and the little house
So fair among the blossomed apple-boughs,

And once again her spirit was aware
Of midmost summer's roses present there.

Within the house she heard a woman sing.
Eleanor knocked the signal of the King.

The chain undid, the bolt was drawn, the key
Turned, and the door was opened; it was she . . .

A girl more beautiful than summer's rose
That in the mid June's beauty burns and glows;

A golden lady graced from foot to tress,
With every simpleness and loveliness,

Who, in the second when she saw the Queen,
Knew that her death had come, for what had been.

Eleanor like a striking python seized
That golden child and dragged her as she pleased.

"O darling of the King," she said, "behold . . .
I, who am Queen, have brought this flask of gold,

"Also the common hangman and his crew.
I, being royal, give a choice to you.

"Either you drink this poison, and so end . . .
Or I will call the hangmen who attend

"And they shall strip you naked and so hoot
And beat you to the Woodstock gallows-foot

"Where they shall hang you: choose, then, sweetest heart."
The girl beheld Death present with his dart.

The present Death with which man cannot strive.
Death that makes beauty be no more alive,

And is so strange the hot blood can but shrink.
"Threaten me not," she said, "for I will drink.

"I, too, am royal: and no way remains."
She drank the golden flasket to its drains,

And straight the savage poison in her side
Thrust on her heart-strings that she sank and died.

*   *   *

Eleanor dragged the body to the bed,
"Lie there and welcome Henry, Golden Head."

Then forth the grim Queen went, and licked her lips
To think of June's bright beauty in eclipse

And Henry going to his love to find
The candle quenched that shone behind the blind.

"He will thrust in and find her lying cold."
So Henry did and found the flask of gold

And knew the Queen's contrivance in the death.
That night the Queen cried: "Open . . . give me breath . . .

"Open the window, for I cannot breathe,
The golden roses' tendrils wreathe and wreathe

"Over my mouth. Oh who has crushed a rose?
The perfume stifles me: unclose, unclose!"

They told her that she dreamed; but she replied:
"The roses choke me: open windows wide.

"Someone has crushed a white rose or a red . . .
Can you not smell the perfume that is shed?

"It comes so close, I cannot breathe the air."
Thenceforward every day and everywhere

The grim Queen cowered from the haunting scent
Of roses crushed, of sweet rose-petals blent,

Red, white and golden, coming where she trod.
Henry and Eleanor are now with God,

Whose Face is in all beauty, as I say.
The pure White Nuns took Rosamund away.

Within their quire they showed for many years
A little chest or scatolin of hers,

Painted with birds, that Henry once had given.
There the White Sisters prayed her into Heaven

That is the rest for lovers: there they wrought
A white-rose tomb for her from loving thought

So that none thought of her, nor ever will
Save as a lovely thing that suffered ill.

There every May the grass above her bosom
Is strown with hawthorn bloom and apple-blossom.

And on the wild-rose spray the blackbirds sing
"O Rose of all the World, O lovely thing."

CHARLOTTE MEW

1869–1928

The Farmer's Bride

Three summers since I chose a maid,
　Too young maybe—but more's to do
At harvest-time than bide and woo.
　When us was wed she turned afraid
Of love and me and all things human;
Like the shut of a winter's day
Her smile went out, and 'twadn't a woman—
　More like a little frightened fay.
　　One night, in the Fall, she runned away.

"Out 'mong the sheep, her be," they said,
'Should properly have been abed;
But sure enough she wadn't there
Lying awake with her wide brown stare.
So over seven-acre field and up-along across the down
　We chased her, flying like a hare
Before our lanterns. To Church-Town
　All in a shiver and a scare
We caught her, fetched her home at last
　And turned the key upon her, fast.

She does the work about the house
As well as most, but like a mouse:
　Happy enough to chat and play
　With birds and rabbits and such as they,
　So long as men-folk keep away.
"Not near, not near!" her eyes beseech
When one of us comes within reach.
　The women say that beasts in stall
　Look round like children at her call.
　I've hardly heard her speak at all.

Shy as a leveret, swift as he,
Straight and slight as a young larch tree,

Sweet as the first wild violets, she,
To her wild self. But what to me?

The short days shorten and the oaks are brown,
    The blue smoke rises to the low grey sky,
One leaf in the still air falls slowly down,
    A magpie's spotted feathers lie
On the black earth spread white with rime,
The berries redden up to Christmas-time.
    What's Christmas-time without there be
    Some other in the house than we!
    She sleeps up in the attic there
    Alone, poor maid. 'Tis but a stair
Betwixt us. Oh my God! the down,
The soft young down of her, the brown,
The brown of her—her eyes, her hair, her hair!

The Rambling Sailor

In the old back streets o' Pimlico,
On the docks at Monte Video,
At the Ring o' Bells on Plymouth Hoe
He'm arter me now wheerever I go.
An' dirty nights when the wind do blow
I can hear him sing-songin' up from sea:
Oh no man nor woman's bin friend to me
An' today I'm feared wheer tomorrow I'll be,
Sin' the night the moon lay whist and white
On the road goin' down to the Lizard Light
When I heard him hummin' behind me.

"Oh look, boy, look in your sweetheart's eyes
    So deep as sea an' so blue as skies;
An' 'tis better to kiss than to chide her.
If they tell 'ee no tales, they'll tell 'ee no lies
        Of the little brown mouse
        That creeps into the house
To lie sleepin' so quiet beside her.

"O hold 'ee long, but hold 'ee light
Your true man's hand when you find him,
He'll help 'ee home on a darksome night
        Wi' a somethin' bright
        That he'm holdin' tight
In the hand that he keeps behind him.

"Oh sit 'ee down to your whack o' pies,
So hot's the stew and the brew likewise,
But whiles you'm scrapin' the plates and dishes,
A'gapin' down in the shiversome sea
For the delicate mossels inside o' we
Theer's a passel o' hungry fishes."

At the *Halte des Marins* at Saint Nazaire
I cussed him, sittin' astride his chair;
An' Christmas Eve on the "Mary Clare"
I pitched him a'down the hatchway stair.
But "Shoutin' and cloutin's nothing to me,
Nor the hop nor the skip nor the jump," says he,
"For I be walkin' on every quay—"

"So look, boy, look in the dear maid's eyes
And take the true man's hand
And eat your fill o' your whack o' pies
Till you'm starin' up wheer the sea-crow flies
Wi' your head lyin' soft in the sand."

EDNA ST. VINCENT MILLAY

1892–1950

Exiled

Searching my heart for its true sorrow,
    This is the thing I find to be:
That I am weary of words and people,
    Sick of the city, wanting the sea;

Wanting the sticky, salty sweetness
    Of the strong wind and shattered spray;
Wanting the loud sound and the soft sound
    Of the big surf that breaks all day.

Always before about my dooryard,
    Marking the reach of the winter sea,
Rooted in sand and dragging driftwood,
    Straggled the purple wild sweetpea;

Always I climbed the wave at morning,
   Shook the sand from my shoes at night,
That now am caught beneath great buildings,
   Stricken with noise, confused with light.

If I could hear the green piles groaning
   Under the windy wooden piers,
See once again the bobbing barrels,
   And the black sticks that fence the weirs,

If I could see the weedy mussels
   Crusting the wrecked and rotting hulls,
Hear once again the hungry crying
   Overhead, of the wheeling gulls,

Feel once again the shanty straining
   Under the turning of the tide,
Fear once again the rising freshet,
   Dread the bell in the fog outside—

I should be happy—that was happy
   All day long on the coast of Maine!
I have need to hold and handle
   Shells and anchors and ships again!

I should be happy, that am happy
   Never at all since I came here.
I am too long away from water.
   I have a need of water near.

Elegy

Let them bury your big eyes
In the secret earth securely,
Your thin fingers, and your fair,
Soft, indefinite-colored hair—
All of these in some way, surely,
From the secret earth shall rise.
Not for these I sit and stare,
Broken and bereft completely;
Your young flesh that sat so neatly
On your little bones will sweetly
Blossom in the air.

But your voice—never the rushing
Of a river underground,
Not the rising of the wind
In the trees before the rain,
Not the woodcock's watery call,
Not the note the white-throat utters,
Not the feet of children pushing
Yellow leaves along the gutters
In the blue and bitter fall,
Shall content my musing mind
For the beauty of that sound
That in no new way at all
Ever will be heard again.

Sweetly through the sappy stalk
Of the vigorous weed,
Holding all it held before,
Cherished by the faithful sun,
On and on eternally
Shall your altered fluid run,
Bud and bloom and go to seed;
But your singing days are done;
But the music of your talk
Never shall the chemistry
Of the secret earth restore.
All your lovely words are spoken.
Once the ivory box is broken,
Beats the golden bird no more.

And You As Well Must Die, Belovéd Dust

And you as well must die, belovéd dust,
And all your beauty stand you in no stead;
This flawless, vital hand, this perfect head,
This body of flame and steel, before the gust
Of Death, or under his autumnal frost,
Shall be as any leaf, be no less dead
Than the first leaf that fell—this wonder fled,
Altered, estranged, disintegrated, lost.
Nor shall my love avail you in your hour.
In spite of all my love, you will arise
Upon that day and wander down the air

Obscurely as the unattended flower,
It mattering not how beautiful you were,
Or how belovéd above all else that dies.

JOHN MILTON
1608–1674

On Shakespeare

What needs my Shakespeare for his honored bones
The labor of an age in piléd stones?
Or that his hallowed reliques should be hid
Under a star-ypointing pyramid?
Dear son of memory, great heir of fame,
What need'st thou such weak witness of thy name?
Thou in our wonder and astonishment
Hast built thyself a livelong monument.
For whilst, to the shame of slow-endeavoring art,
Thy easy numbers flow, and that each heart
Hath from the leaves of thy unvalued book
Those Delphic lines with deep impression took,
Then thou, our fancy of itself bereaving,
Dost make us marble with too much conceiving,
And so sepulchred in such pomp dost lie
That kings for such a tomb would wish to die.

On His Blindness

When I consider how my light is spent,
Ere half my days, in this dark world and wide,
And that one talent which is death to hide
Lodged with me useless, though my soul more bent
To serve therewith my Maker and present
My true account, lest he returning chide.
"Doth God exact day labor, light denied?"
I fondly ask; but Patience, to prevent

That murmur, soon replies: "God doth not need
Either man's work or his own gifts; who best
Bear his mild yoke, they serve him best. His state
Is kingly: thousands at his bidding speed
And post o'er land and ocean without rest.
They also serve who only stand and wait."

HERBERT MORRIS

1929–

This Alice

She, too, the voyaging in doors and Keys,
blue portals to the Indies in the seas,
and cinnamon and sun at Creole teas.
She, too, looked only forward with the ease
of ending Thank You and beginning Please.
One wears the gift of sight before one sees.

The bowls of light arranged beside the limes,
this Alice hewed a house of Haitian dimes
and paper-lace Jamaican valentines.

It was a brittle shack across the beach
with six persimmons and a Cuban peach
strung from a perch of whisper each to each
and clinking in the breeze their fruitful speech,
a shack which any wind or wave would teach
such touch of loveliness as in its reach.

Nightly she played marimba from the pines
and, knowing all the meters and the rimes,
composed the darkness to her own designs.

This Alice took a lover in the sea
and proffered gifts of anklebone and knee.
In loving partially, she eagerly
announced a fuller offering of three
brown fingers on each hand if he would be
a further love and hers entirely.

She learned in yearning for his central sea
that we commit ourselves to the degree
we hunger, that commission sets us free.

Should you be walking evening on that shore,
or steer a deepest ship in sailing for
that shack with every sea for sunken door,
persimmons and a peach upon the floor,
listen for her marimba bass before
you wear the gold calypso Alice wore.

WILLIAM MORRIS

1834–1896

Two Red Roses Across the Moon

There was a lady lived in a hall,
Large of her eyes, and slim and tall;
And ever she sung from noon to noon,
Two red roses across the moon.

There was a knight came riding by
In early spring, when the roads were dry;
And he heard that lady sing at the noon,
Two red roses across the moon.

Yet none the more he stopped at all,
But he rode a-gallop past the hall;
And left that lady singing at noon,
Two red roses across the moon.

Because, forsooth, the battle was set,
And the scarlet and blue had got to be met,
He rode on the spur till the next warm noon—
Two red roses across the moon.

But the battle was scattered from hill to hill,
From the windmill to the watermill;

214

And he said to himself, as it neared the noon,
Two red roses across the moon.

You scarce could see for the scarlet and blue,
A golden helm or a golden shoe:
So he cried, as the fight grew thick at the noon,
Two red roses across the moon!

Verily then the gold bore through
The huddled spears of the scarlet and blue;
And they cried, as they cut them down at the noon,
Two red roses across the moon!

I trow he stopped when he rode again
By the hall, though draggled sore with the rain;
And his lips were pinched to kiss at the noon
Two red roses across the moon

Under the may she stooped to the crown,
All was gold, there was nothing of brown;
And the horns blew up in the hall at noon,
Two red roses across the moon

The Haystack in the Floods

Had she come all the way for this,
To part at last without a kiss?
Yea, had she borne the dirt and rain
That her own eyes might see him slain
Beside the haystack in the floods?

Along the dripping leafless woods,
The stirrup touching either shoe,
She rode astride as troopers do;
With kirtle kilted to her knee,
To which the mud splashed wretchedly;
And the wet dripped from every tree
Upon her head and heavy hair,
And on her eyelids broad and fair;
The tears and rain ran down her face.
By fits and starts they rode apace,
And very often was his place
Far off from her; he had to ride
Ahead, to see what might betide

When the roads crossed; and sometimes, when
There rose a murmuring from his men,
Had to turn back with promises.
Ah me! she had but little ease;
And often for pure doubt and dread
She sobbed, made giddy in the head
By the swift riding; while, for cold,
Her slender fingers scarce could hold
The wet reins; yea, and scarcely, too,
She felt the foot within her shoe
Against the stirrup: all for this,
To part at last without a kiss
Beside the haystack in the floods.

For when they neared that old soaked hay,
They saw across the only way
That Judas, Godmar, and the three
Red running lions dismally
Grinned from his pennon, under which
In one straight line along the ditch,
They counted thirty heads.
                              So then
While Robert turned round to his men,
She saw at once the wretched end,
And, stooping down, tried hard to rend
Her coif the wrong way from her head,
And hid her eyes; while Robert said:
"Nay, love, 'tis scarcely two to one;
At Poictiers where we made them run
So fast—why, sweet my love, good cheer,
The Gascon frontier is so near,
Nought after us."
                    But, "O!" she said,
"My God! my God! I have to tread
The long way back without you; then
The court at Paris; those six men;
The gratings of the Chatelet;
The swift Seine on some rainy day
Like this, and people standing by,
And laughing, while my weak hands try
To recollect how strong men swim.
All this, or else a life with him,
For which I should be damned at last—
Would God that this next hour were past!"

He answered not, but cried his cry,
"St. George for Marny!" cheerily;
And laid his hand upon her rein.
Alas! no man of all his train
Gave back that cheery cry again;
And, while for rage his thumb beat fast
Upon his sword-hilt, someone cast
About his neck a kerchief long,
And bound him.
          Then they went along
To Godmar; who said: "Now, Jehane,
Your lover's life is on the wane
So fast, that, if this very hour
You yield not as my paramour,
He will not see the rain leave off—
Nay, keep your tongue from gibe and scoff,
Sir Robert, or I slay you now."

She laid her hand upon her brow,
Then gazed upon the palm, as though
She thought her forehead bled, and—"No!"
She said, and turned her head away,
As there was nothing else to say,
And everything was settled: red
Grew Godmar's face from chin to head:
"Jehane, on yonder hill there stands
My castle, guarding well my lands;
What hinders me from taking you,
And doing that I list to do
To your fair wilful body, while
Your knight lies dead?"
          A wicked smile
Wrinkled her face, her lips grew thin,
A long way out she thrust her chin:
"You know that I should strangle you
While you were sleeping; or bite through
Your throat, by God's help—Ah!" she said,
"Lord Jesus, pity your poor maid!
For in such wise they hem me in,
I cannot choose but sin and sin,
Whatever happens: yet I think
They could not make me eat or drink,
And so should I just reach my rest."
"Nay, if you do not my behest,

O Jehane! though I love you well,"
Said Godmar, "would I fail to tell
All that I know?" "Foul lies," she said.
"Eh? lies, my Jehane? by God's head,
At Paris folks would deem them true!
Do you know, Jehane, they cry for you:
'Jehane the brown! Jehane the brown!
Give us Jehane to burn or drown!'
Eh!—gag me Robert!—sweet my friend,
This were indeed a piteous end
For those long fingers, and long feet,
And long neck, and smooth shoulders sweet;
An end that few men would forget
That saw it—So, an hour yet:
Consider, Jehane, which to take
Of life or death!"

            So, scarce awake,
Dismounting, did she leave that place,
And totter some yards: with her face
Turned upward to the sky she lay,
Her head on a wet heap of hay,
And fell asleep: and while she slept,
And did not dream, the minutes crept
Round to the twelve again; but she,
Being waked at last, sighed quietly,
And strangely childlike came, and said:
"I will not." Straightway Godmar's head,
As though it hung on strong wires, turned
Most sharply round, and his face burned.

For Robert, both his eyes were dry,
He could not weep, but gloomily
He seemed to watch the rain; yea, too,
His lips were firm; he tried once more
To touch her lips; she reached out, sore
And vain desire so tortured them,
The poor grey lips, and now the hem
Of his sleeve brushed them.

             With a start
Up Godmar rose, thrust them apart;
From Robert's throat he loosed the bands
Of silk and mail; with empty hands
Held out, she stood and gazed, and saw,
The long bright blade without a flaw

Glide out from Godmar's sheath, his hand
In Robert's hair; she saw him bend
Back Robert's head; she saw him send
The thin steel down; the blow told well,
Right backward the knight Robert fell,
And moaned as dogs do, being half dead,
Unwitting, as I deem: so then
Godmar turned grinning to his men,
Who ran, some five or six, and beat
His head to pieces at their feet.

Then Godmar turned again and said:
"So, Jehane, the first fitte is read!
Take note, my lady, that your way
Lies backward to the Chatelet!"
She shook her head and gazed awhile
At her cold hands with a rueful smile,
As though this thing had made her mad.

This was the parting that they had
Beside the haystack in the floods.

OGDEN NASH

1902–

The Tale of Custard, the Dragon

Belinda lived in a little white house,
With a little black kitten and a little grey mouse,
And a little yellow dog and a little red wagon,
And a realio, trulio, little pet dragon.

Now the name of the little black kitten was Ink,
And the little grey mouse, she called her Blink,
And the little yellow dog was sharp as Mustard,
But the dragon was a coward, and she called him Custard.

Custard the dragon had big sharp teeth,
And spikes on top of him and scales underneath,
Mouth like a fireplace, chimney for a nose,
And realio, trulio, daggers on his toes.

Belinda was as brave as a barrel full of bears,
And Ink and Blink chased lions down the stairs,
Mustard was as brave as a tiger in a rage,
But Custard cried for a nice safe cage.

Belinda tickled him, she tickled him unmerciful,
Ink, Blink and Mustard, they rudely called him Percival,
They all sat laughing in the little red wagon
At the realio, trulio, cowardly dragon.

Belinda giggled till she shook the house,
And Blink said, "Weeek!" (which is giggling for a mouse),
Ink and Mustard rudely asked his age
When Custard cried for a nice safe cage.

Suddenly, suddenly they heard a nasty sound,
And Mustard growled, and they all looked around.
"Meowch!" cried Ink, and "Ooh!" cried Belinda,
For there was a pirate, climbing in the winda.

Pistol in his left hand, pistol in his right,
And he held in his teeth a cutlass bright,
His beard was black, one leg was wood;
It was clear that the pirate meant no good.

Belinda paled, and she cried, "Help! help!"
But Mustard fled with a terrified yelp,
Ink trickled down to the bottom of the household,
And little mouse Blink strategically mouseholed.

But up jumped Custard, snorting like an engine,
Clashed his tail like irons in a dungeon.
With a clatter and a clank and a jangling squirm
He went at the pirate like a robin at a worm.

The pirate gaped at Belinda's dragon,
And gulped some grog from his pocket flagon.
He fired two bullets, but they didn't hit,
And Custard gobbled him, every bit.

Belinda embraced him, Mustard licked him,
No one mourned for his pirate victim.
Ink and Blink in glee did gyrate
Around the dragon that ate the pirate.

Belinda still lives in her little white house,
With her little black kitten and her little grey mouse,
And her little yellow dog and her little red wagon,
And her realio, trulio, little pet dragon.

Belinda is as brave as a barrel full of bears,
And Ink and Blink chase lions down the stairs.
Mustard is as brave as a tiger in a rage,
But Custard keeps crying for a nice safe cage.

THOMAS NASHE

1567–1601

Spring, the Sweet Spring

Spring, the sweet spring, is the year's pleasant king;
Then blooms each thing, then maids dance in a ring,
Cold doth not sting, the pretty birds do sing:
   "Cuckoo, jug-jug, pu-we, to-witta-woo!"

The palm and may make country houses gay,
Lambs frisk and play, the shepherds pipe all day,
And we hear aye birds tune this merry lay:
   "Cuckoo, jug-jug, pu-we, to-witta-woo!"

The fields breathe sweet, the daisies kiss our feet,
Young lovers meet, old wives a-sunning sit,
In every street these tunes our ears do greet:
   "Cuckoo, jug-jug, pu-we, to-witta-woo!"
      Spring, the sweet spring!

Litany in Time of Plague

Adieu, farewell earth's bliss,
This world uncertain is;
Fond are life's lustful joys,
Death proves them all but toys,
None from his darts can fly.
I am sick, I must die.
   Lord, have mercy on us!

Rich men, trust not in wealth,
Gold cannot buy you health;

Physic himself must fade,
All things to end are made,
The plague full swift goes by.
I am sick, I must die.
  Lord, have mercy on us!

Beauty is but a flower
Which wrinkles will devour:
Brightness falls from the air,
Queens have died young and fair,
Dust hath closed Helen's eye.
I am sick, I must die.
  Lord, have mercy on us!

Strength stoops unto the grave,
Worms feed on Hector brave,
Swords may not fight with fate;
Earth still holds ope her gate;
"Come! come!" the bells do cry.
I am sick, I must die.
  Lord, have mercy on us!

Wit with his wantonness
Tasteth death's bitterness;
Hell's executioner
Hath no ears for to hear
What vain art can reply.
I am sick, I must die.
  Lord, have mercy on us!

Haste, therefore, each degree,
To welcome destiny.
Heaven is our heritage,
Earth but a player's stage;
Mount we unto the sky.
I am sick, I must die.
  Lord, have mercy on us!

SIR HENRY NEWBOLT

1862–1938

Drake's Drum

Drake he's in his hammock an' a thousand mile away,
    (Capten, art tha sleepin' there below?)
Slung atween the round shot in Nombre Dios Bay,
    An' dreamin' arl the time o' Plymouth Hoe.
Yarnder lumes the Island, yarnder lie the ships,
    Wi' sailor-lads a-dancin' heel-an'-toe,
An' the shore-lights flashin', an' the night-tide dashin',
    He sees et arl so plainly as he saw et long ago.

Drake he was a Devon man, an' ruled the Devon seas,
    (Capten, art tha sleepin' there below?)
Rovin' tho' his death fell, he went wi' heart at ease,
    An' dreamin' arl the time o' Plymouth Hoe.
"Take my drum to England, hang et by the shore,
    Strike et when your powder's runnin' low;
If the Dons sight Devon, I'll quit the port o' Heaven,
    An' drum them up the Channel as we drummed them long ago."

Drake he's in his hammock till the great Armadas come,
    (Capten, art tha sleepin' there below?)
Slung atween the round shot, listenin' for the drum,
    An' dreamin' arl the time o' Plymouth Hoe.
Call him on the deep sea, call him up the Sound,
    Call him when ye sail to meet the foe;
Where the old trade's plyin' an' the old flag flyin'
    They shall find him ware an' wakin', as they found him long ago!

ALFRED NOYES

1880–

The Barrel-Organ *

There's a barrel-organ caroling across a golden street
  In the City as the sun sinks low;
And the music's not immortal; but the world has made it sweet
  And fulfilled it with the sunset glow;
And it pulses through the pleasures of the City and the pain
  That surround the singing organ like a large eternal light;
And they've given it a glory and a part to play again
  In the Symphony that rules the day and night.

And now it's marching onward through the realms of old romance,
  And trolling out a fond familiar tune,
And now it's roaring cannon down to fight the King of France,
  And now it's prattling softly to the moon,
And all around the organ there's a sea without a shore
  Of human joys and wonders and regrets;
To remember and to recompense the music evermore
  For what the cold machinery forgets. . . .

      Yes; as the music changes,
        Like a prismatic glass,
      It takes the light and ranges
        Through all the moods that pass;
      Dissects the common carnival
        Of passions and regrets,
      And gives the world a glimpse of all
        The colors it forgets.

      And there *La Traviata* sighs
        Another sadder song;
      And there *Il Trovatore* cries
        A tale of deeper wrong;
      And bolder knights to battle go
        With sword and shield and lance,

---

* From *Collected Poems, Volume I* by Alfred Noyes, copyright, 1906, 1934, by Alfred Noyes. Selection reprinted by permission of J. B. Lippincott Company.

224

Than ever here on earth below
Have whirled into—*a dance!*

Go down to Kew in lilac-time, in lilac-time, in lilac-time;
 Go down to Kew in lilac-time (it isn't far from London!)
And you shall wander hand in hand with love in summer's wonder-
 land;
 Go down to Kew in lilac-time (it isn't far from London!)

The cherry-trees are seas of bloom and soft perfume and sweet
 perfume,
 The cherry-trees are seas of bloom (and oh so near to London!)
And there they say, when dawn is high and all the world's a blaze
 of sky
 The cuckoo, though he's very shy, will sing a song for London.

The Dorian nightingale is rare and yet they say you'll hear him
 there
 At Kew, at Kew in lilac-time (and oh so near to London!)
The linnet and the throstle, too, and after dark the long halloo
 And golden-eyed *tu-whit, tu-whoo* of owls that ogle London.

For Noah hardly knew a bird of any kind that isn't heard
 At Kew, at Kew in lilac-time (and oh so near to London!)
And when the rose begins to pout and all the chestnut spires are
 out,
 You'll hear the rest without a doubt, all chorusing for London:

Come down to Kew in lilac-time, in lilac-time, in lilac-time;
 Come down to Kew in lilac-time (it isn't far from London!)
And you shall wander hand in hand with love in summer's wonder-
 land;
 Come down to Kew in lilac-time (it isn't far from London!)

And then the troubadour begins to thrill the golden street,
 In the City as the sun sinks low;
And in all the gaudy busses there are scores of weary feet
Marking time, sweet time, with a dull mechanic beat,
And a thousand hearts are plunging to a love they'll never meet,
Through the meadows of the sunset, through the poppies and the
 wheat,
 In the land where the dead dreams go.

Verdi, Verdi, when you wrote *Il Trovatore* did you dream
 Of the City when the sun sinks low,
Of the organ and the monkey and the many-colored stream
On the Piccadilly pavement, of the myriad eyes that seem

To be litten for a moment with a wild Italian gleam
As *A che la morte* parodies the world's eternal theme
   And pulses with the sunset-glow?

There's a thief, perhaps, that listens with a face of frozen stone
   In the City as the sun sinks low;
There's a portly man of business with a balance of his own,
There's a clerk and there's a butcher of a soft reposeful tone,
And they're all of them returning to the heavens they have known:
They are crammed and jammed in busses and—they're each of
      them alone
   In the land where the dead dreams go.

There's a very modish woman and her smile is very bland
   In the City as the sun sinks low;
And her hansom jingles onward, but her little jeweled hand
Is clenched a little tighter and she cannot understand
What she wants or why she wanders to that undiscovered land,
For the parties there are not at all the sort of thing she planned,
   In the land where the dead dreams go.

There's a rowing man that listens and his heart is crying out
   In the City as the sun sinks low;
For the barge, the eight, the Isis, and the coach's whoop and shout,
For the minute-gun, the counting and the long disheveled rout,
For the howl along the tow-path and a fate that's still in doubt,
For a roughened oar to handle and a race to think about
   In the land where the dead dreams go.

There's a laborer that listens to the voices of the dead
   In the City as the sun sinks low;
And his hand begins to tremble and his face to smoulder red
As he sees a loafer watching him and—there he turns his head
And stares into the sunset where his April love is fled,
For he hears her softly singing and his lonely soul is led
   Through the land where the dead dreams go.

There's an old and haggard demi-rep, it's ringing in her ears,
   In the City as the sun sinks low;
With the wild and empty sorrow of the love that blights and sears,
Oh and if she hurries onward, then be sure, be sure she hears,
Hears and bears the bitter burden of the unforgotten years,
And her laugh's a little harsher and her eyes are brimmed with tears
   For the land where the dead dreams go.

There's a barrel-organ caroling across a golden street
   In the City as the sun sinks low;

Though the music's only Verdi there's a world to make it sweet
Just as yonder yellow sunset where the earth and heaven meet
Mellows all the sooty City! Hark, a hundred thousand feet
Are marching on to glory through the poppies and the wheat
    In the land where the dead dreams go.

          So it's Jeremiah, Jeremiah,
             What have you to say
          When you meet the garland girls
             Tripping on their way?

          All around my gala hat
             I wear a wreath of roses
          (A long and lonely year it is
             I've waited for the May!)
          If anyone should ask you,
             The reason why I wear it is—
          My own love, my true love, is coming home today.

And it's buy a bunch of violets for the lady
    (*It's lilac-time in London; it's lilac-time in London!*)
Buy a bunch of violets for the lady;
    While the sky burns blue above:
On the other side the street you'll find it shady
    (*It's lilac-time in London; it's lilac-time in London!*)
But buy a bunch of violets for the lady,
    And tell her she's your own true love.

There's a barrel-organ caroling across a golden street
    In the City as the sun sinks glittering and slow;
And the music's not immortal; but the world has made it sweet
And enriched it with the harmonies that make a song complete
In the deeper heavens of music where the night and morning meet,
    As it dies into the sunset-glow;
And it pulses through the pleasures of the City and the pain
    That surround the singing organ like a large eternal light,
And they've given it a glory and a part to play again
    In the Symphony that rules the day and night.

          And there, as the music changes,
             The song runs round again.
          Once more it turns and ranges
             Through all its joy and pain,
          Dissects the common carnival
             Of passions and regrets;
          And the wheeling world remembers all
             The wheeling song forgets.

Once more *La Traviata* sighs
  Another sadder song:
Once more *Il Trovatore* cries
  A tale of deeper wrong;
Once more the knights to battle go
  With sword and shield and lance
Till once, once more, the shattered foe
  Has whirled into—*a dance!*

Come down to Kew in lilac-time, in lilac-time, in lilac-time;
  Come down to Kew in lilac-time (it isn't far from London!)
And you shall wander hand in hand with love in summer's wonder-
  land;
  Come down to Kew in lilac-time (it isn't far from London!)

ARTHUR O'SHAUGHNESSY

1844–1881

Would I Might Go Far over Sea

Would I might go far over sea,
My love, or high above the air,
And come to land or heaven with thee,
Where no law is, and none shall be,
Against beholding the most rare
Strange beauty that thou hast for me.

Alas, for in this bitter land
Full many a written curse doth stand
Against the kiss thy lips should bear,
Against the sweet gift of thy hands,
Against the knowing that thou art fair,
And too fond loving of thy hair.

                (after Marie de France)

DOROTHY PARKER

1893–

Godmother

The day that I was christened—
  It's a hundred years, and more!—
A hag came and listened
  At the white church door,
A-hearing her that bore me
  And all my kith and kin
Considerately, for me,
  Renouncing sin.
While some gave me corals,
  And some gave me gold
And porringers, with morals
  Agreeably scrolled,
The hag stood, buckled
  In a dim grey cloak;
Stood there and chuckled,
  Spat, and spoke:
"There's few enough in life'll
  Be needing my help,
But I've got a trifle
  For your fine young whelp.
I give her sadness,
  And the gift of pain,
The new-moon madness,
  And the love of rain."
And little good to lave me
  In their holy silver bowl
After what she gave me—
  Rest her soul!

GEORGE PEELE

1558?–1597?

Farewell to Arms

(*To Queen Elizabeth I*)

His golden locks time hath to silver turned;
   O time too swift, O swiftness never ceasing!
His youth 'gainst time and age hath ever spurned,
   But spurned in vain; youth waneth by increasing.
Beauty, strength, youth are flowers but fading seen;
Duty, faith, love are roots, and ever green.

His helmet now shall make a hive for bees,
   And, lovers' sonnets turned to holy psalms,
A man-at-arms must now serve on his knees,
   And feed on prayers, which are age his alms:
But though from court to cottage he depart,
His saint is sure of his unspotted heart.

And when he saddest sits in homely cell,
   He'll teach his swains this carol for a song—
"Blest be the hearts that wish my sovereign well,
   Curst be the souls that think her any wrong."
Goddess, allow this agéd man his right,
To be your beadsman now that was your knight.

RUTH PITTER

1897–

Time's Fool

Time's fool, but not heaven's: yet hope not for any return.
The rabbit-eaten dry branch and the halfpenny candle

Are lost with the other treasure: the sooty kettle
Thrown away, become redbreast's home in the hedge, where the
    nettle
Shoots up, and bad bindweed wreathes rust-fretted handle.
Under that broken thing no more shall the dry branch burn.

Poor comfort all comfort: once what the mouse had spared
Was enough, was delight, there where the heart was at home;
The hard cankered apple holed by the wasp and the bird,
The damp bed, with the beetle's tap in the headboard heard,
The dim bit of mirror, three inches of comb:
Dear enough, when with youth and with fancy shared.

I knew that the roots were creeping under the floor,
That the toad was safe in his hole, the poor cat by the fire,
The starling snug in the roof, each slept in his place:
The lily in splendor, the vine in her grace,
The fox in the forest, all had their desire,
As then I had mine, in the place that was happy and poor.

VICTOR PLARR

1863–1929

Stand Not Uttering Sedately

Stand not uttering sedately
    Trite oblivious praise above her!
Rather say you saw her lately
    Lightly kissing her last lover.

Whisper not, "There is a reason
    Why we bring her no white blossom";
Since the snowy bloom's in season,
    Strow it on her sleeping bosom.

Oh for it would be a pity
    To o'erpraise her or to flout her:
She was wild, and sweet, and witty—
    Let's not say dull things about her.

EDGAR ALLAN POE

1809–1849

The Raven

Once upon a midnight dreary, while I pondered, weak and weary,
Over many a quaint and curious volume of forgotten lore—
While I nodded, nearly napping, suddenly there came a tapping,
As of someone gently rapping, rapping at my chamber door.
" 'Tis some visitor," I muttered, "tapping at my chamber door—
    Only this and nothing more."

Ah distinctly I remember it was in the bleak December,
And each separate dying ember wrought its ghost upon the floor.
Eagerly I wished the morrow—vainly I had sought to borrow
From my books surcease of sorrow—sorrow for the lost Lenore—
For the rare and radiant maiden whom the angels name Lenore—
    Nameless *here* for evermore.

And the silken, sad, uncertain rustling of each purple curtain
Thrilled me—filled me with fantastic terrors never felt before;
So that now, to still the beating of my heart, I stood repeating,
" 'Tis some visitor entreating entrance at my chamber door—
Some late visitor entreating entrance at my chamber door—
    This it is and nothing more."

Presently my soul grew stronger; hesitating then no longer,
"Sir," said I, "or Madam, truly your forgiveness I implore;
But the fact is I was napping, and so gently you came rapping,
And so faintly you came tapping, tapping at my chamber door,
That I scarce was sure I heard you"—here I opened wide the door—
    Darkness there and nothing more.

Deep into that darkness peering, long I stood there wondering,
      fearing,
Doubting, dreaming dreams no mortal ever dared to dream before;
But the silence was unbroken, and the stillness gave no token,
And the only word there spoken was the whispered word, "Lenore!"
This I whispered, and an echo murmured back the word, "Lenore!"
    Merely this and nothing more.

Back into the chamber turning, all my soul within me burning,
Soon again I heard a tapping somewhat louder than before.
"Surely," said I, "surely that is something at my window lattice.
Let me see, then, what thereat is, and this mystery explore—
Let my heart be still a moment and this mystery explore—
    'Tis the wind and nothing more!"

Open here I flung the shutter, when, with many a flirt and flutter,
In there stepped a stately Raven of the saintly days of yore.
Not the least obeisance made he, not a minute stopped or stayed he,
But with mien of lord or lady, perched above my chamber door—
Perched upon a bust of Pallas just above my chamber door—
    Perched, and sat, and nothing more.

Then this ebony bird beguiling my sad fancy into smiling,
By the grave and stern decorum of the countenance it wore,
"Though thy crest be shorn and shaven, thou," I said, "art sure
    no craven,
Ghastly grim and ancient Raven wandering from the nightly
    shore—
Tell me what thy lordly name is on the Night's Plutonian
    shore."
    Quoth the Raven, "Nevermore."

Much I marvelled this ungainly fowl to hear discourse so plainly,
Though its answer little meaning—little relevancy bore;
For we cannot help agreeing that no living human being
Ever yet was blessed with seeing bird above his chamber door—
Bird or beast upon the sculptured bust above his chamber door,
    With such name as 'Nevermore.'

But the Raven, sitting lonely on the placid bust, spoke only
That one word, as if his soul in that one word he did outpour.
Nothing further then he uttered—not a feather then he fluttered—
Till I scarcely more than muttered, "Other friends have flown
    before—
On the morrow *he* will leave me, as my hopes have flown before."
    Then the bird said, "Nevermore."

Startled at the stillness broken by reply so aptly spoken,
"Doubtless," said I, "what it utters is its only stock and store,
Caught from some unhappy master whom unmerciful disaster
Followed fast and followed faster till his songs one burden bore—
Till the dirges of his hope that melancholy burden bore
    Of 'Never—nevermore.' "

But the Raven still beguiling my sad fancy into smiling,
Straight I wheeled a cushioned seat in front of bird and bust and
      door;
Then upon the velvet sinking, I betook myself to linking
Fancy unto fancy, thinking what this ominous bird of yore—
What this grim, ungainly, ghastly, gaunt, and ominous bird of
      yore
      Meant in croaking, "Nevermore."

This I sat engaged in guessing, but no syllable expressing
To the fowl whose fiery eyes now burned into my bosom's core;
This and more I sat divining, with my head at ease reclining
On the cushion's velvet lining that the lamplight gloated o'er—
But whose velvet-violet lining with the lamplight gloating o'er,
      She shall press, ah, nevermore!

Then, methought, the air grew denser, perfumed from an unseen
      censer
Swung by seraphim whose footfalls tinkled on the tufted floor.
"Wretch," I cried, "thy God hath lent thee—by these angels He
      hath sent thee
Respite—respite and nepenthe from thy memories of Lenore;
Quaff, oh, quaff this kind nepenthe and forget this lost Lenore!"
      Quoth the Raven, "Nevermore."

"Prophet!" said I, "thing of evil!—prophet still, if bird or devil!—
Whether Tempter sent, or whether tempest tossed thee here
      ashore,
Desolate yet all undaunted, on this desert land enchanted—
On this home by horror haunted—tell me truly, I implore—
Is there—*is* there balm in Gilead?—tell me—tell me, I implore!"
      Quoth the Raven, "Nevermore."

"Prophet!" said I, "thing of evil!—prophet still, if bird or devil!
By that Heaven that bends above us—by that God we both adore—
Tell this soul with sorrow laden if, within the distant Aidenn,
It shall clasp a sainted maiden whom the angels name Lenore—
Clasp a rare and radiant maiden whom the angels name Lenore."
      Quoth the Raven, "Nevermore."

'Be that word our sign of parting, bird or fiend!" I shrieked,
      upstarting.
"Get thee back into the tempest and the Night's Plutonian shore!
Leave no black plume as a token of that lie thy soul hath spoken!
Leave my loneliness unbroken!—quit the bust above my door!
Take thy beak from out my heart, and take thy form from off my
      door!"
      Quoth the Raven, "Nevermore."

234

And the Raven, never flitting, still is sitting, *still* is sitting
On the pallid bust of Pallas just above my chamber door;
And his eyes have all the seeming of a demon's that is dreaming,
And the lamplight o'er him streaming throws his shadow on the
   floor;
And my soul from out that shadow that lies floating on the floor
  Shall be lifted—*nevermore!*

To Helen

Helen, thy beauty is to me
 Like those Nicean barks of yore,
That gently, o'er a perfumed sea,
 The weary, wayworn wanderer bore
 To his own native shore.

On desperate seas long wont to roam,
 Thy hyacinth hair, thy classic face,
Thy Naiad airs have brought me home
 To the glory that was Greece
And the grandeur that was Rome.

Lo! in yon brilliant window-niche
 How statuelike I see thee stand!
 The agate lamp within thy hand,
Ah! Psyche, from the regions which
 Are Holy Land!

ALEXANDER POPE

1688–1744

Ode on Solitude

Happy the man whose wish and care
A few paternal acres bound,
Content to breathe his native air
  In his own ground:

Whose herds with milk, whose fields with bread,
Whose flocks supply him with attire;
Whose trees in summer yield him shade,
    In winter fire:

Blest, who can unconcernedly find
Hours, days, and years slide soft away
In health of body, peace of mind,
    Quiet by day:

Sound sleep by night; study and ease
Together mixed, sweet recreation,
And innocence, which most does please
    With meditation.

Thus let me live, unseen, unknown;
Thus unlamented let me die;
Steal from the world, and not a stone
    Tell where I lie.

EZRA POUND

1885–

Ballad of the Goodly Fere *

(Simon Zelotes speaketh it somewhile after the Crucifixion)

Ha' we lost the goodliest fere o' all
For the priests and the gallows tree?
Aye, lover he was of brawny men,
O' ships and the open sea.

When they came wi' a host to take Our Man
His smile was good to see,
"First let these go!" quo' our Goodly Fere,
"Or I'll see ye damned," says he.

Aye, he sent us out through the crossed high spears,
And the scorn of his laugh rang free,

* Fere: companion.

"Why took ye not me when I walked about
Alone in the town?" says he.

Oh we drank his "Hale" in the good red wine
When we last made company,
No capon priest was the Goodly Fere
But a man o' men was he.

I ha' seen him drive a hundred men
Wi' a bundle o' cords swung free,
When they took the high and holy house
For their pawn and treasury.

They'll no get him a' in a book I think
Though they write it cunningly;
No mouse of the scrolls was the Goodly Fere
But aye loved the open sea.

If they think they ha' snared our Goodly Fere
They are fools to the last degree.
"I'll go to the feast," quo' our Goodly Fere,
"Though I go to the gallows tree."

"Ye ha' seen me heal the lame and the blind,
And wake the dead," says he,
"Ye shall see one thing to master all:
'Tis how a brave man dies on the tree."

A son of God was the Goodly Fere
That bade us his brothers be.
I ha' seen him cow a thousand men.
I ha' seen him upon the tree.

He cried no cry when they drave the nails
And the blood gushed hot and free,
The hounds of the crimson sky gave tongue
But never a cry cried he.

I ha' seen him cow a thousand men
On the hills o' Galilee,
They whined as he walked out calm between,
Wi' his eyes like the grey o' the sea.

Like the sea that brooks no voyaging
With the winds unleashed and free,
Like the sea that he cowed at Gennesaret
Wi' twey words spoke' suddenly.

A master of men was the Goodly Fere,
A mate of the wind and sea,
If they think they ha' slain our Goodly Fere
They are fools eternally.

I ha' seen him eat o' the honeycomb
Sin' they nailed him to the tree.

JOHN PRESS

1920–

Farewell

*(Mary, daughter of King James I, dying at the age
of three, cried aloud: "I go, I go, away I go.")*

The smell of death was in the air
And, as the candles guttered low,
Her pain became a mounting tide
Which dragged her in its undertow.
She watched the world recede and cried:
"I go, I go, away I go."

This was a cry of pure despair
From one too innocent to know
That web of words we spin to cloak
The nakedness which Truth would show.
It was her dying wisdom spoke:
"I go, I go, away I go."

Even the glibbest courtier there
Was dumb to say it was not so.
How strange that, in a moment's space,
A child should into knowledge grow
And cry, by God's, or terror's, grace:
"I go, I go, away I go."

MATTHEW PRIOR
1664–1721

An Ode

The merchant, to secure his treasure,
  Conveys it in a borrowed name:
Euphelia serves to grace my measure,
  But Chloe is my real flame.

My softest verse, my darling lyre
  Upon Euphelia's toilet lay,
When Chloe noted her desire
  That I should sing, that I should play.

My lyre I tune, my voice I raise;
  But with my numbers mix my sighs;
And whilst I sing Euphelia's praise,
  I fix my soul on Chloe's eyes.

Fair Chloe blushed, Euphelia frowned,
  I sang and gazed, I played and trembled:
And Venus to the Loves around
  Remarked how ill we all dissembled.

SIR WALTER RALEIGH
1552?–1618

Even Such Is Time

Even such is time, which takes in trust
Our youth, our joys, our all we have,
And pays us but with earth and dust;
Who, in the dark and silent grave,

When we have wandered all our ways,
Shuts up the story of our days.
But from this earth, and grave, and dust,
My God shall raise me up, I trust!

Give Me My Scallop-Shell of Quiet

Give me my scallop-shell of quiet,
  My staff of faith to walk upon,
My scrip of joy, immortal diet,
  My bottle of salvation,
My gown of glory, hope's true gauge;
And thus I'll take my pilgrimage.

Blood must be my body's balmer—
  No other balm will there be given;
Whilst my soul, like a quiet palmer,
  Travels to the land of heaven,
Over the silver mountains,
Where spring the nectar fountains;
            And there I'll kiss
            The bowl of bliss,
Drinking my eternal fill
Upon every milken hill.
My soul will be a-dry before,
But after, it will thirst no more.

And by the happy, blissful way
  More peaceful pilgrims I shall see,
That have shook off their gowns of clay,
  And go appareled fresh like me.
            I'll take them first,
            To slake their thirst
And then taste those nectar suckets,
            At the clear wells
            Where sweetness dwells,
  Drawn up by saints in crystal buckets.

And when our bottles and all we
Are filled with immortality,
Then the holy paths we'll travel,
Strewed with rubies thick as gravel—
Ceilings of diamonds, sapphire floors,
High walls of coral, and pearly bowers.

From thence to heaven's bribeless hall,
Where no corrupted voices brawl,
No conscience molten into gold,
No forged accusers bought and sold;
No cause deferred, no vain-spent journey,
For there Christ is the King's attorney,
Who pleads for all, without degrees,
And he hath angels, but no fees.

And when the grand twelve-million jury
Of our sins, with direful fury,
'Gainst our souls black verdicts give,
Christ pleads His death; and then we live.
Be Thou my speaker, taintless pleader!
Unblotted lawyer, true proceeder!
Thou giv'st salvation, even for alms,
Not with a bribéd lawyer's palms.

And this is my eternal plea
To Him that made heaven, earth, and sea:
That since my flesh must die so soon,
And want a head to dine next noon,
Just at the stroke, when my veins start and spread,
Set on my soul an everlasting head!
Then am I ready, like a palmer fit,
To tread those blest paths, which before I writ.

JOHN CROWE RANSOM

1888–

Here Lies a Lady

Here lies a lady of beauty and high degree.
Of chills and fever she died, of fever and chills,
The delight of her husband, her aunts, and infant of three,
And of medicos marveling sweetly on her ills.

For either she burned, and her confident eyes would blaze,
And her fingers fly in a manner to puzzle their heads—

What was she making? Why, nothing; she sat in a maze
Of old scraps of laces, snipped into curious shreds—

Or this would pass, and the light of her fire decline
Till she lay discouraged and cold, like a stalk white and blown,
And would not open her eyes, to kisses, to wine;
The sixth of these states was her last; the cold settled down.

Sweet ladies, long may ye bloom, and toughly I hope ye may thole,
But was she not lucky? In flowers and lace and mourning,
In love and great honor we bade God rest her soul
After six little spaces of chill, and six of burning.

Blackberry Winter

If the lady hath any loveliness, let it die.
For being drunken with the steam of Cuban cigars,
I find no pungence in the odor of stars,
And all my music goes out of me on a sigh.

But still would I sing to my maidenly apple-tree,
Before she has borne me a single apple of red;
The pictures of silver and apples of gold are dead;
But one more apple ripeneth yet maybe.

The garnished house of the Daughter of Heaven is cold.
I have seen her often, she stood all night on the hill,
Fiercely the pale youth clambered to her, till—
Hoarsely the rooster awakened him, footing the mould.

The breath of a girl is music—fall and swell—
The trumpets convolve in the warrior's chambered ear,
But I have listened, there is no one breathing here,
And all of the wars have dwindled since Troy fell.

But still I will haunt beneath my apple-tree,
Heedful again to star-looks and wind-words,
Anxious for the flash of whether eyes or swords,
And hoping a little, a little, that either may be.

EDWIN ARLINGTON ROBINSON
1869–1935

Miniver Cheevy

Miniver Cheevy, child of scorn,
   Grew lean while he assailed the seasons;
He wept that he was ever born,
   And he had reasons.

Miniver loved the days of old
   When swords were bright and steeds were prancing;
The vision of a warrior bold
   Would set him dancing.

Miniver sighed for what was not,
   And dreamed, and rested from his labors;
He dreamed of Thebes and Camelot,
   And Priam's neighbors.

Miniver mourned the ripe renown
   That made so many a name so fragrant;
He mourned Romance, now on the town,
   And Art, a vagrant.

Miniver loved the Medici,
   Albeit he had never seen one;
He would have sinned incessantly
   Could he have been one.

Miniver cursed the commonplace
   And eyed a khaki suit with loathing;
He missed the medieval grace
   Of iron clothing.

Miniver scorned the gold he sought,
   But sore annoyed was he without it;
Miniver thought, and thought, and thought,
   And thought about it.

Miniver Cheevy, born too late,
   Scratched his head and kept on thinking;

Miniver coughed, and called it fate,
And kept on drinking.

Richard Cory

Whenever Richard Cory went down town,
We people on the pavement looked at him:
He was a gentleman from sole to crown,
Clean favored, and imperially slim.

And he was always quietly arrayed,
And he was always human when he talked;
But still he fluttered pulses when he said,
"Good morning," and he glittered when he walked.

And he was rich—yes, richer than a king—
And admirably schooled in every grace:
In fine, we thought that he was everything
To make us wish that we were in his place.

So on we worked, and waited for the light,
And went without the meat, and cursed the bread;
And Richard Cory, one calm summer night,
Went home and put a bullet through his head.

Luke Havergal

Go to the western gate, Luke Havergal,
There where the vines cling crimson on the wall,
And in the twilight wait for what will come.
The leaves will whisper there of her, and some,
Like flying words, will strike you as they fall;
But go, and if you listen, she will call.
Go to the western gate, Luke Havergal—
Luke Havergal.

No, there is not a dawn in eastern skies
To rift the fiery night that's in your eyes;
But there, where western glooms are gathering,
The dark will end the dark, if anything:
God slays Himself with every leaf that flies,

244

And hell is more than half of paradise.
No, there is not a dawn in eastern skies—
In eastern skies.

Out of a grave I come to tell you this,
Out of a grave I come to quench the kiss
That flames upon your forehead with a glow
That blinds you to the way that you must go.
Yet, there is yet one way to where she is,
Bitter, but one that faith may never miss.
Out of a grave I come to tell you this—
To tell you this.

There is the western gate, Luke Havergal,
There are the crimson leaves upon the wall.
Go, for the winds are tearing them away—
Nor think to riddle the dead words they say,
Nor any more to feel them as they fall;
But go, and if you trust her she will call.
There is the western gate, Luke Havergal—
Luke Havergal.

For a Dead Lady

No more with overflowing light
Shall fill the eyes that now are faded,
Nor shall another's fringe with night
Their woman-hidden world as they did.
No more shall quiver down the days
The flowing wonder of her ways,
Whereof no language may requite
The shifting and the many-shaded.

The grace, divine, definitive,
Clings only as a faint forestalling;
The laugh that love could not forgive
Is hushed, and answers to no calling;
The forehead and the little ears
Have gone where Saturn keeps the years;
The breast where roses could not live
Has done with rising and with falling.

The beauty, shattered by the laws
That have creation in their keeping,

No longer trembles at applause,
Or over children that are sleeping;
And we who delve in beauty's lore
Know all that we have known before
Of what inexorable cause
Makes Time so vicious in his reaping.

Mr. Flood's Party

Old Eben Flood, climbing alone one night
Over the hill between the town below
And the forsaken upland hermitage
That held as much as he should ever know
On earth again of home, paused warily.
The road was his with not a native near;
And Eben, having leisure, said aloud,
For no man else in Tilbury Town to hear:

"Well, Mr. Flood, we have the harvest moon
Again, and we may not have many more;
The bird is on the wing, the poet says,
And you and I have said it here before.
Drink to the bird." He raised up to the light
The jug that he had gone so far to fill,
And answered huskily: "Well, Mr. Flood,
Since you propose it, I believe I will."

Alone, as if enduring to the end
A valiant armor of scarred hopes outworn,
He stood there in the middle of the road
Like Roland's ghost winding a silent horn.
Below him, in the town among the trees,
Where friends of other days had honored him,
A phantom salutation of the dead
Rang thinly till old Eben's eyes were dim.

Then, as a mother lays her sleeping child
Down tenderly, fearing it may awake,
He set the jug down slowly at his feet
With trembling care, knowing that most things break;
And only when assured that on firm earth
It stood, as the uncertain lives of men
Assuredly did not, he paced away,
And with his hand extended paused again:

246

"Well, Mr. Flood, we have not met like this
In a long time; and many a change has come
To both of us, I fear, since last it was
We had a drop together. Welcome home!"
Convivially returning with himself,
Again he raised the jug up to the light;
And with an acquiescent quaver said:
"Well, Mr. Flood, if you insist, I might.

"Only a very little, Mr. Flood—
For auld lang syne. No more, sir; that will do."
So, for the time, apparently it did,
And Eben evidently thought so too;
For soon amid the silver loneliness
Of night he lifted up his voice and sang,
Secure, with only two moons listening,
Until the whole harmonious landscape rang—

"For auld lang syne." The weary throat gave out,
The last word wavered; and the song being done,
He raised again the jug regretfully
And shook his head, and was again alone.
There was not much that was ahead of him,
And there was nothing in the town below—
Where strangers would have shut the many doors
That many friends had opened long ago.

CHRISTINA ROSSETTI
1830–1894

Song

When I am dead, my dearest,
   Sing no sad songs for me;
Plant thou no roses at my head,
   Nor shady cypress tree:
Be the green grass above me
   With showers and dewdrops wet;
And if thou wilt, remember,
   And if thou wilt, forget.

I shall not see the shadows,
   I shall not feel the rain;
I shall not hear the nightingale
   Sing on as if in pain:
And dreaming through the twilight
   That doth not rise nor set,
Haply I may remember,
   And haply may forget.

Remember

Remember me when I am gone away,
   Gone far away into the silent land;
   When you can no more hold me by the hand,
Nor I half turn to go, yet turning stay.
Remember me when no more day by day,
   You tell me of our future that you planned:
   Only remember me; you understand
It will be late to counsel then or pray.
Yet if you should forget me for a while
   And afterwards remember, do not grieve:
   For if the darkness and corruption leave
   A vestige of the thoughts that once I had,
Better by far you should forget and smile
   Than that you should remember and be sad.

Mirage

The hope I dreamed of was a dream,
   Was but a dream; and now I wake
Exceeding comfortless and worn and old,
   For a dream's sake.

I hang my harp upon a tree,
   A weeping willow in a lake;
I hang my silenced harp there, wrung and snapped,
   For a dream's sake.

Lie still, lie still, my breaking heart;
   My silent heart, lie still and break:
Life and the world and mine own self are changed,
   For a dream's sake.

248

Up-hill

"Does the road wind up-hill all the way?"
   "Yes, to the very end."
"Will the day's journey take the whole long day?"
   "From morn to night, my friend."

"But is there for the night a resting-place?
   A roof for when the slow dark hours begin?
May not the darkness hide it from my face?"
   "You cannot miss that inn."

"Shall I meet other wayfarers at night?"
   "Those who have gone before."
"Then must I knock, or call when just in sight?"
   "They will not keep you standing at that door."

"Shall I find comfort, travel-sore and weak?"
   "Of labor you shall find the sum."
"Will there be beds for me and all who seek?"
   "Yea, beds for all who come."

DANTE GABRIEL ROSSETTI

1828–1882

The Ballade of Dead Ladies

Tell me now in what hidden way is
   Lady Flora the lovely Roman?
Where's Hipparchia, and where is Thaïs,
   Neither of them the fairer woman?
   Where is Echo, beheld of no man,
Only heard on river and mere—
   She whose beauty was more than human? . . .
But where are the snows of yester-year?

Where's Héloïse, the learnéd nun,
   For whose sake Abeillard, I ween,
Lost manhood and put priesthood on?
   (From Love he won such dule and teen!)

And where, I pray you, is the Queen
Who willed that Buridan should steer
  Sewed in a sack's mouth down the Seine? . . .
But where are the snows of yester-year?

White Queen Blanche, like a queen of lilies,
  With a voice like any mermaiden—
Bertha Broadfoot, Beatrice, Alice,
  And Ermengarde the lady of Maine—
  And that good Joan whom Englishmen
At Rouen doomed and burned her there—
  Mother of God, where are they then? . . .
But where are the snows of yester-year?

Nay, never ask this week, fair lord,
  Where they are gone, nor yet this year,
Except with this for an overword—
  But where are the snows of yester-year?

                         (*after* **Villon**)

SIR WALTER SCOTT

1771–1832

Coronach

He is gone on the mountain,
  He is lost to the forest,
Like a summer-dried fountain,
  When our need was the sorest.
The font, reappearing,
  From the raindrops shall borrow,
But to us comes no cheering,
  To Duncan no morrow!

The hand of the reaper
  Takes the ears that are hoary,
But the voice of the weeper
  Wails manhood in glory.
The autumn winds rushing

Waft the leaves that are searest,
But our flower was in flushing
    When blighting was nearest.

Fleet foot on the correi,
    Sage counsel in cumber,
Red hand in the foray,
    How sound is thy slumber!
Like the dew on the mountain,
    Like the foam on the river,
Like the bubble on the fountain,
    Thou art gone, and forever!

Soldier, Rest!

Soldier, rest! thy warfare o'er,
    Sleep the sleep that knows not breaking;
Dream of battled fields no more,
    Days of danger, nights of waking.
In our isle's enchanted hall,
    Hands unseen thy couch are strewing,
Fairy strains of music fall,
    Every sense in slumber dewing.
Soldier, rest! thy warfare o'er,
Dream of fighting fields no more:
Sleep the sleep that knows not breaking,
Morn of toil, nor night of waking.

No rude sound shall reach thine ear,
    Armor's clang, or war-steed champing,
Trump nor pibroch summon here
    Mustering clan, or squadron tramping.
Yet the lark's shrill fife may come
    At the daybreak from the fallow,
And the bittern sound his drum,
    Booming from the sedgy shallow.
Ruder sounds shall none be near,
Guards nor warders challenge here;
Here's no war-steed's neigh and champing,
Shouting clans or squadrons stamping.

Huntsman, rest! thy chase is done;
    While our slumbrous spells assail ye,

Dream not, with the rising sun,
    Bugles here shall sound reveillé.
Sleep! the deer is in his den;
    Sleep! thy hounds are by thee lying;
Sleep! nor dream in yonder glen
    How thy gallant steed lay dying.
Huntsman, rest! thy chase is done;
Think not of the rising sun,
For at dawning to assail ye,
Here no bugles sound reveillé.

Lochinvar

Oh young Lochinvar is come out of the west,
Through all the wide Border his steed was the best;
And save his good broadsword he weapons had none.
He rode all unarmed, and he rode all alone.
So faithful in love and so dauntless in war,
There never was knight like the young Lochinvar.

He stayed not for brake and he stopped not for stone,
He swam the Eske River where ford there was none,
But ere he alighted at Netherby gate
The bride had consented, the gallant came late:
For a laggard in love and a dastard in war
Was to wed the fair Ellen of brave Lochinvar.

So boldly he entered the Netherby Hall,
Among bridesmen, and kinsmen, and brothers, and all:
Then spoke the bride's father, his hand on his sword—
For the poor craven bridegroom said never a word—
"Oh come ye in peace here, or come ye in war,
Or to dance at our bridal, young Lord Lochinvar?"

"I long wooed your daughter, my suit you denied;
Love swells like the Solway, but ebbs like its tide—
And now am I come, with this lost love of mine,
To lead but one measure, drink one cup of wine.
There are maidens in Scotland more lovely by far,
That would gladly be bride to the young Lochinvar."

The bride kissed the goblet; the knight took it up,
He quaffed off the wine, and he threw down the cup.
She looked down to blush, and she looked up to sigh,

With a smile on her lips and a tear in her eye.
He took her soft hand ere her mother could bar—
"Now tread we a measure!" said young Lochinvar.

So stately his form, and so lovely her face,
That never a hall such a galliard did grace;
While her mother did fret, and her father did fume,
And the bridegroom stood dangling his bonnet and plume;
And the bride-maidens whispered, " 'Twere better by far
To have matched our fair cousin with young Lochinvar."

One touch to her hand and one word in her ear,
When they reached the hall-door, and the charger stood near;
So light to the croupe the fair lady he swung,
So light to the saddle before her he sprung!
"She is won! We are gone, over bank, bush, and scaur;
They'll have fleet steeds that follow," quoth young Lochinvar.

There was mounting 'mong Graemes of the Netherby clan;
Forsters, Fenwicks, and Musgraves, they rode and they ran:
There was racing and chasing on Cannobie Lee,
But the lost bride of Netherby ne'er did they see.
So daring in love and so dauntless in war,
Have ye e'er heard of gallant like young Lochinvar?

Edmund's Song

Oh Brignall banks are wild and fair,
    And Greta woods are green,
And you may gather garlands there,
    Would grace a summer queen.
And as I rode by Dalton-hall,
    Beneath the turrets high,
A maiden on the castle wall
    Was singing merrily.

"Oh Brignall banks are fresh and fair,
    And Greta woods are green;
I'd rather rove with Edmund there,
    Than reign our English queen."

"If, maiden, thou wouldst wend with me,
    To leave both tower and town,
Thou first must guess what life lead we,

That dwell by dale and down.
And if thou canst that riddle read,
　　As read full well you may,
Then to the greenwood shalt thou speed,
　　As blithe as Queen of May."

Yet sung she, "Brignall banks are fair,
　　And Greta woods are green;
I'd rather rove with Edmund there,
　　Than reign our English queen.

"I read you by your bugle-horn
　　And by your palfrey good,
I read you for a Ranger sworn
　　To keep the king's greenwood."
"A Ranger, lady, winds his horn,
　　And 'tis at peep of light;
His blast is heard at merry morn,
　　And mine at dead of night."

Yet sung she, "Brignall banks are fair,
　　And Greta woods are gay;
I would I were with Edmund there,
　　To reign his Queen of May!

"With burnished brand and musketoon,
　　So gallantly you come,
I read you for a bold dragoon,
　　That lists the tuck of drum."
"I list no more the tuck of drum,
　　No more the trumpet hear;
But when the beetle sounds his hum,
　　My comrades take the spear.

"And, oh though Brignall banks be fair,
　　And Greta woods be gay,
Yet mickle must the maiden dare,
　　Would reign my Queen of May!

"Maiden! a nameless life I lead,
　　A nameless death I'll die;
The fiend whose lantern lights the mead
　　Were better mate than I!
And when I'm with my comrades met
　　Beneath the greenwood bough,
What once we were we all forget,
　　Nor think what we are now.

"Yet Brignall banks are fresh and fair,
    And Greta woods are green,
And you may gather garlands there
    Would grace a summer queen."

ROBERT SERVICE

1874–

The Shooting of Dan McGrew

A bunch of the boys were whooping it up in the Malamute saloon;
The kid that handles the music-box was hitting a jag-time tune;
Back of the bar, in a solo game, sat Dangerous Dan McGrew,
And watching his luck was his light-o'-love, the lady that's known as
    Lou.

When out of the night, which was fifty below, and into the din and
    the glare,
There stumbled a miner fresh from the creeks, dog-dirty, and loaded
    for bear.
He looked like a man with a foot in the grave and scarcely the
    strength of a louse,
Yet he tilted a poke of dust on the bar, and he called for drinks for
    the house.
There was none could place the stranger's face, though we searched
    ourselves for a clue;
But we drank his health, and the last to drink was Dangerous Dan
    McGrew.

There's men that somehow just grip your eyes, and hold them hard
    like a spell;
And such was he, and he looked to me like a man who had lived in
    hell;
With a face most hair, and the dreary stare of a dog whose day is
    done,
As he watered the green stuff in his glass, and the drops fell one by
    one.
Then I got to figgering who he was, and wondering what he'd do,

And I turned my head—and there watching him was the lady that's
known as Lou.

His eyes went rubbering round the room, and he seemed in a kind
of daze,
Till at last that old piano fell in the way of his wandering gaze.
The rag-time kid was having a drink; there was no one else on the
stool,
So the stranger stumbles across the room, and flops down there like
a fool.
In a buckskin shirt that was glazed with dirt he sat, and I saw him
sway;
Then he clutched the keys with his talon hands—my God! but that
man could play.

Were you ever out in the Great Alone, when the moon was awful
clear,
And the icy mountains hemmed you in with a silence you most
could *hear*;
With only the howl of a timber wolf, and you camped there in the
cold,
A half-dead thing in a stark, dead world, clean mad for the muck
called gold;
While high overhead, green, yellow and red, the North Lights swept
in bars?—
Then you've a hunch what the music meant . . . hunger and night
and the stars.

And hunger not of the belly kind, that's banished with bacon and
beans,
But the gnawing hunger of lonely men for a home and all that it
means;
For a fireside far from the cares that are, four walls and a roof above;
But oh so cramful of cosy joy, and crowned with a woman's love—
A woman dearer than all the world, and true as Heaven is true—
(God! how ghastly she looks through her rouge—the lady that's
known as Lou.)

Then on a sudden the music changed, so soft that you scarce could
hear;
But you felt that your life had been looted clean of all that it once
held dear;
That someone had stolen the woman you loved; that her love was a
devil's lie;
That your guts were gone, and the best for you was to crawl away
and die.

POEMS TO READ ALOUD

'Twas the crowning cry of a heart's despair, and it thrilled you
    through and through—
"I guess I'll make it a spread misère," said Dangerous Dan McGrew.

The music almost died away . . . then it burst like a pent-up flood;
And it seemed to say, "Repay, repay," and my eyes were blind with
    blood.
The thought came back of an ancient wrong, and it stung like a
    frozen lash,
And the lust awoke to kill, to kill . . . then the music stopped with
    a crash,
And the stranger turned, and his eyes they burned in a most peculiar
    way;
In a buckskin shirt that was glazed with dirt he sat, and I saw him
    sway;
Then his lips went in, in a kind of grin, and he spoke, and his voice
    was calm,
And "Boys," says he, "you don't know me, and none of you care a
    damn;
But I want to state, and my words are straight, and I'll bet my poke
    they're true,
That one of you is a hound of hell . . . and that one is Dan
    McGrew."

Then I ducked my head, and the lights went out, and two guns
    blazed in the dark,
And a woman screamed, and the lights went up, and two men lay
    stiff and stark.
Pitched on his head, and pumped full of lead, was Dangerous Dan
    McGrew,
While the man from the creeks lay clutched to the breast of the
    lady that's known as Lou.

These are the simple facts of the case, and I guess I ought to know.
They say that the stranger was crazed with hooch, and I'm not
    denying it's so.
I'm not so wise as the lawyer guys, but strictly between us two—
The woman that kissed him—and pinched his poke—was the lady
    that's known as Lou.

WILLIAM SHAKESPEARE

1564–1616

It Was a Lover and His Lass

It was a lover and his lass
  (With a hey, and a ho, and hey nonino)
That o'er the green cornfield did pass
  In springtime, the only pretty ring-time,
When birds do sing, hey ding a ding, ding:
Sweet lovers love the spring.

Between the acres of the rye
  (With a hey, and a ho, and a hey nonino)
These pretty country folk would lie,
  In springtime, the only pretty ring-time,
When birds do sing, hey ding a ding, ding:
Sweet lovers love the spring.

This carol they began that hour
  (With a hey, and a ho, and a hey nonino),
How that a life was but a flower
  In springtime, the only pretty ring-time,
When birds do sing, hey ding a ding, ding:
Sweet lovers love the spring.

And therefore take the present time
  (With a hey, and a ho, and a hey nonino),
For love is crownéd with the prime
  In springtime, the only pretty ring-time,
When birds do sing, hey ding a ding, ding:
Sweet lovers love the spring.

O Mistress Mine

O mistress mine, where are you roaming?
Oh stay and hear! your true love's coming,
  That can sing both high and low.

258

Trip no further, pretty sweeting,
Journeys end in lovers meeting,
   Every wise man's son doth know.

What is love? 'Tis not hereafter;
Present mirth hath present laughter;
   What's to come is still unsure:
In delay there lies no plenty;
Then come kiss me, sweet and twenty!
   Youth's a stuff will not endure.

When Daisies Pied

When daisies pied and violets blue
   And lady-smocks all silver-white
And cuckoo buds of yellow hue
   Do paint the meadows with delight,
The cuckoo then, on every tree,
Mocks married men; for thus sings he,
    "Cuckoo!
Cuckoo, cuckoo!" Oh word of fear,
Unpleasing to a married ear!

When shepherds pipe on oaten straws,
   And merry larks are ploughmen's clocks,
When turtles tread, and rooks, and daws,
   And maidens bleach their summer smocks,
The cuckoo then, on every tree,
Mocks married men; for thus sings he,
    "Cuckoo!
Cuckoo, cuckoo!" Oh word of fear,
Unpleasing to a married ear!

When Icicles Hang by the Wall

When icicles hang by the wall,
   And Dick the shepherd blows his nail,
And Tom bears logs into the hall,
   And milk comes frozen home in pail,
When blood is nipped and ways be foul,
Then nightly sings the staring owl,

"Tu-whit, tu-who!" a merry note,
While greasy Joan doth keel the pot.

When all aloud the wind doth blow,
    And coughing drowns the parson's saw,
And birds sit brooding in the snow,
    And Marian's nose looks red and raw,
When roasted crabs hiss in the bowl,
Then nightly sings the staring owl,
"Tu-whit, tu-who!" a merry note,
    While greasy Joan doth keel the pot.

How Should I Your True-Love Know?

How should I your true-love know
    From another one?
By his cockle hat and staff,
    And his sandal shoon.

He is dead and gone, lady,
    He is dead and gone;
At his head a grass-green turf,
    At his heels a stone.

White his shroud as the mountain snow,
    Larded with sweet flowers;
Which bewept to the grave did go
    With true-love showers.

Come Away, Death

Come away, come away, death,
    And in sad cypress let me be laid;
Fly away, fly away, breath;
    I am slain by a fair cruel maid.
My shroud of white, stuck all with yew,
        Oh prepare it!
My part of death, no one so true
        Did share it.

Not a flower, not a flower sweet,
    On my black coffin let there be strown;

Not a friend, not a friend greet
   My poor corpse, where my bones shall be thrown.
A thousand thousand sighs to save,
     Lay me, oh where
Sad true lover never find my grave,
     To weep there!

Full Fathom Five

Full fathom five thy father lies:
   Of his bones are coral made;
Those are pearls that were his eyes;
   Nothing of him that doth fade
But doth suffer a sea-change
Into something rich and strange.
Sea nymphs hourly ring his knell:
             Ding-dong!
Hark! now I hear them—Ding-dong, bell!

When That I Was and a Little Tiny Boy

When that I was and a little tiny boy,
   With hey, ho, the wind and the rain,
A foolish thing was but a toy,
   For the rain it raineth every day.

But when I came to man's estate
   With hey, ho, the wind and the rain,
'Gainst knaves and thieves men shut their gate,
   For the rain it raineth every day.

But when I came, alas! to wive,
   With hey, ho, the wind and the rain,
By swaggering could I never thrive,
   For the rain it raineth every day.

But when I came unto my beds,
   With hey, ho, the wind and the rain,
With toss-pots still had drunken heads,
   For the rain it raineth every day.

A great while ago the world begun,
   With hey, ho, the wind and the rain,
But that's all one, our play is done,
   And we'll strive to please you every day.

Fear No More the Heat o' the Sun

Fear no more the heat o' the sun,
   Nor the furious winter's rages;
Thou thy worldly task hath done,
   Home art gone, and ta'en thy wages:
Golden lads and girls all must,
As chimney-sweepers, come to dust.

Fear no more the frown o' the great;
   Thou art past the tyrant's stroke;
Care no more to clothe and eat;
   To thee the reed is as the oak:
The sceptre, learning, physic, must
All follow this, and come to dust.

Fear no more the lightning-flash,
   Nor th' all-dreaded thunder-stone;
Fear not slander, censure rash;
   Thou hast finished joy and moan:
All lovers young, all lovers must
Consign to thee, and come to dust.

No exorciser harm thee!
Nor no witchcraft charm thee!
Ghost unlaid forbear thee!
Nothing ill come near thee!
Quiet consummation have;
And renownéd be thy grave!

You Spotted Snakes

You spotted snakes with double tongue,
   Thorny hedgehogs, be not seen;
Newts and blind-worms, do no wrong;
   Come not near our fairy queen.

Philomel, with melody,
Sing in our sweet lullaby;
Lulla, lulla, lullaby; lulla, lulla, lullaby!
Never harm,
Nor spell nor charm,
Come our lovely lady nigh;
So, good night, with lullaby.

Weaving spiders, come not here;
Hence, you long-legged spinners, hence!
Beetles black, approach not near;
Worm nor snail, do no offence.

Philomel, with melody,
Sing in our sweet lullaby;
Lulla, lulla, lullaby; lulla, lulla, lullaby!
Never harm,
Nor spell nor charm,
Come our lovely lady nigh;
So, good night, with lullaby.

Sonnets

18

Shall I compare thee to a summer's day?
Thou art more lovely and more temperate:
Rough winds do shake the darling buds of May,
And summer's lease hath all too short a date;
Sometime too hot the eye of heaven shines,
And often is his gold complexion dimmed;
And every fair from fair sometime declines,
By chance or nature's changing course untrimmed;
But thy eternal summer shall not fade
Nor lose possession of that fair thou ow'st;
Nor shall Death brag thou wand'rest in his shade
When in eternal lines to time thou grow'st:
So long as men can breathe, or eyes can see,
So long lives this, and this gives life to thee.

29

When, in disgrace with fortune and men's eyes,
I all alone beweep my outcast state
And trouble deaf heaven with my bootless cries

And look upon myself and curse my fate,
Wishing me like to one more rich in hope,
Featured like him, like him with friends possessed,
Desiring this man's art and that man's scope,
With what I most enjoy contented least:
Yet in these thoughts myself almost despising,
Haply I think on thee, and then my state,
Like to the lark at break of day arising
From sullen earth, sings hymns at heaven's gate:
   For thy sweet love remembered such wealth brings
   That then I scorn to change my state with kings.

30

When to the sessions of sweet silent thought
I summon up remembrance of things past,
I sigh the lack of many a thing I sought,
And with old woes new wail my dear time's waste.
Then can I drown an eye, unused to flow,
For precious friends hid in death's dateless night,
And weep afresh love's long since canceled woe,
And moan th' expense of many a vanished sight.
Then can I grieve at grievances foregone,
And heavily from woe to woe tell o'er
The sad account of fore-bemoanéd moan,
Which I new pay as if not paid before.
   But if the while I think on thee, dear friend,
   All losses are restored and sorrows end.

33

Full many a glorious morning have I seen
Flatter the mountain-tops with sovereign eye,
Kissing with golden face the meadows green,
Gilding pale streams with heavenly alchemy;
Anon permit the basest clouds to ride
With ugly rack on his celestial face,
And from the forlorn world his visage hide,
Stealing unseen to west with this disgrace.
Even so my sun one early morn did shine
With all-triumphant splendor on my brow;
But out, alack! he was but one hour mine;
The region cloud hath masked him from me now.
   Yet him for this my love no whit disdaineth;
   Suns of the world may stain when heaven's sun staineth.

55

Not marble, nor the gilded monuments
Of princes, shall outlive this powerful rime;
But you shall shine more bright in these contents
Than unswept stone, besmeared with sluttish time.
When wasteful war shall statues overturn,
And broils root out the work of masonry,
Nor Mars his sword nor war's quick fire shall burn
The living record of your memory.
'Gainst death and all-oblivious enmity
Shall you pace forth; your praise shall still find room
Even in the eyes of all posterity
That wear this world out to the ending doom.
   So, till the judgment that yourself arise,
   You live in this, and dwell in lovers' eyes.

60

Like as the waves make towards the pebbled shore,
So do our minutes hasten to their end;
Each changing place with that which goes before,
In sequent toil all forwards do contend.
Nativity, once in the main of light,
Crawls to maturity, wherewith being crowned,
Crooked eclipses 'gainst his glory fight,
And Time that gave doth now his gift confound.
Time doth transfix the flourish set on youth
And delves the parallels in beauty's brow,
Feeds on the rarities of nature's truth,
And nothing stands but for his scythe to mow:
   And yet to times in hope my verse shall stand,
   Praising thy worth, despite his cruel hand.

64

When I have seen by Time's fell hand defaced
The rich-proud cost of outworn buried age;
When sometime lofty towers I see down-razed,
And brass eternal slave to mortal rage;
When I have seen the hungry ocean gain
Advantage on the kingdom of the shore,
And the firm soil win of the wat'ry main,
Increasing store with loss, and loss with store;
When I have seen such interchange of state,
Or state itself confounded to decay,

Ruin hath taught me thus to ruminate,
That Time will come and take my love away.
   This thought is as a death, which cannot choose
   But weep to have that which it fears to lose.

65

Since brass, nor stone, nor earth, nor boundless sea,
But sad mortality o'er-sways their power,
How with this rage shall beauty hold a plea,
Whose action is no stronger than a flower?
Oh how shall summer's honey breath hold out
Against the wrackful siege of batt'ring days,
When rocks impregnable are not so stout,
Nor gates of steel so strong, but Time decays?
Oh fearful meditation! Where, alack,
Shall Time's best jewel from Time's chest lie hid?
Or what strong hand can hold his swift foot back?
Or who his spoil of beauty can forbid?
   Oh none!—unless this miracle have might,
   That in black ink my love may still shine bright.

71

No longer mourn for me when I am dead
Than you shall hear the surly sullen bell
Give warning to the world that I am fled
From this vile world, with vilest worms to dwell.
Nay, if you read this line, remember not
The hand that writ it; for I love you so
That I in your sweet thoughts would be forgot
If thinking on me then should make you woe.
Oh if, I say, you look upon this verse
When I, perhaps, compounded am with clay,
Do not so much as my poor name rehearse,
But let your love even with my life decay:
   Lest the wise world should look into your moan
   And mock you with me after I am gone.

73

That time of year thou mayst in me behold
When yellow leaves, or none, or few, do hang
Upon those boughs which shake against the cold—
Bare ruined choirs, where late the sweet birds sang.
In me thou seest the twilight of such day
As after sunset fadeth in the west,

Which by and by black night doth take away,
Death's second self, that seals up all in rest.
In me thou seest the glowing of such fire
That on the ashes of his youth doth lie,
As the deathbed whereon it must expire,
Consumed with that which it was nourished by.
This thou perceivest, which makes thy love more strong,
To love that well which thou must leave ere long.

97

How like a winter hath my absence been
From thee, the pleasure of the fleeting year!
What freezings have I felt, what dark days seen!
What old December's bareness everywhere!
And yet this time removed was summer's time,
The teeming autumn, big with rich increase,
Bearing the wanton burthen of the prime,
Like widowed wombs after their lords' decease.
Yet this abundant issue seemed to me
But hope of orphans and unfathered fruit;
For summer and his pleasures wait on thee,
And, thou away, the very birds are mute;
Or, if they sing, 'tis with so dull a cheer
That leaves look pale, dreading the winter's near.

106

When in the chronicles of wasted time
I see descriptions of the fairest wights,
And beauty making beautiful old rime
In praise of ladies dead and lovely knights,
Then, in the blazon of sweet beauty's best,
Of hand, of foot, of lip, of eye, of brow,
I see their antique pen would have expressed
Even such a beauty as you master now.
So all their praises are but prophecies
Of this our time, all you prefiguring;
And, for they looked but with divining eyes,
They had not skill enough your worth to sing:
For we, which now behold these present days,
Have eyes to wonder, but lack tongues to praise.

116

Let me not to the marriage of true minds
Admit impediments. Love is not love

Which alters when it alteration finds
Or bends with the remover to remove,
Oh no! it is an ever-fixéd mark
That looks on tempests and is never shaken;
It is the star to every wand'ring bark,
Whose worth's unknown, although his height be taken.
Love's not Time's fool, though rosy lips and cheeks
Within his bending sickle's compass come;
Love alters not with his brief hours and weeks,
But bears it out even to the edge of doom.
    If this be error and upon me proved,
    I never writ, nor no man ever loved.

PERCY BYSSHE SHELLEY

1792–1822

Ozymandias

I met a traveler from an antique land
Who said: Two vast and trunkless legs of stone
Stand in the desert. Near them, on the sand,
Half sunk, a shattered visage lies, whose frown,
And wrinkled lip, and sneer of cold command,
Tell that its sculptor well those passions read
Which yet survive, stamped on these lifeless things,
The hand that mocked them and the heart that fed.
And on the pedestal these words appear:
"My name is Ozymandias, king of kings;
Look on my works, ye mighty, and despair!"
Nothing beside remains. Round the decay
Of that colossal wreck, boundless and bare
The lone and level sands stretch far away.

Ode to the West Wind

I

O wild West Wind, thou breath of Autumn's
    being,
Thou, from whose unseen presence the leaves
    dead
Are driven, like ghosts from an enchanter fleeing,

Yellow, and black, and pale, and hectic red,
Pestilence-stricken multitudes! O thou
Who chariotest to their dark wintry bed

The wingéd seeds, where they lie cold and low,
Each like a corpse within its grave, until
Thine azure sister of the Spring shall blow

Her clarion o'er the dreaming earth, and fill
(Driving sweet buds like flocks to feed in air)
With living hues and odors plain and hill:

Wild Spirit, which art moving everywhere,
Destroyer and preserver, hear, oh hear!

II

Thou on whose stream, 'mid the steep sky's com-
    motion,
Loose clouds like earth's decaying leaves are shed,
Shook from the tangled boughs of heaven and
    ocean,

Angels of rain and lightning! there are spread
On the blue surface of thine airy surge,
Like the bright hair uplifted from the head

Of some fierce Mænad even from the dim verge
Of the horizon to the zenith's height,
The locks of the approaching storm. Thou dirge

Of the dying year, to which this closing night
Will be the dome of a vast sepulchre,
Vaulted with all thy congregated might

Of vapors, from whose solid atmosphere
Black rain, and fire, and hail, will burst: oh hear!

III

Thou who didst waken from his summerdreams
The blue Mediterranean, where he lay,
Lulled by the coil of his crystalline streams

Beside a pumice isle in Baiae's bay,
And saw in sleep old palaces and towers
Quivering within the wave's intenser day,

All overgrown with azure moss and flowers
So sweet, the sense faints picturing them! Thou
For whose path the Atlantic's level powers

Cleave themselves into chasms, while far below
The sea-blooms and the oozy woods which wear
The sapless foliage of the ocean know

Thy voice, and suddenly grow grey with fear
And tremble and despoil themselves: oh hear!

IV

If I were a dead leaf thou mightest bear,
If I were a swift cloud to fly with thee,
A wave to pant beneath thy power, and share

The impulse of thy strength, only less free
Than thou, O uncontrollable! If even
I were as in my boyhood and could be

The comrade of thy wanderings over heaven,
As then, when to outstrip thy skyey speed
Scarce seemed a vision, I would ne'er have striven

As thus with thee in prayer in my sore need.
Oh lift me as a wave, a leaf, a cloud!
I fall upon the thorns of life! I bleed!

A heavy weight of hours has chained and bowed
One too like thee—tameless, and swift, and
    proud.

V

Make me thy lyre, even as the forest is:
What if my leaves are falling like its own!
The tumult of thy mighty harmonies

Will take from both a deep, autumnal tone,
Sweet though in sadness. Be thou, Spirit fierce,
My spirit! Be thou me, impetuous one!

Drive my dead thoughts over the universe
Like withered leaves, to quicken a new birth!
And by the incantation of this verse,

Scatter, as from an unextinguished hearth
Ashes and sparks, my words among mankind!
Be through my lips to unawakened earth

The trumpet of a prophecy! O wind,
If Winter comes, can Spring be far behind?

Stanzas Written in Dejection near Naples

The sun is warm, the sky is clear,
    The waves are dancing fast and bright,
Blue isles and snowy mountains wear
    The purple noon's transparent might;
    The breath of the moist earth is light
Around its unexpanded buds;
    Like many a voice of one delight,
The winds', the birds', the ocean-floods',
The city's voice itself is soft like solitude's.

I see the deep's untrampled floor
    With green and purple seaweeds strown;
I see the waves upon the shore
    Like light dissolved in star-showers thrown;
    I sit upon the sands alone.
The lightning of the noon-tide ocean
    Is flashing round me, and a tone
Arises from its measured motion—
How sweet! did any heart now share in my emotion.

Alas! I have nor hope nor health,
    Nor peace within nor calm around,
Nor that content, surpassing wealth,
    The sage in meditation found,
    And walked with inward glory crowned—
Nor fame, nor power, nor love, nor leisure;

Others I see whom these surround—
  Smiling they live, and call life pleasure;
To me that cup has been dealt in another measure.

Yet now despair itself is mild,
   Even as the winds and waters are;
I could lie down like a tired child,
   And weep away the life of care
   Which I have borne, and yet must bear,
Till death like sleep might steal on me,
   And I might feel in the warm air
My cheek grow cold, and hear the sea
Breathe o'er my dying brain its last monotony.

Some might lament that I were cold,
   As I, when this sweet day is gone,
Which my lost heart, too soon grown old,
   Insults with this untimely moan;
   They might lament—for I am one
Whom men love not—and yet regret,
   Unlike this day, which, when the sun
Shall on its stainless glory set,
Will linger, though enjoyed, like joy in memory
      yet.

To Night

Swiftly walk o'er the western wave,
     Spirit of Night!
Out of the misty eastern cave,
Where all the long and lone daylight
Thou wovest dreams of joy and fear,
Which make thee terrible and dear—
     Swift be thy flight!

Wrap thy form in a mantle grey,
     Star-inwrought!
Blind with thine hair the eyes of Day,
Kiss her until she be wearied out;
Then wander o'er city, and sea, and land,
Touching all with thine opiate wand—
     Come, long-sought!

When I arose and saw the dawn,
          I sighed for thee;
When light rode high, and the dew was gone,
And noon lay heavy on flower and tree,
And the weary Day turned to his rest,
Lingering like an unloved guest,
          I sighed for thee.

Thy brother Death came, and cried,
          "Wouldst thou me?"
Thy sweet child Sleep, the filmy-eyed,
Murmured like a noontide bee,
"Shall I nestle near thy side?
Wouldst thou me?" And I replied,
          "No, not thee!"

Death will come when thou art dead,
          Soon, too soon;
Sleep will come when thou art fled;
Of neither would I ask the boon
I ask of thee, belovéd Night—
Swift be thine approaching flight,
          Come soon, soon!

A Lament

O world! O life! O time!
On whose last steps I climb,
   Trembling at that where I had stood before;
When will return the glory of your prime?
         No more—Oh never more!

Out of the day and night
A joy has taken flight;
   Fresh spring, and summer, and winter hoar,
Move my faint heart with grief, but with delight
         No more—Oh never more!

A Dirge

    Rough wind, that moanest loud
      Grief too sad for song;

Wild wind, when sullen cloud
  Knells all the night long;
Sad storm, whose tears are vain,
Bare woods, whose branches strain,
Deep caves and dreary main—
  Wail, for the world's wrong!

RICHARD BRINSLEY SHERIDAN
1751–1816

Song

Here's to the maiden of bashful fifteen;
  Here's to the widow of fifty;
Here's to the flaunting extravagant quean,
  And here's to the housewife that's thrifty.
      Let the toast pass,
      Drink to the lass,
I'll warrant she'll prove an excuse for the glass.

Here's to the charmer whose dimples we prize;
  Now to the maid who has none, sir;
Here's to the girl with a pair of blue eyes,
  And here's to the nymph with but one, sir.
      Let the toast pass, etc.

Here's to the maid with a bosom of snow;
  Now to her that's as brown as a berry;
Here's to the wife with a face full of woe,
  And now to the damsel that's merry.
      Let the toast pass, etc.

For let 'em be clumsy, or let 'em be slim,
  Young or ancient, I care not a feather;
So fill a pint bumper quite up to the brim,
  And let us e'en toast them together.
      Let the toast pass, etc.

JAMES SHIRLEY
1596–1666

The Glories of Our Blood and State

The glories of our blood and state
    Are shadows, not substantial things;
There is no armor against fate;
    Death lays his icy hand on kings:
        Sceptre and crown
        Must tumble down,
And in the dust be equal made
With the poor crookéd scythe and spade.

Some men with swords may reap the field,
    And plant fresh laurels where they kill:
But their strong nerves at last must yield;
    They tame but one another still:
        Early or late
        They stoop to fate,
And must give up their murmuring breath
When they, pale captives, creep to death.

The garlands wither on your brow;
    Then boast no more your mighty deeds;
Upon death's purple altar now
    See where the victor-victim bleeds:
        Your heads must come
        To the cold tomb;
Only the actions of the just
Smell sweet and blossom in their dust.

SIR PHILIP SIDNEY

1554–1586

With How Sad Steps, O Moon

With how sad steps, O Moon, thou climb'st the
    skies!
How silently, and with how wan a face!
What, may it be that even in heavenly place
That busy archer his sharp arrows tries?
Sure, if that long-with-love-acquainted eyes
Can judge of love, thou feel'st a lover's case;
I read it in thy looks; thy languished grace,
To me, that feel the like, thy state descries.
Then, even of fellowship, O Moon, tell me,
Is constant love deemed there but want of wit?
Are beauties there as proud as here they be?
Do they above love to be loved, and yet
Those lovers scorn whom that love doth possess?
Do they call virtue there ungratefulness?

Come, Sleep!

Come, Sleep! O Sleep, the certain knot of peace,
The baiting-place of wit, the balm of woe,
The poor man's wealth, the prisoner's release,
Th' indifferent judge between the high and low;
With shield of proof shield me from out the
    prease
Of those fierce darts Despair at me doth throw;
Oh make in me those civil wars to cease;
I will good tribute pay, if thou do so.
Take thou of me smooth pillows, sweetest bed,
A chamber deaf to noise and blind to light,
A rosy garland and a weary head:
And if these things, as being thine in right,

Move not thy heavy grace, thou shalt in me,
Livelier than elsewhere, Stella's image see.

Leave Me, O Love

Leave me, O Love, which reachest but to dust,
And thou, my mind, aspire to higher things!
Grow rich in that which never taketh rust:
Whatever fades but fading pleasure brings.
Draw in thy beams, and humble all thy might
To that sweet yoke where lasting freedoms be,
Which breaks the clouds and opens forth the
    light
That doth both shine and give us sight to see.
Oh take fast hold! Let that light be thy guide
In this small course which birth draws out to
    death;
And think how evil becometh him to slide
Who seeketh heaven and comes of heavenly
    breath.
Then farewell, world; thy uttermost I see:
Eternal Love, maintain thy life in me.

EDITH SITWELL

1887–

Aubade

Jane, Jane,
Tall as a crane,
The morning light creaks down again.

Comb your cockscomb-ragged hair;
Jane, Jane, come down the stair.

Each dull blunt wooden stalactite
Of rain creaks, hardened by the light,

Sounding like an overtone
From some lonely world unknown.

But the creaking empty light
Will never harden into sight,

Will never penetrate your brain
With overtones like the blunt rain.

The light would show (if it could harden)
Eternities of kitchen-garden,

Cockscomb flowers that none will pluck,
And wooden flowers that 'gin to cluck.

In the kitchen you must light
Flames as staring, red and white

As carrots or as turnips, shining
Where the cold dawn light lies whining.

Cockscomb hair on the cold wind
Hangs limp, turns the milk's weak mind. . . .

> Jane, Jane,
> Tall as a crane,
> The morning light creaks down again!!

JOHN SKELTON

1460?–1529

To Mistress Margaret Hussey

> Merry Margaret,
> As midsummer flower,
> Gentle as falcon
> Or hawk of the tower;
>   With solace and gladness,
> Much mirth and no madness,
> All good and no badness,
> So joyously,
> So maidenly,

So womanly
Her demeaning
In every thing—
Far, far passing
That I can endite
Or suffice to write
Of merry Margaret,
As midsummer flower,
Gentle as falcon
Or hawk of the tower.
   As patient and as still,
And as full of good will,
As fair Isiphill,
Coliander,
Sweet pomander,
Good Cassander;
Steadfast of thought,
Well made, well wrought;
Far may be sought
Erst that ye can find
So curteise, so kind
As merry Margaret,
This midsummer flower,
Gentle as falcon,
Or hawk of the tower.

KENNETH SLESSOR

1901–

Five Bells

Time that is moved by little fidget wheels
Is not my Time, the flood that does not flow.
Between the double and the single bell
Of a ship's hour, between a round of bells
From the dark warship riding there below,
I have lived many lives, and this one life
Of Joe, long dead, who lives between five bells.

Deep and dissolving verticals of light
Ferry the falls of moonshine down. Five bells
Coldly rung out in a machine's voice. Night and water
Pour to one rip of darkness, the Harbor floats
In air, the Cross hangs upside-down in water.

Why do I think of you, dead man, why thieve
These profitless lodgings from the flukes of thought
Anchored in Time? You have gone from the earth,
Gone even from the meaning of a name;
Yet something's there, yet something forms its lips
And hits and cries against the ports of space,
Beating their sides to make its fury heard.

Are you shouting at me, dead man, squeezing your face
In agonies of speech on speechless panes?
Cry louder, beat the windows, bawl your name!

But I hear nothing, nothing . . . only bells,
Five bells, the bumpkin calculus of Time.
Your echoes die, your voice is dowsed by Life,
There's not a mouth can fly the pygmy strait—
Nothing except the memory of some bones
Long shoved away, and sucked away, in mud;
And unimportant things you might have done,
Or once I thought you did; but you forgot,
And all have now forgotten—looks and words
And slops of beer; your coat with buttons off,
Your gaunt chin and pricked eye, and raging tales
Of Irish kings and English perfidy,
And dirtier perfidy of publicans
Groaning to God from Darlinghurst.

Five bells.

Then I saw the road, and I heard the thunder
Tumble, and felt the talons of the rain
The night we came to Moorebank in slab-dark,
So dark you bore no body, had no face,
But a sheer voice that rattled out of air
(As now you'd cry if I could break the glass),
A voice that spoke beside me in the bush,
Loud for a breath or bitten off by wind,
Of Milton, melons and the Rights of Man,
And blowing flutes, and how Tahitian girls
Are brown and angry-tongued, and Sydney girls
Are white and angry-tongued, or so you'd found.

280

But all I heard was words that didn't join,
So Milton became melons, melons girls,
And fifty mouths, it seemed, were all that night,
And in each tree an ear was bending down,
Or something had just run, gone behind grass,
When, blank and bone-white, like a maniac's thought,
The naphtha-flash of lightning slit the sky,
Knifing the dark with deathly photographs.
There's not so many with so poor a purse
Or fierce a need, must fare by night like that,
Five miles in darkness on a country track,
But when you do, that's what you think.

Five bells.

In Melbourne, your appetite had gone,
Your angers too; they had been leeched away
By the soft archery of summer rains
And the sponge-paws of wetness, the slow damp
That stuck the leaves of living, snailed the mind,
And showed your bones, that had been sharp with rage,
The sodden ecstasies of rectitude.
I thought of what you'd written in faint ink,
Your journal with the sawn-off lock, that stayed behind
With other things you left, all without use,
All without meaning now, except a sign
That someone had been living who now was dead:
"At Labassa. Room 6 x 8
On top of the tower; because of this, very dark
And cold in winter. Everything has been stowed
Into this room—500 books all shapes
And colors, dealt across the floor
And over sills and on the laps of chairs;
Guns, photos of many different things
And different curios that I obtained. . . ."

In Sydney, by the spent aquarium-flare
Of penny gaslight on pink wallpaper,
We argued about blowing up the world,
But you were living backward, so each night
You crept a moment closer to the breast,
And they were living, all of them, those frames
And shapes of flesh that had perplexed your youth,
And most your father, the old man gone blind,
With fingers always round a fiddle's neck,
That graveyard mason whose fair monuments

And tablets cut with dreams of piety
Rest on the bosoms of a thousand men
Staked bone by bone, in quiet astonishment
At cargoes they had never thought to bear,
These funeral-cakes of sweet and sculptured stone.

Where have you gone? The tide is over you,
The turn of midnight water's over you,
As Time is over you, and mystery,
And memory, the flood that does not flow.
You have no suburb, like those easier dead
In private berths of dissolution laid—
The tide goes over, the waves ride over you
And let their shadows down like shining hair,
But they are Water; and the sea-pinks bend
Like lilies in your teeth, but they are Weed;
And you are only part of an Idea.

I felt the wet push its black thumb-balls in,
The night you died, I felt your eardrums crack,
And the short agony, the longer dream,
The Nothing that was neither long nor short;
But I was bound, and could not go that way,
But I was blind, and could not feel your hand.
If I could find an answer, could only find
Your meaning, or could say why you were here
Who now are gone, what purpose gave you breath
Or seized it back, might I not hear your voice?

I looked out of my window in the dark
At waves with diamond quills and combs of light
That arched their mackerel-backs and smacked the sand
In the moon's drench, that straight enormous glaze,
And ships far off asleep, and harbor-buoys
Tossing their fire-balls wearily each to each,
And tried to hear your voice, but all I heard
Was a boat's whistle, and the scraping squeal
Of seabird's voices far away, and bells,
Five bells. Five bells coldly ringing out.

Five bells.

STEPHEN SPENDER

1909–

I Think Continually of Those Who Were Truly Great

I think continually of those who were truly great.
Who, from the womb, remembered the soul's history
Through corridors of light where the hours are suns,
Endless and singing. Whose lovely ambition
Was that their lips, still touched with fire,
Should tell of the Spirit, clothed from head to foot in
  song.
And who hoarded from the Spring branches
The desires falling across their bodies like blossoms.

What is precious is never to forget
The essential delight of the blood drawn from ageless
  springs
Breaking through rocks in worlds before our earth.
Never to deny its pleasure in the morning simple light
Nor its grave evening demand for love.
Never to allow gradually the traffic to smother,
With noise and fog, the flowering of the spirit.

Near the snow, near the sun, in the highest fields,
See how these names are fêted by the waving grass
And by the streamers of white cloud
And whispers of wind in the listening sky.
The names of those who in their lives fought for life,
Who wore at their hearts the fire's center.
Born of the sun, they traveled a short while towards
  the sun,
And left the vivid air signed with their honor.

JAMES STEPHENS

1882–1950

Deirdre

Do not let any woman read this verse!
It is for men, and after them their sons,
And their sons' sons!

The time comes when our hearts sink utterly;
When we remember Deirdre and her tale,
And that her lips are dust.

Once she did tread the earth: men took her hand;
They looked into her eyes and said their say,
And she replied to them.

More than two thousand years it is since she
Was beautiful: she trod the waving grass;
She saw the clouds.

Two thousand years! The grass is still the same;
The clouds as lovely as they were that time
When Deirdre was alive.

But there has never been a woman born
Who was so beautiful; not one so beautiful
Of all the women born.

Let all men go apart and mourn together!
No man can ever love her! not a man
Can dream to be her lover!

No man can bend before her! No man say—
What could one say to her? There are no words
That one could say to her!

Now she is but a story that is told
Beside the fire! No man can ever be
The friend of that poor queen!

WALLACE STEVENS

1879–1956

Dry Loaf

It is equal to living in a tragic land
To live in a tragic time.
Regard now the sloping, mountainous rocks
And the river that batters its way over stones,
Regard the hovels of those that live in this land.

That was what I painted behind the loaf,
The rocks not even touched by snow,
The pines along the river and the dry men blown
Brown as the bread, thinking of birds
Flying from burning countries and brown sand shores,

Birds that came like dirty water in waves
Flowing above the rocks, flowing over the sky,
As if the sky was a current that bore them along,
Spreading them as waves spread flat on the shore,
One after another washing the mountains bare.

It was the battering of drums I heard
It was hunger, it was the hungry that cried
And the waves, the waves were soldiers moving,
Marching and marching in a tragic time
Below me, on the asphalt, under the trees.

It was soldiers went marching over the rocks
And still the birds came, came in watery flocks,
Because it was spring and the birds had to come.
No doubt that soldiers had to be marching
And that drums had to be rolling, rolling, rolling.

The Candle   A Saint

Green is the night, green kindled and apparelled.
It is she that walks among astronomers.

She strides above the rabbit and the cat,
Like a noble figure, out of the sky,

Moving among the sleepers, the men,
Those that lie chanting *green is the night.*

Green is the night and out of madness woven,
The self-same madness of the astronomers

And of him that sees, beyond the astronomers,
The topaz rabbit and the emerald cat,

That sees above them, that sees rise up above them,
The noble figure, the essential shadow,

Moving and being, the image at its source,
The abstract, the archaic queen. Green is the night.

ROBERT LOUIS STEVENSON

1850–1894

Romance

I will make you brooches and toys for your delight
Of bird-song at morning and star-shine at night.
I will make a palace fit for you and me,
Of green days in forests and blue days at sea.

I will make my kitchen, and you shall keep your room,
Where white flows the river and bright blows the broom,
And you shall wash your linen and keep your body white
In rainfall at morning and dewfall at night.

And this shall be for music when no one else is near,
The fine song for singing, the rare song to hear!
That only I remember, that only you admire,
Of the broad road that stretches and the roadside fire.

Windy Nights

Whenever the moon and stars are set,
   Whenever the wind is high,
All night long in the dark and wet,
   A man goes riding by.
Late in the night when the fires are out,
Why does he gallop and gallop about?

Whenever the trees are crying aloud,
   And ships are tossed at sea,
By on the highway low and loud,
   By at the gallop goes he.
By at the gallop he goes, and then
By he comes back at the gallop again.

Requiem

Under the wide and starry sky,
Dig the grave and let me lie.
Glad did I live and gladly die,
   And I laid me down with a will.

This be the verse you grave for me:
Here he lies where he longed to be;
Home is the sailor, home from sea,
   And the hunter home from the hill.

Go, Little Book

Go, little book, and wish to all
Flowers in the garden, meat in the hall,
A bin of wine, a spice of wit,
A house with lawns enclosing it,
A living river by the door,
A nightingale in the sycamore.

SIR JOHN SUCKLING
1609–1642

Out upon It!

Out upon it! I have loved
  Three whole days together,
And am like to love three more,
  If it prove fair weather.

Time shall moult away his wings,
  Ere he shall discover
In the whole wide world again
  Such a constant lover.

But the spite on 't is, no praise
  Is due at all to me;
Love with me had made no stays
  Had it any been but she.

Had it any been but she
  And that very face,
There had been at least ere this
  A dozen dozen in her place.

Why So Pale and Wan?

Why so pale and wan, fond lover?
  Prithee, why so pale?
Will, when looking well can't move her,
  Looking ill prevail?
  Prithee, why so pale?

Why so dull and mute, young sinner?
  Prithee, why so mute?
Will, when speaking well can't win her,
  Saying nothing do 't?
  Prithee, why so mute?

Quit, quit for shame! This will not move;
   This cannot take her.
If of herself she will not love,
   Nothing can make her.
   The devil take her!

ALGERNON SWINBURNE

1837–1909

A Ballad of François Villon

Prince of All Ballad-Makers

Bird of the bitter bright grey golden morn,
   Scarce risen upon the dusk of dolorous years,
First of us all and sweetest singer born,
   Whose far shrill note the world of new men hears
   Cleave the cold shuddering shade as twilight clears;
When song new-born put off the old world's attire
And felt its tune on her changed lips expire,
   Writ foremost on the roll of them that came
Fresh girt for service of the latter lyre,
   Villon, our sad bad glad mad brother's name!

Alas, the joy, the sorrow, and the scorn,
   That clothed thy life with hopes and sins and fears,
And gave thee stones for bread and tares for corn
   And plume-plucked jail-birds for thy starveling peers,
   Till death clipped close their flight with shameful
      shears;
Till shifts came short and loves were hard to hire,
When lilt of song nor twitch of twangling wire
   Could buy thee bread or kisses; when light fame
Spurned like a ball and haled through brake and briar,
   Villon, our sad bad glad mad brother's name!

Poor splendid wings so frayed and soiled and torn!
   Poor kind wild eyes so dashed with light quick tears!
Poor perfect voice, most blithe when most forlorn,

That rings athwart the sea whence no man steers,
   Like joy-bells crossed with death-bells in our ears!
What far delight has cooled the fierce desire
   That, like some ravenous bird, was strong to tire
   On that frail flesh and soul consumed with flame,
But left more sweet than roses to respire,
   Villon, our sad bad glad mad brother's name?

ENVOI

Prince of sweet songs made out of tears and fire,
A harlot was thy nurse, a God thy sire;
   Shame soiled thy song, and song assoiled thy shame.
But from thy feet now death has washed the mire,
Love reads out first at head of all our quire,
   Villon, our sad bad glad mad brother's name.

The Garden of Proserpine

Here, where the world is quiet,
   Here, where all trouble seems
Dead winds' and spent waves' riot
   In doubtful dreams of dreams,
I watch the green field growing
For reaping folk and sowing,
For harvest-time and mowing,
   A sleepy world of streams.

I am tired of tears and laughter,
   And men that laugh and weep;
Of what may come hereafter
   For men that sow to reap.
I am weary of days and hours,
Blown buds of barren flowers,
Desires and dreams and powers
   And everything but sleep.

Here life has death for neighbor,
   And far from eye or ear
Wan waves and wet winds labor,
   Weak ships and spirits steer;
They drive adrift, and whither
They wot not who make thither;

But no such winds blow hither,
    And no such things grow here.

No growth of moor or coppice,
    No heather-flower or vine,
But bloomless buds of poppies,
    Green grapes of Proserpine,
Pale beds of blowing rushes,
    Where no leaf blooms or blushes
Save this whereout she crushes
    For dead men deadly wine.

Pale, without name or number,
    In fruitless fields of corn,
They bow themselves and slumber
    All night till light is born;
And like a soul belated,
In hell and heaven unmated,
By cloud and mist abated
    Comes out of darkness morn.

Though one were strong as seven,
    He too with death shall dwell,
Nor wake with wings in heaven,
    Nor weep for pains in hell;
Though one were fair as roses,
His beauty clouds and closes;
And well though love reposes,
    In the end it is not well.

Pale, beyond porch and portal,
    Crowned with calm leaves, she stands
Who gathers all things mortal
    With cold, immortal hands;
Her languid lips are sweeter
Than love's who fears to greet her,
To men that mix and meet her
    From many times and lands.

She waits for each and other,
    She waits for all men born;
Forgets the earth her mother,
    The life of fruits and corn;
And spring and seed and swallow
Take wing for her and follow

Where summer song rings hollow
  And flowers are put to scorn.

There go the loves that wither,
  The old loves with wearier wings;
And all dead years draw thither,
  And all disastrous things;
Dead dreams of days forsaken,
Blind buds that snows have shaken,
Wild leaves that winds have taken,
  Red strays of ruined springs.

We are not sure of sorrow,
  And joy was never sure;
Today will die tomorrow;
  Time stoops to no man's lure;
And love, grown faint and fretful,
With lips but half regretful
Sighs, and with eyes forgetful
  Weeps that no loves endure.

From too much love of living,
  From hope and fear set free,
We thank with brief thanksgiving
  Whatever gods may be
That no life lives forever,
That dead men rise up never,
That even the weariest river
  Winds somewhere safe to sea.

Then star nor sun shall waken,
  Nor any change of light;
Nor sound of waters shaken,
  Nor any sound or sight;
Nor wintry leaves nor vernal,
Nor days nor things diurnal—
Only the sleep eternal
  In an eternal night.

GENEVIEVE TAGGARD

1894–1948

Song for Unbound Hair

Oh never marry Ishmael!
Marry another and prosper well;
But not, but never Ishmael . . .

What has he ever to buy or sell?
He only owns what his strength can keep,
Only a vanishing knot of sheep,
A goat or two. Does he sow or reap?
In the hanging rocks rings his old ram's bell—
Who would marry Ishmael?

What has he to give to a bride?
Only trouble, little beside,
Only his arm like a little cave
To cover a woman and keep her safe;
A rough fierce kiss, and the wind and the rain,
A child, perhaps, and another again—
Who would marry Ishmael?

The arrogant Lucifer when he fell
Bequeathed his wrath to Ishmael;
The hand of every man is set
Against this lad, and this lad's hand
Is cruel and quick—forget, forget
The nomad boy on his leagues of sand. . . .

Marry another and prosper well,
But not, but never Ishmael.

ALFRED, LORD TENNYSON

1809–1892

Ulysses

It little profits that, an idle king,
By this still hearth, among these barren crags,
Matched with an agéd wife, I mete and dole
Unequal laws unto a savage race
That hoard, and sleep, and feed, and know not me.
I cannot rest from travel—I will drink
Life to the lees. All times I have enjoyed
Greatly, have suffered greatly, both with those
That loved me, and alone; on shore, and when
Through scudding drifts the rainy Hyades
Vexed the dim sea. I am become a name;
For always roaming with a hungry heart
Much have I seen and known; cities of men
And manners, climates, councils, governments,
Myself not least, but honored of them all;
And drunk delight of battle with my peers,
Far on the ringing plains of windy Troy.
I am a part of all that I have met;
Yet all experience is an arch wherethrough
Gleams that untraveled world, whose margin fades
For ever and for ever when I move.
How dull it is to pause, to make an end,
To rust unburnished, not to shine in use!
As though to breathe were life! Life piled on life
Were all too little, and of one to me
Little remains: but every hour is saved
From that eternal silence, something more,
A bringer of new things; and vile it were
For some three suns to store and hoard myself,
And this grey spirit yearning in desire
To follow knowledge like a sinking star,
Beyond the utmost bound of human thought.

    This is my son, mine own Telemachus,
To whom I leave the scepter and the isle—

Well-loved of me, discerning to fulfill
This labor, by slow prudence to make mild
A rugged people, and through soft degrees
Subdue them to the useful and the good.
Most blameless is he, centered in the sphere
Of common duties, decent not to fail
In offices of tenderness, and pay
Meet adoration to my household gods,
When I am gone. He works his work, I mine.

There lies the port; the vessel puffs her sail;
There gloom the dark broad seas. My mariners,
Souls that have toiled, and wrought, and thought with me—
That ever with a frolic welcome took
The thunder and the sunshine, and opposed
Free hearts, free foreheads—you and I are old;
Old age hath yet his honor and his toil.
Death closes all; but something ere the end,
Some work of noble note, may yet be done,
Not unbecoming men that strove with gods.
The lights begin to twinkle from the rocks;
The long day wanes; the slow moon climbs; the deep
Moans round with many voices. Come, my friends,
'Tis not too late to seek a newer world.
Push off, and sitting well in order smite
The sounding furrows; for my purpose holds
To sail beyond the sunset and the baths
Of all the western stars, until I die.
It may be that the gulfs will wash us down;
It may be that we shall touch the Happy Isles,
And see the great Achilles, whom we knew.
Though much is taken, much abides; and though
We are not now that strength which in old days
Moved earth and heaven, that which we are, we are:
One equal temper of heroic hearts,
Made weak by time and fate, but strong in will
To strive, to seek, to find, and not to yield.

The Revenge

At Flores in the Azores Sir Richard Grenville lay,
And a pinnace, like a fluttered bird, came flying from far away:

"Spanish ships of war at sea! we have sighted fifty-three!"
Then sware Lord Thomas Howard: "'Fore God I am no
    coward;
But I cannot meet them here, for my ships are out of gear,
And the half my men are sick. I must fly, but follow quick.
We are six ships of the line; can we fight with fifty-three?"

Then spake Sir Richard Grenville: "I know you are no coward;
You fly them for a moment to fight with them again.
But I've ninety men and more that are lying sick ashore.
I should count myself the coward if I left them, my Lord
    Howard,
To these Inquisition dogs and the devildoms of Spain."

So Lord Howard passed away with five ships of war that day,
Till he melted like a cloud in the silent summer heaven;
But Sir Richard bore in hand all his sick men from the land
Very carefully and slow,
Men of Bideford in Devon,
And we laid them on the ballast down below;
For we brought them all aboard,
And they blessed him in their pain, that they were not left to
    Spain,
To the thumb-screw and the stake, for the glory of the Lord.

He had only a hundred seamen to work the ship and to fight,
And he sailed away from Flores till the Spaniard came in sight,
With his huge sea-castles heaving upon the weather bow.
"Shall we fight or shall we fly?
Good Sir Richard, tell us now,
For to fight is but to die!
There'll be little of us left by the time this sun be set."
And Sir Richard said again: "We be all good English men.
Let us bang these dogs of Seville, the children of the devil,
For I never turned my back upon Don or devil yet."

Sir Richard spoke and he laughed, and we roared a hurrah,
    and so
The little *Revenge* ran on sheer into the heart of the foe,
With her hundred fighters on deck, and her ninety sick below;
For half of their fleet to the right and half to the left were
    seen,
And the little *Revenge* ran on through the long sea-lane
    between.

Thousands of their soldiers looked down from their decks and
    laughed,
Thousands of their seamen made mock at the mad little craft
Running on and on, till delayed
By their mountain-like *San Philip* that, of fifteen hundred tons,
And up-shadowing high above us with her yawning tiers of
    guns,
Took the breath from our sails, and we stayed.

And while now the great *San Philip* hung above us like a
    cloud
Whence the thunderbolt will fall
Long and loud,
Four galleons drew away
From the Spanish fleet that day,
And two upon the larboard and two upon the starboard lay,
And the battle-thunder broke from them all.

But anon the great *San Philip*, she bethought herself and went,
Having that within her womb that had left her ill content;
And the rest they came aboard us, and they fought us hand
    to hand.
For a dozen times they came with their pikes and musketeers,
And a dozen times we shook 'em off as a dog that shakes his
    ears
When he leaps from the water to the land.

And the sun went down, and the stars came out far over the
    summer sea,
But never a moment ceased the fight of the one and the fifty-
    three.
Ship after ship, the whole night long, their high-built galleons
    came,
Ship after ship, the whole night long, with her battle-thunder
    and flame;
Ship after ship, the whole night long, drew back with her dead
    and her shame.
For some were sunk and many were shattered, and so could
    fight us no more—
God of battles, was ever a battle like this in the world before?

For he said, "Fight on! fight on!"
Though his vessel was all but a wreck;
And it chanced that, when half of the short summer night was
    gone,

With a grisly wound to be dressed he had left the deck,
But a bullet struck him that was dressing it suddenly dead,
And himself he was wounded again in the side and the head,
And he said, "Fight on! fight on!"

And the night went down, and the sun smiled out far over the
 summer sea,
And the Spanish fleet with broken sides lay round us all in a
 ring;
But they dared not touch us again, for they feared that we still
 could sting,
So they watched what the end would be.
And we had not fought them in vain,
But in perilous plight were we,
Seeing forty of our poor hundred were slain,
And half of the rest of us maimed for life
In the crash of the cannonades and the desperate strife;
And the sick men down in the hold were most of them stark
 and cold,
And the pikes were all broken or bent, and the powder was all
 of it spent;
And the masts and the rigging were lying over the side;
But Sir Richard cried in his English pride:
"We have fought such a fight for a day and a night
As may never be fought again!
We have won great glory, my men!
And a day less or more
At sea or ashore,
We die—does it matter when?
Sink me the ship, Master Gunner—sink her, split her in twain!
Fall into the hands of God, not in the hands of Spain!"

And the gunner said, "Ay, ay," but the seamen made reply:
"We have children, we have wives,
And the Lord hath spared our lives.
We will make the Spaniard promise, if we yield, to let us go;
We shall live to fight again and to strike another blow."
And the lion there lay dying, and they yielded to the foe.

And the stately Spanish men to their flagship bore him then,
Where they laid him by the mast, old Sir Richard caught at
 last,
And they praised him to his face with their courtly foreign
 grace;
But he rose upon their decks, and he cried:

"I have fought for Queen and Faith like a valiant man and
   true;
I have only done my duty as a man is bound to do.
With a joyful spirit I Sir Richard Grenville die!"
And he fell upon their decks, and he died.

And they stared at the dead that had been so valiant and true,
And had holden the power and glory of Spain so cheap
That he dared her with one little ship and his English few;
Was he devil or man? He was devil for aught they knew,
But they sank his body with honor down into the deep,
And they manned the *Revenge* with a swarthier alien crew,
And away she sailed with her loss and longed for her own;
When a wind from the lands they had ruined awoke from
   sleep,
And the water began to heave and the weather to moan,
And or ever that evening ended, a great gale blew,
And a wave like the wave that is raised by an earthquake grew,
Till it smote on their hulls and their sails and their masts and
   their flags,
And the whole sea plunged and fell on the shot-shattered navy
   of Spain,
And the little *Revenge* herself went down by the island crags
To be lost evermore in the main.

Break, Break, Break

Break, break, break,
   On thy cold grey stones, O Sea!
And I would that my tongue could utter
   The thoughts that arise in me.

Oh well for the fisherman's boy,
   That he shouts with his sister at play!
Oh well for the sailor lad,
   That he sings in his boat on the bay!

And the stately ships go on
   To their haven under the hill;
But oh for the touch of a vanished hand,
   And the sound of a voice that is still!

Break, break, break,
   At the foot of thy crags, O Sea!

But the tender grace of a day that is dead
Will never come back to me.

Crossing the Bar

Sunset and evening star,
   And one clear call for me!
And may there be no moaning of the bar,
   When I put out to sea,

But such a tide as moving seems asleep,
   Too full for sound and foam,
When that which drew from out the boundless deep
   Turns again home.

Twilight and evening bell,
   And after that the dark!
And may there be no sadness of farewell,
   When I embark;

For though from out our bourne of Time and Place
   The flood may bear me far,
I hope to see my Pilot face to face
   When I have crossed the bar.

ERNEST LAWRENCE THAYER

1863–1940

Casey at the Bat

It looked extremely rocky for the Mudville nine that day,
The score stood four to six with but an inning left to play.
And so, when Cooney died at first, and Burrows did the same,
A pallor wreathed the features of the patrons of the game.
A straggling few got up to go, leaving there the rest
With that hope which springs eternal within the human breast.
For they thought if only Casey could get a whack at that,

They'd put up even money with Casey at the bat.
But Flynn preceded Casey, and likewise so did Blake,
And the former was a pudding and the latter was a fake;
So on that stricken multitude a death-like silence sat,
For there seemed but little chance of Casey's getting to the bat.

But Flynn let drive a single to the wonderment of all,
And the much despised Blakey tore the cover off the ball,
And when the dust had lifted and they saw what had occurred,
There was Blakey safe on second, and Flynn a-hugging third.
Then from the gladdened multitude went up a joyous yell;
It bounded from the mountain top and rattled in the dell,
It struck upon the hillside and rebounded on the flat,
For Casey, mighty Casey, was advancing to the bat.
There was ease in Casey's manner as he stepped into his place,
There was pride in Casey's bearing and a smile on Casey's face,
And when responding to the cheers he lightly doffed his hat,
No stranger in the crowd could doubt, 'twas Casey at the bat.

Ten thousand eyes were on him as he rubbed his hands with dirt,
Five thousand tongues applauded as he wiped them on his shirt;
And while the writhing pitcher ground the ball into his hip,
Defiance gleamed from Casey's eye, a sneer curled Casey's lip.
And now the leather-covered sphere came hurtling through the air,
And Casey stood a-watching it in haughty grandeur there;
Close by the sturdy batsman the ball unheeded sped—
"That hain't my style," said Casey. "Strike one!" the Umpire said.
From the bleachers black with people there rose a sullen roar,
Like the beating of the storm waves on a stern and distant shore.
"Kill him! kill the Umpire!" shouted someone from the stand—
And it's likely they'd have done it had not Casey raised his hand.

With a smile of Christian charity great Casey's visage shone,
He stilled the rising tumult and he bade the game go on;
He signalled to the pitcher and again the spheroid flew,
But Casey still ignored it, and the Umpire said, "Strike two!"
"Fraud!" yelled the maddened thousands, and the echo answered,
    "Fraud!"
But one scornful look from Casey, and the audience was awed;
They saw his face grow stern and cold, they saw his muscles strain,
And they knew that Casey would not let that ball go by again.
The sneer is gone from Casey's lip; his teeth are clenched with hate;
He pounds with cruel violence his bat upon the plate.
And now the pitcher holds the ball, and now he lets it go,
And now the air is shattered by the force of Casey's blow.—

Oh somewhere in this favored land the sun is shining bright,
The band is playing somewhere, and somewhere hearts are light,
And somewhere men are laughing, and somewhere children shout:
But there is no joy in Mudville—mighty Casey has struck out!

DYLAN THOMAS

1914–1953

Fern Hill

Now as I was young and easy under the apple boughs
About the lilting house and happy as the grass was green,
    The night above the dingle starry,
      Time let me hail and climb
    Golden in the heydays of his eyes,
And honored among wagons I was prince of the apple towns
And once below a time I lordly had the trees and leaves
      Trail with daisies and barley
    Down the rivers of the windfall light.

And as I was green and carefree, famous among the barns
About the happy yard and singing as the farm was home,
    In the sun that is young once only,
      Time let me play and be
    Golden in the mercy of his means,
And green and golden I was huntsman and herdsman, the calves
Sang to my horn, the foxes on the hills barked clear and cold,
      And the sabbath rang slowly
    In the pebbles of the holy streams.

All the sun long it was running, it was lovely, the hay-
Fields high as the house, the tunes from the chimneys, it was air
    And playing, lovely and watery
      And fire green as grass.
    And nightly under the simple stars
As I rode to sleep the owls were bearing the farm away,
All the moon long I heard, blessed among stables, the nightjars
      Flying with the ricks, and the horses
        Flashing into the dark.

302

And then to awake, and the farm, like a wanderer white
With the dew, come back, the cock on his shoulder: it was all
      Shining, it was Adam and maiden,
        The sky gathered again
      And the sun grew round that very day.
So it must have been after the birth of the simple light
In the first, spinning place, the spellbound horses walking warm
      Out of the whinnying green stable
        On to the fields of praise.

And honored among foxes and pheasants by the gay house
Under the new made clouds and happy as the heart was long,
      In the sun born over and over,
        I ran my heedless ways,
      My wishes raced through the house-high hay
And nothing I cared, at my sky blue trades, that time allows
In all his tuneful turnings so few and such morning songs
      Before the children green and golden
        Follow him out of grace,

Nothing I cared, in the lamb white days, that time would take me
Up to the swallow thronged loft by the shadow of my hand,
      In the moon that is always rising,
        Nor that riding to sleep
      I should hear him fly with the high fields
And wake to the farm forever fled from the childless land.
Oh as I was young and easy in the mercy of his means,
      Time held me green and dying
      Though I sang in my chains like the sea.

Poem in October

      It was my thirtieth year to heaven
Woke to my hearing from harbor and neighbor wood
      And the mussel pooled and the heron
        Priested shore
        The morning beckon
With water praying and call of seagull and rook
And the knock of sailing boats on the net-webbed wall
      Myself to set foot
        That second
      In the still sleeping town and set forth.

My birthday began with the water-
Birds and the birds of the winged trees flying my name
          Above the farms and the white horses
                    And I rose
                In rainy autumn
And walked abroad in a shower of all my days.
High tide and the heron dived when I took the road
                    Over the border
                    And the gates
          Of the town closed as the town awoke.

          A springful of larks in a rolling
Cloud and the roadside bushes brimming with whistling
          Blackbirds and the sun of October
                    Summery
                On the hill's shoulder,
Here were fond climates and sweet singers suddenly
Come in the morning where I wandered and listened
                To the rain wringing
                    Wind blow cold
          In the wood faraway under me.

          Pale rain over the dwindling harbor
And over the sea-wet church the size of a snail
          With its horns through mist and the castle
                    Brown as owls
                But all the gardens
Of spring and summer were blooming in the tall tales
Beyond the border and under the lark-full cloud.
                There could I marvel
                    My birthday
          Away but the weather turned around.

          It turned away from the blithe country
And down the other air and the blue altered sky
          Streamed again a wonder of summer
                    With apples
                Pears and red currants
And I saw in the turning so clearly a child's
Forgotten mornings when he walked with his mother
                Through the parables
                    Of sunlight
          And the legends of the green chapels

          And the twice-told fields of infancy
That his tears burned my cheeks and his heart moved in mine.

These were the woods the river and sea
Where a boy
In the listening
Summertime of the dead whispered the truth of his joy
To the trees and the stones and the fish in the tide.
And the mystery
Sang alive
Still in the water and singingbirds.

And there could I marvel my birthday
Away but the weather turned around. And the true
Joy of the long dead child sang burning
In the sun.
It was my thirtieth
Year to heaven stood there then in the summer noon
Though the town below lay leaved with October blood.
Oh may my heart's truth
Still be sung
On this high hill in a year's turning.

W. J. TURNER

1889?–1946

Romance

When I was but thirteen or so
    I went into a golden land,
Chimborazo, Cotopaxi
    Took me by the hand.

My father died, my brother too,
    They passed like fleeting dreams,
I stood where Popocatapetl
    In the sunlight gleams.

I dimly heard the master's voice
    And boys far-off at play—
Chimborazo, Cotopaxi
    Had stolen me away.

I walked in a great golden dream
 To and fro from school—
Shining Popocatapetl
 The dusty streets did rule.

I walked home with a gold dark boy
 And never a word I'd say,
Chimborazo, Cotopaxi
 Had taken my speech away.

I gazed entranced upon his face
 Fairer than any flower—
O shining Popocatapetl,
 It was thy magic hour:

The houses, people, traffic seemed
 Thin fading dreams by day;
Chimborazo, Cotopaxi,
 They had stolen my soul away!

MARK VAN DOREN

1894–

The Runaways

Upon a summer Sunday: sweet the sound
Of noon's high warmness flowing to the ground;

Upon a summer Sunday: wide the song
Of strengthless wings that bore the sky along;

Upon a summer Sunday: strange the power,
Inaudible, that opened every flower;

On Sunday, in the summer, through the white
Mid-world they wandered, meditating flight.

With every boundary melted, still they ran,
Still looked for where the end of earth began;

Still truant; but, dissolving far ahead,
The edge of day as effortlessly fled,

As innocently distanced all they were
Of quick-eared dog and fat philosopher.

On Sunday, in the summer, down a field,
Leader and led, alternately they wheeled

Till the great grass possessed them, and the sky
No longer was a map to measure by;

Till round and round they floated, lost and small,
Like butterflies that afterward will fall

But now between the great sky and the ground,
Sun-tethered, dance all morning meadow-bound.

Upon a summer Sunday, when the light
Of perfect noon was everywhere and white—

Pure death of place and color—then the pair
Grew sudden-silent, hungry for home's air;

Paused, turned; remembered shadows in a yard;
And had again their own high wall and hard.

Proper Clay

Their little room grew light with cries;
He woke and heard them thread the dark,
He woke and felt them like the rays
Of some unlawful dawn at work:

Some random sunrise, lost and small,
That found the room's heart, vein by vein.
But she was whispering to the wall,
And he must see what she had seen.

He asked her gently, and she wept.
"Oh I have dreamed the ancient dream.
My time was on me, and I slept;
And I grew greater than I am;

"And lay like dead; but when I lived,
Three wingéd midwives wrapped the child.
It was a god that I had loved,
It was a hero I had held.

"Stretch out your mortal hands, I beg.
Say common sentences to me.
Lie cold and still, that I may brag
How close I am to proper clay.

"Let this within me hear the truth.
Speak loud to it." He stopped her lips.
He smoothed the covers over both.
It was a dream perhaps, perhaps;

Yet why this radiance round the room,
And why this trembling at her waist?
And then he smiled. It was the same
Undoubted flesh that he had kissed;

She lay unchanged from what she was,
She cried as ever woman cried.
Yet why this light along his brows?
And whence the music no one made?

HENRY VAUGHAN

1622–1695

The Retreat

Happy those early days when I
Shined in my angel-infancy!
Before I understood this place
Appointed for my second race,
Or taught my soul to fancy aught
But a white, celestial thought;
When yet I had not walked above
A mile or two from my first love,
And looking back, at that short space,
Could see a glimpse of His bright face;
When on some gilded cloud or flow'r
My gazing soul would dwell an hour,
And in those weaker glories spy
Some shadows of eternity;
Before I taught my tongue to wound

My conscience with a sinful sound,
Or had the black art to dispense,
A sev'ral sin to ev'ry sense;
But felt through all this fleshly dress
Bright shoots of everlastingness.
    Oh how I long to travel back,
And tread again that ancient track!
That I might once more reach that plain,
Where first I left my glorious train;
From whence th' enlightened spirit sees
That shady city of palm trees.
But ah! my soul with too much stay
Is drunk and staggers in the way!
Some men a forward motion love,
But I by backward steps would move;
And when this dust falls to the urn,
In that state I came, return.

PETER VIERECK
1916–

Kilroy Was Here

I

Also Ulysses once—that other war.
        (Is it because we find his scrawl
        Today on every privy door
        That we forget his ancient role?)
Also was there—he did it for the wages—
When a Cathay-drunk Genoese set sail.
Whenever "longen folk to goon on pilgrimages,"
Kilroy is there;
            he tells The Miller's Tale.

II

At times he seems a paranoiac king
Who stamps his crest on walls and says, "My own!"

But in the end he fades like a lost tune,
Tossed here and there, whom all the breezes sing.
"Kilroy was here"; these words sound wanly gay.
        Haughty yet tired with long marching.
He is Orestes—guilty of what crime?—
        For whom the Furies still are searching;
        When they arrive, they find their prey
(Leaving his name to mock them) went away.
Sometimes he does not flee from them in time:
"*Kilroy was*—"
            (*with his blood a dying man*
            Wrote half the phrase out in Bataan.)

III

Kilroy, beware. "HOME" is the final trap
That lurks for you in many a wily shape:
In pipe-and-slippers plus a Loyal Hound
        Or fooling around, just fooling around.
Kind to the old (their warm Penelope)
But fierce to boys,
            thus "home" becomes that sea,
Horribly disguised, where you were always drowned—
        (How could suburban Crete condone
The yarns you would have V-mailed from the sun?)—
And folksy fishes sip Icarian tea.

One stab of hopeless wings imprinted your
            Exultant Kilroy-signature
Upon sheer sky for the world to stare:
        "*I was there! I was there! I was there!*"

IV

God is like Kilroy; He, too, sees it all;
That's how he knows of every sparrow's fall;
That's why we prayed each time the tightropes cracked
On which our loveliest clowns contrived their act.
The G.I. Faustus who was
                        everywhere
Strolled home again. "What was it like outside?"
Asked Can't, with his good neighbors Ought and But
And pale Perhaps and grave-eyed Better Not;
For "Kilroy" means: the world is very wide.
        He was there, he was there, he was there!

And in the suburbs Can't sat down and cried.

EDMUND WALLER

1606–1687

Go, Lovely Rose

Go, lovely rose!
Tell her that wastes her time and me
That now she knows,
When I resemble her to thee,
How sweet and fair she seems to be.

Tell her that's young,
And shuns to have her graces spied,
That hadst thou sprung
In deserts where no men abide,
Thou must have uncommended died.

Small is the worth
Of beauty from the light retired;
Bid her come forth,
Suffer herself to be desired,
And not blush so to be admired,

Then die—that she
The common fate of all things rare
May read in thee:
How small a part of time they share
That are so wondrous sweet and fair!

On a Girdle

That which her slender waist confined
Shall now my joyful temples bind;
No monarch but would give his crown,
His arms might do what this has done.

It was my heaven's extremest sphere,
The pale which held that lovely deer.

My joy, my grief, my hope, my love,
Did all within this circle move!

A narrow compass! and yet there
Dwelt all that's good and all that's fair;
Give me but what this ribband bound,
Take all the rest the sun goes round!

JOHN WEBSTER

1580?–1625?

Call for the Robin-Redbreast

Call for the robin-redbreast and the wren,
   Since o'er shady groves they hover,
   And with leaves and flowers do cover
The friendless bodies of unburied men.
   Call unto his funeral dole
   The ant, the field-mouse, and the mole
To rear him hillocks that shall keep him warm,
And (when gay tombs are robbed) sustain no harm;
But keep the wolf far thence, that's foe to men,
For with his nails he'll dig them up again.

All the Flowers of the Spring

All the flowers of the spring
Meet to perfume our burying;
These have but their growing prime,
And man doth flourish but his time.
Survey our progress from our birth—
We are set, we grow, we turn to earth.
Courts adieu, and all delights,
All bewitching appetites.
Sweetest breath and clearest eye,
Like perfumes, go out and die;

And consequently this is done
As shadows wait upon the sun.
Vain the ambitiön of kings
Who seek by trophies and dead things
To leave a living name behind,
And weave but nets to catch the wind.

WALT WHITMAN

1819–1892

When Lilacs Last in the Dooryard Bloomed

1

When lilacs last in the dooryard bloomed
And the great star early drooped in the western sky in the night,
I mourned, and yet shall mourn with ever-returning spring.

Ever-returning spring, trinity sure to me you bring,
Lilac blooming perennial and drooping star in the west,
And thought of him I love.

2

O powerful western fallen star!
O shades of night—O moody, tearful night!
O great star disappeared—O the black murk that hides the star!
O cruel hands that hold me powerless—O helpless soul of me!
O harsh surrounding cloud that will not free my soul.

3

In the dooryard fronting an old farmhouse near the whitewashed
palings
Stands the lilac-bush tall-growing with heart-shaped leaves of rich
green,
With many a pointed blossom rising delicate, with the perfume
strong I love,
With every leaf a miracle—and from this bush in the dooryard,
With delicate-colored blossoms and heart-shaped leaves of rich
green,
A sprig with its flower I break.

4

In the swamp in secluded recesses,
A shy and hidden bird is warbling a song.

Solitary the thrush,
The hermit withdrawn to himself, avoiding the settlements,
Sings by himself a song.

Song of the bleeding throat,
Death's outlet song of life, (for well dear brother I know,
If thou wast not granted to sing thou would'st surely die.)

5

Over the breast of the spring, the land, amid cities,
Amid lanes and through old woods, where lately the violets peeped
     from the ground, spotting the grey debris,
Amid the grass in the fields each side of the lanes, passing the end-
     less grass,
Passing the yellow-speared wheat, every grain from its shroud in the
     dark-brown fields uprisen,
Passing the apple-tree blows of white and pink in the orchards,
Carrying a corpse to where it shall rest in the grave,
Night and day journeys a coffin.

6

Coffin that passes through lanes and streets,
Through day and night with the great cloud darkening the land,
With the pomp of the inlooped flags, with the cities draped in
     black,
With the show of the States themselves as of crape-veiled women
     standing,
With processions long and winding and the flambeaus of the night,
With the countless torches lit, with the silent sea of faces and the
     unbared heads,
With the waiting depot, the arriving coffin, and the sombre faces,
With dirges through the night, with the thousand voices rising
     strong and solemn,
With the mournful voices of the dirges poured around the coffin,
The dim-lit churches and the shuddering organs—where amid these
     you journey,
With the tolling tolling bells' perpetual clang,
Here, coffin that slowly passes,
I give you my sprig of lilac.

7

(Nor for you, for one alone,
Blossoms and branches green to coffins all I bring,

For fresh as the morning, thus would I chant a song for you, O sane
and sacred death.

All over bouquets of roses,
O death, I cover you over with roses and early lilies,
But mostly and now the lilac that blooms the first,
Copious I break, I break the sprigs from the bushes,
With loaded arms I come, pouring for you,
For you and the coffins all of you, O death.)

8

O western orb sailing the heaven,
Now I know what you must have meant as a month since I walked,
As I walked in silence the transparent shadowy night,
As I saw you had something to tell as you bent to me night after
night,
As you drooped from the sky low down as if to my side, (while the
other stars all looked on,)
As we wandered together the solemn night, (for something I know
not what kept me from sleep,)
As the night advanced, and I saw on the rim of the west how full
you were of woe,
As I stood on the rising ground in the breeze in the cool transparent
night,
As I watched where you passed and was lost in the netherward black
of the night,
As my soul in its trouble dissatisfied sank, as where you, sad orb,
Concluded, dropped in the night, and was gone.

9

Sing on there in the swamp,
O singer bashful and tender, I hear your notes, I hear your call,
I hear, I come presently, I understand you,
But a moment I linger, for the lustrous star has detained me,
The star my departing comrade holds and detains me.

10

O how shall I warble myself for the dead one there I loved?
And how shall I deck my song for the large sweet soul that has
gone?
And what shall my perfume be for the grave of him I love?

Sea-winds blown from east and west,
Blown from the Eastern sea and blown from the Western sea, till
there on the prairies meeting,

These and with these and the breath of my chant,
I'll perfume the grave of him I love.

11

O what shall I hang on the chamber walls?
And what shall the pictures be that I hang on the walls,
To adorn the burial-house of him I love?

Pictures of growing spring and farms and homes,
With the Fourth-month eve at sundown, and the grey smoke lucid
    and bright,
With floods of yellow gold of the gorgeous, indolent, sinking sun,
    burning, expanding the air,
With the fresh sweet herbage underfoot, and the pale green leaves
    of the trees prolific,
In the distance the flowing glaze, the breast of the river, with a
    wind-dapple here and there,
With ranging hills on the banks, with many a line against the sky,
    and shadows,
And the city at hand with dwellings so dense, and stacks of chim-
    neys,
And all the scenes of life and the workshops, and the workmen
    homeward returning.

12

Lo, body and soul—this land,
My own Manhattan with spires, and the sparkling and hurrying
    tides, and the ships,
The varied and ample land, the South and the North in the light,
    Ohio's shores and flashing Missouri,
And ever the far-spreading prairies covered with grass and corn.

Lo, the most excellent sun so calm and haughty,
The violet and purple morn with just-felt breezes,
The gentle soft-born measureless light,
The miracle spreading bathing all, the fulfilled noon,
The coming eve delicious, the welcome night and the stars,
Over my cities shining all, enveloping man and land.

13

Sing on, sing on you grey-brown bird,
Sing from the swamps, the recesses, pour your chant from the
    bushes,
Limitless out of the dusk, out of the cedars and pines.

Sing on dearest brother, warble your reedy song,
Loud human song, with voice of uttermost woe.

O liquid and free and tender!
O wild and loose to my soul—O wondrous singer!
You only I hear—yet the star holds me, (but will soon depart,)
Yet the lilac with mastering odor holds me.

14

Now while I sat in the day and looked forth,
In the close of the day with its light and the fields of spring, and the
    farmers preparing their crops,
In the large unconscious scenery of my land with its lakes and
    forests,
In the heavenly aerial beauty, (after the perturbed winds and the
    storms,)
Under the arching heavens of the afternoon swift passing, and the
    voices of children and women,
The many-moving sea-tides, and I saw the ships how they sailed,
And the summer approaching with richness, and the fields all busy
    with labor,
And the infinite separate houses, how they all went on, each with its
    meals and minutia of daily usages,
And the streets how their throbbings throbbed, and the cities pent
    —lo, then and there,
Falling upon them all and among them all, enveloping me with the
    rest,
Appeared the cloud, appeared the long black trail;
And I knew death, its thought, and the sacred knowledge of death.

Then with the knowledge of death as walking one side of me,
And the thought of death close-walking the other side of me,
And I in the middle as with companions, and as holding the hands
    of companions,
I fled forth to the hiding receiving night that talks not,
Down to the shores of the water, the path by the swamp in the
    dimness,
To the solemn shadowy cedars and ghostly pines so still.

And the singer so shy to the rest received me,
The grey-brown bird I know received us comrades three,
And he sang the carol of death, and a verse for him I love.

From deep secluded recesses,
From the fragrant cedars and the ghostly pines so still,
Came the carol of the bird.

And the charm of the carol rapt me,
As I held as if by their hands my comrades in the night,
And the voice of my spirit tallied the song of the bird.

Come lovely and soothing death,
Undulate round the world, serenely arriving, arriving,
In the day, in the night, to all, to each,
Sooner or later delicate death.

Praised be the fathomless universe,
For life and joy, and for objects and knowledge curious,
And for love, sweet love—but praise! praise! praise!
For the sure-enwinding arms of cool-enfolding death.

Dark mother always gliding near with soft feet,
Have none chanted for thee a chant of fullest welcome?
Then I chant it for thee, I glorify thee above all,
I bring thee a song that when thou must indeed come, come un-
falteringly.

Approach strong deliveress,
When it is so, when thou hast taken them I joyously sing the dead,
Lost in the loving floating ocean of thee,
Laved in the flood by thy bliss O death.

From me to thee glad serenades,
Dances for thee I propose saluting thee, adornments and feastings
for thee,
And the sights of the open landscape and the high-spread sky are
fitting,
And life and the fields, and the huge and thoughtful night.

The night in silence under many a star,
The ocean shore and the husky whispering wave whose voice I
know,
And the soul turning to thee, O vast and well-veiled death,
And the body gratefully nestling close to thee.

Over the tree-tops I float thee a song,
Over the rising and sinking waves, over the myriad fields and the
prairies wide,
Over the dense-packed cities all and the teeming wharves and ways,
I float this carol with joy, with joy to thee, O death!

15

To the tally of my soul,
Loud and strong kept up the grey-brown bird,
With pure, deliberate notes spreading filling the night.

Loud in the pines and cedars dim,
Clear in the freshness moist and the swamp-perfume,
And I with my comrades there in the night.
While my sight that was bound in my eyes unclosed,
As to long panoramas of visions.

And I saw askant the armies,
I saw as in noiseless dreams hundreds of battle-flags,
Borne through the smoke of the battles and pierced with missiles I
  saw them,
And carried hither and yon through the smoke, and torn and
  bloody,
And at last but a few shreds left on the staffs, (and all in silence,)
And the staffs all splintered and broken.

I saw battle-corpses, myriads of them,
And the white skeletons of young men, I saw them,
I saw the debris and debris of all the slain soldiers of the war,
But I saw they were not as was thought,
They themselves were fully at rest, they suffered not,
The living remained and suffered, the mother suffered,
And the wife and the child and the musing comrade suffered,
And the armies that remained suffered.

16

Passing the visions, passing the night,
Passing, unloosing the hold of my comrades' hands,
Passing the song of the hermit bird and the tallying song of my
  soul,
Victorious song, death's outlet song, yet varying ever-altering song,
As low and wailing, yet clear the notes, rising and falling, flooding
  the night,
Sadly sinking and fainting, as warning and warning, and yet again
  bursting with joy,
Covering the earth and filling the spread of the heaven,
As that powerful psalm in the night I heard from recesses,
Passing, I leave thee lilac with heart-shaped leaves,
I leave thee there in the dooryard, blooming, returning with spring.

I cease from my song for thee,
From my gaze on thee in the west, fronting the west, communing
  with thee,
O comrade lustrous with silver face in the night.
Yet each to keep and all, retrievements out of the night,
The song, the wondrous chant of the grey-brown bird,
And the tallying chant, the echo aroused in my soul,

With the lustrous and drooping star with the countenance full of
    woe,
With the holders holding my hand nearing the call of the bird,
Comrades mine and I in the midst, and their memory ever to keep,
    for the dead I loved so well,
For the sweetest, wisest soul of all my days and lands—and this for
    his dear sake,
Lilac and star and bird twined with the chant of my soul,
There in the fragrant pines and the cedars dusk and dim.

RICHARD WILBUR

1921–

Love Calls Us to the Things of This World

      The eyes open to a cry of pulleys,
And spirited from sleep, the astounded soul
Hangs for a moment bodiless and simple
As false dawn.
             Outside the open window
The morning air is all awash with angels.

      Some are in bed-sheets, some are in blouses,
Some are in smocks: but truly there they are.
Now they are rising together in calm swells
Of halcyon feeling, filling whatever they wear
With the deep joy of their impersonal breathing;

      Now they are flying in place, conveying
The terrible speed of their omnipresence, moving
And staying like white water; and now of a sudden
They swoon down into so rapt a quiet
That nobody seems to be there.
                 The soul shrinks

      From all that it is about to remember,
From the punctual rape of every blessed day,
And cries,
         "Oh let there be nothing on earth but laundry,

320

Nothing but rosy hands in the rising steam
And clear dances done in the sight of heaven."

  Yet, as the sun acknowledges
With a warm look the world's hunks and colors,
The soul descends once more in bitter love
To accept the waking body, saying now
In a changed voice as the man yawns and rises,

  "Bring them down from their ruddy gallows;
Let there be clean linen for the backs of thieves;
Let lovers go fresh and sweet to be undone,
And the heaviest nuns walk in a pure floating
Of dark habits,
    keeping their difficult balance."

OSCAR WILDE

1856–1900

The Garden

The lily's withered chalice falls
 Around its rod of dusty gold,
 And from the beech-trees in the wold
The last wood-pigeon coos and calls.

The gaudy leonine sunflower
 Hangs black and barren on its stalk,
 And down the windy garden walk
The dead leaves scatter—hour by hour.

Pale privet-petals white as milk
 Are blown into a snowy mass:
 The roses lie upon the grass
Like little shreds of crimson silk.

CHARLES WOLFE

1791–1823

The Burial of Sir John Moore at Corunna

Not a drum was heard, not a funeral note,
    As his corse to the rampart we hurried;
Not a soldier discharged his farewell shot
    O'er the grave where our hero we buried.

We buried him darkly at dead of night,
    The sods with our bayonets turning;
By the struggling moonbeam's misty light
    And the lantern dimly burning.

No useless coffin enclosed his breast,
    Not in sheet or in shroud we wound him;
But he lay like a warrior taking his rest
    With his martial cloak around him.

Few and short were the prayers we said,
    And we spoke not a word of sorrow;
But we steadfastly gazed on the face that was dead,
    And we bitterly thought of the morrow.

We thought, as we hollowed his narrow bed
    And smoothed down his lonely pillow,
That the foe and the stranger would tread o'er his head,
    And we far away on the billow!

Lightly they'll talk of the spirit that's gone
    And o'er his cold ashes upbraid him—
But little he'll reck, if they let him sleep on
    In the grave where a Briton has laid him.

But half of our heavy task was done
    When the clock struck the hour for retiring;
And we heard the distant and random gun
    That the foe was sullenly firing.

Slowly and sadly we laid him down,
    From the field of his fame fresh and gory;

322

We carved not a line, and we raised not a stone—
But we left him alone with his glory.

WILLIAM WORDSWORTH

1770–1850

The Solitary Reaper

Behold her, single in the field,
Yon solitary Highland lass!
Reaping and singing by herself;
Stop here, or gently pass!
Alone she cuts and binds the grain
And sings a melancholy strain;
Oh listen! for the vale profound
Is overflowing with the sound.

No nightingale did ever chaunt
More welcome notes to weary bands
Of travelers in some shady haunt
Among Arabian sands.
A voice so thrilling ne'er was heard
In springtime from the cuckoo-bird,
Breaking the silence of the seas
Among the farthest Hebrides.

Will no one tell me what she sings?—
Perhaps the plaintive numbers flow
For old, unhappy, far-off things
And battles long ago.
Or is it some more humble lay,
Familiar matter of today?
Some natural sorrow, loss, or pain
That has been, and may be again?

Whate'er the theme, the maiden sang
As if her song could have no ending;
I saw her singing at her work,
And o'er the sickle bending—

I listened, motionless and still;
And as I mounted up the hill,
The music in my heart I bore,
Long after it was heard no more.

I Wandered Lonely as a Cloud

I wandered lonely as a cloud
That floats on high o'er vales and hills,
When all at once I saw a crowd,
A host, of golden daffodils—
Beside the lake, beneath the trees,
Fluttering and dancing in the breeze.

Continuous as the stars that shine
And twinkle on the milky way,
They stretched in never-ending line
Along the margin of a bay:
Ten thousand saw I at a glance,
Tossing their heads in sprightly dance.

The waves beside them danced; but they
Outdid the sparkling waves in glee:
A poet could not but be gay
In such a jocund company:
I gazed—and gazed—but little thought
What wealth the show to me had brought:

For oft, when on my couch I lie
In vacant or in pensive mood,
They flash upon that inward eye
Which is the bliss of solitude;
And then my heart with pleasure fills,
And dances with the daffodils.

A Slumber Did My Spirit Seal

A slumber did my spirit seal;
    I had no human fears:
She seemed a thing that could not feel
    The touch of earthly years.

324

No motion has she now, no force;
  She neither hears nor sees;
Rolled round in earth's diurnal course
  With rocks, and stones, and trees.

To Toussaint L'Ouverture

Toussaint, the most unhappy man of men!
Whether the whistling rustic tend his plough
Within thy hearing, or thy head be now
Pillowed in some deep dungeon's earless den—
O miserable chieftain! where and when
Wilt thou find patience? Yet die not; do thou
Wear rather in thy bonds a cheerful brow:
Though fallen thyself, never to rise again,
Live, and take comfort. Thou hast left behind
Powers that will work for thee—air, earth, and skies.
There's not a breathing of the common wind
That will forget thee; thou hast great allies:
Thy friends are exultations, agonies,
And love, and man's unconquerable mind.

Westminster Bridge

Earth has not anything to show more fair:
Dull would he be of soul who could pass by
A sight so touching in its majesty:
This city now doth like a garment wear
The beauty of the morning; silent, bare,
Ships, towers, domes, theaters, and temples lie
Open unto the fields and to the sky,
All bright and glittering in the smokeless air.
Never did sun more beautifully steep
In his first splendor valley, rock, or hill;
Ne'er saw I, never felt, a calm so deep!
The river glideth at his own sweet will.
Dear God! the very houses seem asleep;
And all that mighty heart is lying still!

London, 1802

Milton! thou shouldst be living at this hour:
England hath need of thee; she is a fen
Of stagnant waters; altar, sword and pen,
Fireside, the heroic wealth of hall and bower
Have forfeited their ancient English dower
Of inward happiness. We are selfish men;
Oh raise us up, return to us again
And give us manners, virtue, freedom, power.
Thy soul was like a star and dwelt apart;
Thou hadst a voice whose sound was like the sea:
Pure as the naked heavens, majestic, free,
So didst thou travel on life's common way,
In cheerful godliness; and yet thy heart
The lowliest duties on herself did lay.

The World Is Too Much With Us

The world is too much with us: late and soon,
Getting and spending, we lay waste our powers.
Little we see in nature that is ours;
We have given our hearts away, a sordid boon!
This sea that bares her bosom to the moon,
The winds that will be howling at all hours,
And are up-gathered now like sleeping flowers—
For this, for everything, we are out of tune;
It moves us not.—Great God! I'd rather be
A pagan suckled in a creed outworn;
So might I, standing on this pleasant lea,
Have glimpses that would make me less forlorn,
Have sight of Proteus rising from the sea,
Or hear old Triton blow his wreathéd horn.

Yarrow Unvisited

From Sterling Castle we had seen
The mazy Forth unraveled,
Had trod the banks of Clyde and Tay,
And with the Tweed had traveled;

And when we came to Clovenford,
Then said my winsome Marrow,
"Whate'er betide, we'll turn aside,
And see the Braes of Yarrow."

"Let Yarrow folk frae Selkirk town,
Who have been buying, selling,
Go back to Yarrow, 't is their own,
Each maiden to her dwelling!
On Yarrow's banks let herons feed,
Hares couch, and rabbits burrow!
But we will downward with the Tweed,
Nor turn aside to Yarrow.

"There's Gala Water, Leader Haughs,
Both lying right before us;
And Dryborough, where with chiming Tweed
The lintwhites sing in chorus;
There's pleasant Teviot-dale, a land
Made blithe with plough and harrow:
Why throw away a needful day
To go in search of Yarrow?

"What's Yarrow but a river bare,
That glides the dark hills under?
There are a thousand such elsewhere
As worthy of your wonder."—
Strange words they seemed of slight and scorn:
My true-love sighed for sorrow,
And looked me in the face, to think
I thus could speak of Yarrow!

"Oh green," said I, "are Yarrow's holms,
And sweet is Yarrow flowing!
Fair hangs the apple frae the rock,
But we will leave it growing.
O'er hilly path and open Strath,
We'll wander Scotland thorough;
But though so near, we will not turn
Into the dale of Yarrow.

"Let beeves and home-bred kine partake
The sweets of Burn-mill meadow;
The swan on still St. Mary's Lake
Float double, swan and shadow!
We will not see them, will not go

Today, nor yet tomorrow;
Enough if in our hearts we know
There's such a place as Yarrow.

"Be Yarrow stream unseen, unknown!
It must, or we shall rue it:
We have a vision of our own;
Ah! why should we undo it?
The treasured dreams of times long past,
We'll keep them, winsome Marrow!
For when we're there, although 'tis fair,
'Twill be another Yarrow!

"If care with freezing years should come,
And wandering seem but folly,
Should we be loath to stir from home,
And yet be melancholy;
Should life be dull, and spirits low,
'Twill soothe us in our sorrow
That earth has something yet to show,
The bonny holms of Yarrow!"

SIR THOMAS WYATT

1503?–1542

The Lover Showeth How He Is Forsaken

They flee from me that sometime did me seek,
  With naked foot stalking in my chamber.
I have seen them gentle, tame, and meek,
  That now are wild, and do not remember
  That some time they put themselves in danger
    To take bread at my hand; and now they range,
    Busily seeking with a continual change.

Thanked be Fortune, it hath been otherwise
  Twenty times better; but once in special,
In thin array, after a pleasant guise,
  When her loose gown from her shoulders did fall,
  And she me caught in her arms long and small,

328

Therewith all sweetly did me kiss,
And softly said, "Dear heart, how like you this?"

It was no dream; I lay broad waking.
But all is turnéd, thorough my gentleness,
Into a strange fashion of forsaking;
And I have leave to go, of her goodness,
And she also to use newfangleness.
But since that I so kindély am servéd,
I fain would know what *she* hath deservéd.

ELINOR WYLIE

1885–1928

The Puritan's Ballad

My love came up from Barnegat,
  The sea was in his eyes;
He trod as softly as a cat
  And told me terrible lies.

His hair was yellow as new-cut pine
  In shavings curled and feathered;
I thought how silver it would shine
  By cruel winters weathered.

But he was in his twentieth year,
  This time I'm speaking of;
We were head over heels in love with fear
  And half a-feared of love.

His feet were used to treading a gale
  And balancing thereon;
His face was brown as a foreign sail
  Threadbare against the sun.

His arms were thick as hickory logs
  Whittled to little wrists;
Strong as the teeth of terrier dogs
  Were the fingers of his fists.

Within his arms I feared to sink
    Where lions shook their manes,
And dragons drawn in azure ink
    Leapt quickened by his veins.

Dreadful his strength and length of limb
    As the sea to foundering ships;
I dipped my hands in love for him
    No deeper than their tips.

But our palms were welded by a flame
    The moment we came to part,
And on his knuckles I read my name
    Enscrolled within a heart.

And something made our wills to bend
    As wild as trees blown over;
We were no longer friend and friend,
    But only lover and lover.

"In seven weeks or seventy years—
    God grant it may be sooner!—
I'll make a handkerchief for your tears
    From the sails of my captain's schooner.

"We'll wear our loves like wedding rings
    Long polished to our touch;
We shall be busy with other things
    And they cannot bother us much.

"When you are skimming the wrinkled cream
    And your ring clinks on the pan,
You'll say to yourself in a pensive dream,
    'How wonderful a man!'

"When I am slitting a fish's head
    And my ring clanks on the knife,
I'll say with thanks, as a prayer is said,
    'How beautiful a wife!'

"And I shall fold my decorous paws
    In velvet smooth and deep,
Like a kitten that covers up its claws
    To sleep and sleep and sleep.

"Like a little blue pigeon you shall bow
    Your bright alarming crest;
In the crook of my arm you'll lay your brow
    To rest and rest and rest."

330

Will he never come back from Barnegat
With thunder in his eyes,
Treading as soft as a tiger cat,
To tell me terrible lies?

Madman's Song

Better to see your cheek grown hollow,
Better to see your temple worn,
Than to forget to follow, follow,
After the sound of a silver horn.

Better to bind your brow with willow
And follow, follow until you die,
Than to sleep with your head on a golden pillow,
Nor lift it up when the hunt goes by.

Better to see your cheek grown sallow
And your hair grown grey, so soon, so soon,
Than to forget to hallo, hallo,
After the milk-white hounds of the moon.

WILLIAM BUTLER YEATS

1865–1939

The Lake Isle of Innisfree

I will arise and go now, and go to Innisfree,
And a small cabin build there, of clay and wattles made:
Nine bean-rows will I have there, a hive for the honey-bee,
And live alone in the bee-loud glade.

And I shall have some peace there, for peace comes dropping slow,
Dropping from the veils of the morning to where the cricket sings;
There midnight's all a glimmer, and noon a purple glow,
And evening full of the linnet's wings.

I will arise and go now, for always night and day
I hear lake water lapping with low sounds by the shore;

While I stand on the roadway, or on the pavements grey,
I hear it in the deep heart's core.

The Song of Wandering Aengus

I went out to the hazel wood,
Because a fire was in my head,
And cut and peeled a hazel wand,
And hooked a berry to a thread;
And when white moths were on the wing,
And moth-like stars were flickering out,
I dropped the berry in a stream
And caught a little silver trout.

When I had laid it on the floor
I went to blow the fire aflame,
But something rustled on the floor,
And someone called me by my name:
It had become a glimmering girl
With apple blossom in her hair
Who called me by my name and ran
And faded through the brightening air.

Though I am old with wandering
Through hollow lands and hilly lands,
I will find out where she has gone,
And kiss her lips and take her hands;
And walk among long dappled grass,
And pluck till time and times are done,
The silver apples of the moon,
The golden apples of the sun.

September 1913

What need you, being come to sense,
But fumble in a greasy till
And add the halfpence to the pence
And prayer to shivering prayer, until
You have dried the marrow from the bone;
For men were born to pray and save:

Romantic Ireland's dead and gone,
It's with O'Leary in the grave.

Yet they were of a different kind,
The names that stilled your childish play,
They have gone about the world like wind,
But little time had they to pray
For whom the hangman's rope was spun,
And what, God help us, could they save?
Romantic Ireland's dead and gone,
It's with O'Leary in the grave.

Was it for this the wild geese spread
The grey wing upon every tide;
For this that all that blood was shed,
For this Edward Fitzgerald died,
And Robert Emmet and Wolfe Tone—
All that delirium of the brave?
Romantic Ireland's dead and gone,
It's with O'Leary in the grave.

Yet could we turn the years again,
And call those exiles as they were
In all their loneliness and pain,
You'd cry, "Some woman's yellow hair
Has maddened every mother's son":
They weighed so lightly what they gave.
But let them be, they're dead and gone,
They're with O'Leary in the grave.

The Ballad of Father Gilligan

The old priest Peter Gilligan
Was weary night and day;
For half his flock were in their beds,
Or under green sods lay.

Once, while he nodded on a chair,
At the moth-hour of eve,
Another poor man sent for him,
And he began to grieve.

"I have no rest, nor joy, nor peace,
For people die and die;"

And after cried he, "God forgive!
My body spake, not I!"

He knelt, and leaning on the chair
He prayed and fell asleep;
And the moth-hour went from the fields,
And stars began to peep.

They slowly into millions grew,
And leaves shook in the wind;
And God covered the world with shade,
And whispered to mankind.

Upon the time of sparrow-chirp
When moths came once more,
The old priest Peter Gilligan
Stood upright on the floor.

"Mavrone, mavrone! the man has died
While I slept on the chair;"
He roused his horse out of its sleep,
And rode with little care.

He rode now as he never rode,
By rocky lane and fen;
The sick man's wife opened the door:
"Father! you come again!"

"And is the poor man dead?" he cried.
"He died an hour ago."
The old priest Peter Gilligan
In grief swayed to and fro.

"When you were gone, he turned and died
As merry as a bird."
The old priest Peter Gilligan
He knelt him at that word.

"He Who hath made the night of stars
For souls who tire and bleed,
Sent one of His great angels down
To help me in my need.

"He Who is wrapped in purple robes,
With planets in His care,
Had pity on the least of things
Asleep upon a chair."

Some Read-Aloud Poems Children Like

Some Long Poems

If space had permitted, the following poems would have been included in *Poems to Read Aloud*:

Matthew Arnold: The Scholar-Gypsy
Robert Browning: Fra Lippo Lippi
              Andrea del Sarto
Robert Burns: The Cotter's Saturday Night
Samuel Taylor Coleridge: The Rime of the Ancient Mariner
William Cowper: The Diverting History of John Gilpin
T. S. Eliot: The Waste Land
       Ash Wednesday
Edward Fitzgerald: The Rubáiyát of Omar Kháyyám of Naishapur
Oliver Goldsmith: The Deserted Village
Thomas Gray: Elegy Written in a Country Churchyard
John Keats: The Eve of St. Agnes
John Milton: Lycidas
Alexander Pope: The Rape of the Lock
Edwin Arlington Robinson: Ben Jonson Entertains a Man from Stratford
Dante Gabriel Rossetti: Sister Helen
Percy Bysshe Shelley: Adonais
Alfred, Lord Tennyson: The Lotos-Eaters
Francis Thompson: The Hound of Heaven
Walt Whitman: Out of the Cradle Endlessly Rocking

Index of Titles and First Lines *

* Only the title is given when it seems sufficient identification.

339

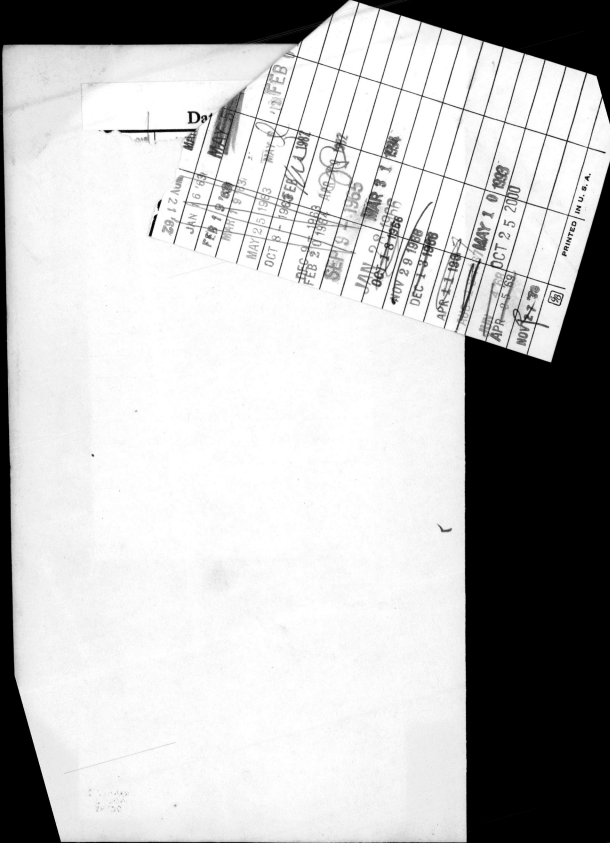